FRONTIER MANHATTAN

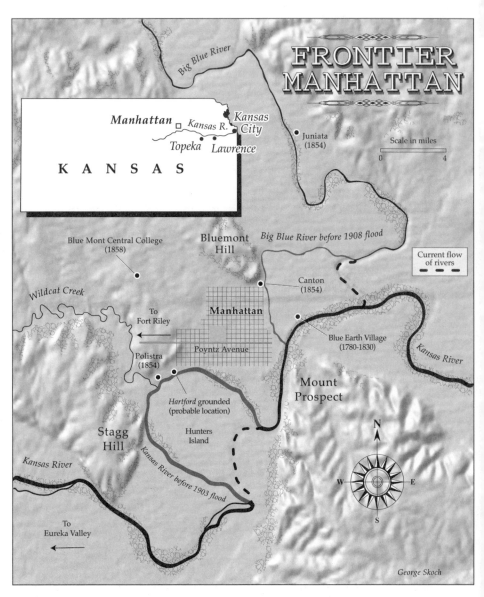

FRONTIER MANHATTAN

KANSAS

Manhattan □ Kansas R. Kansas City
Topeka Lawrence

Juniata
(1854)

Scale in miles

0   4

Blue Mont Central College
(1858)

Bluemont
Hill

Big Blue River before 1908 flood

Big Blue River

Canton
(1854)

Current flow
of rivers

Wildcat Creek

To
Fort Riley

Manhattan

Blue Earth Village
(1780-1830)

Kansas River

Poyntz Avenue

Polistra
(1854)

Hartford grounded
(probable location)

Mount
Prospect

Stagg
Hill

Hunters
Island

Kansas River before 1903 flood

N

Kansas River

W   E

To
Eureka Valley

S

George Skoch

Map by George Skoch.

FRONTIER MANHATTAN

YANKEE SETTLEMENT

TO KANSAS TOWN,

1854–1894

KEVIN G. W. OLSON

UNIVERSITY PRESS OF KANSAS

Published by the University Press of Kansas (Lawrence, Kansas 66045), which was
organized by the Kansas Board of Regents and is operated and funded by Emporia
State University, Fort Hays State University, Kansas State University, Pittsburg State
University, the University of Kansas, and Wichita State University

Library of Congress Cataloging-in-Publication Data

Olson, Kevin G. W.
    Frontier Manhattan : yankee settlement to Kansas town, 1854–1894 /
Kevin G. W. Olson.
        p.   cm.
    ISBN 978-0-7006-1832-3 (cloth : alk. paper) 1. Manhattan (Kan.)—History—
19th century. 2. Frontier and pioneer life—Kansas—Manhattan. I. Title.
    F689.M2O47 2012
    978.1'28—dc23
                    2011047229

British Library Cataloguing-in-Publication Data is available.

Printed in the United States of America
10 9 8 7 6 5 4 3 2 1

The paper used in this publication is recycled and contains 30 percent postconsumer
waste. It is acid free and meets the minimum requirements of the American National
Standard for Permanence of Paper for Printed Library Materials Z39.48-1992.

TO MY PARENTS,

WITH DEEPEST LOVE AND

TREMENDOUS GRATITUDE

FOR ALL THEY HAVE DONE.

TABLE OF CONTENTS

PROLOGUE

On a frosty afternoon in Kansas Territory on March 27, 1855, a stern Rhode Island abolitionist named Isaac Goodnow and five other New Englanders wrestled a bulky canvas tent into shape in a tallgrass prairie at the junction of the Kansas and Big Blue rivers. The prairie was colder than Goodnow had imagined it would be in late March. But he and his party were in good spirits as they moved mattresses and supplies from the wagon into their campsite: the men had finally reached their destination after a three-week trip from Boston, covering 1,500 miles, capped by a struggle to get their overburdened covered wagon through the snowstorms and icy rivers of Kansas Territory. Happily, the first night at the site rewarded them with a splendid moonlit evening.

Only one of the six men who found themselves on the frontier that night was familiar with the conditions. Massachusetts native Luke Lincoln had been to Kansas Territory the summer before, when it originally opened to settlement. The others had rarely been far from New England. Goodnow was a teacher at an academy outside Providence; another, Charles Lovejoy, was a noted preacher from New Hampshire; and a third was Lovejoy's seventeen-year-old son. Yet all were bound and determined to transplant antislavery ideals to the unbroken soils of Kansas Territory.

They were not the first pioneers seeking to settle this site. In fact, a shrewd land speculator had already built a log cabin nearby. But they were the vanguard of a larger group of New Englanders who would transform the spot from open prairie into a frontier settlement. Over the next few days, the six men would further reinforce the walls of their tent with sod bricks while welcoming additional Yankees to their camp. The men would also come face-to-face with a band of fifteen mounted and armed Southerners who made bombastic threats, slashed their tent's ropes, and fired a musket ball through the tent in an effort to scare away the abolitionists.

For many New Englanders who ventured to Goodnow's camp that spring the challenges were too much to bear. Desolation, harassment, and homesickness conspired to drive them back east to the United States. But

Goodnow was resolute — he was a hard worker who adopted the creed "we should die with the harness on" — and he held his ground to establish an antislavery and educational stronghold on the site: the town of Manhattan, Kansas. It was not an easy task.

THE PEOPLE, THE PLACE, THE TIMES

In the spring of 1855 Manhattan was founded as an "ardent, fire-eating" antislavery settlement on the Kansas Territory frontier.[1] The founding of Manhattan was part of the rapid westward expansion of the United States. Less than eighty years had passed since English colonists, clinging to the East Coast, issued a Declaration of Independence from the British king.

In the turbulent era when Manhattan was established — five and a half years before Kansas became a state — Kansas Territory was sparsely populated with Native Americans, woolly frontiersmen, overwhelmed settler families in covered wagons, and fanatics of all stripes, including Yankee abolitionists, southern proslavery reactionaries, and religious missionaries seeking to convert Native Americans. It was not yet the time of saloons and cowboys, though they were coming soon. And although the United States was on the cusp of a new age of travel and communication, Manhattan was founded during a simpler, slower era. As the author Henry Adams later observed, "in essentials like religion, ethics, philosophy; in history, literature, art; in the concepts of all science, except perhaps mathematics, the American boy of 1854 stood nearer the year 1 than to the year 1900."[2] (An illustration of the primitiveness of the era is that the tallest building in the world in 1855 was the Strasbourg Cathedral, built by medieval men.)

The Pony Express, the transcontinental telegraph, and the transcontinental railroad were marvels of speed that still lay in the future when Manhattan was founded. In 1855 it regularly took travelers and news reports, traveling overland at a normal rate, five days to make the "long journey" of 125 miles from Manhattan to Kansas City — the nearest village with a population over 1,000.[3] Communication with the centers of population and commerce on the East Coast could take more than a month. One Manhattan settler, Thomas C. Wells, in regular correspondence with his family in Rhode Island, excitedly wrote in August 1855, "I am happy to say that I get your letters quite regularly now; the last reached me in less than a month after it was written."[4]

Manhattan itself was barely more than a small, remote camp for the first years of its existence. But most of Manhattan's settlers arrived in this faraway place resolved to outlast any inconvenience or danger. The founders of Manhattan were abolitionist New Englanders and other "Free-Staters," who raced to Kansas Territory to cast a vote for antislavery candidates for the Territorial Legislature — a vote that would help determine whether Kansas entered the Union as a free state or a slave state — and who stood firm afterward in the face of widespread proslavery violence. The founders were a zealous, self-selected group of people who risked their personal safety and left behind civilization and family, all to help curb the spread of slavery.

To fully understand the settlers who went to Kansas Territory, it is important to recognize that while all the "Free-Staters" in Kansas opposed the introduction of slavery into the territory, only some were abolitionists. Others insisted they wanted the territory to be free of all African Americans — whether enslaved or free.[5] The editor of the *Manhattan Express* clearly expressed the Free-State line in an editorial on June 30, 1860: "We oppose slavery in the territories, not for love of the negro but the white man, whom we would save from the condition, either as an arrogant slave holder, or as degraded by him, in which we find him in the slave states. Nor do we want the free blacks, for, degraded as they are, they constitute a pernicious element, like other unfortunate subjects of society."

Confusing the matter, some of those in Kansas Territory who were in fact strident abolitionists falsely claimed that their goal was not to fight slavery in all places, but that they merely wished to prevent its spread to Kansas. The *Squatter Sovereign,* a virulently proslavery newspaper printed in Atchison, Kansas Territory, recognized this and wrote in March 1855: "[The Free-State leader] knows how the people abhor the open abolitionist, hence he cunningly makes a platform, false on its face, but which, regarding as he does the (pro-slavery) squatters as his foes, he hopes may deceive them."[6] To simplify the issue, the proslavery editor of the *Herald* in Leavenworth, Kansas Territory, declared in 1855 that "he that is not for us is against us."[7]

Many of Manhattan's first settlers were sent by the foremost Free-State organization, the New England Emigrant Aid Company, which was organized in 1854 to encourage and finance the emigration of New England Free-Staters to Kansas Territory. It was composed of men who were clearly abolitionists under the modern definition, but who often rejected the label for themselves because "abolitionist" was a highly loaded word in the 1850s. For example, the principal founder of the Emigrant Aid Company, Eli Thayer, asserted that the company was *not* an abolitionist organization — equating abolitionism as it was then preached with reckless attacks on the Union by radicals such as newspaperman William Lloyd Garrison.[8] Nevertheless, Thayer saw no contradiction in baldly writing that the Emigrant Aid Company's goal was "TO GO AND PUT AN END TO SLAVERY."[9]

The other main body of Manhattan's founders came from Cincinnati, Ohio, which was also home to abolitionist sentiment (and home to the Underground Railroad, being located directly across the Ohio River from Kentucky). One leader of the Cincinnati party, Judge John Pipher, insisted shortly after arriving in Manhattan that his group was not as ardent as the New Englanders — claiming that his party was composed not of abolitionists but of Free-Staters. Pipher wrote on July 16, 1855, "I do not know the political sentiments of all my associates; but I do know, however, we are not abolitionists."[10] He added, "So far as my own sentiments are concerned, I will vote for making Kansas a free state; and will use all honorable means to accomplish this."[11] Yet, as the similar proclamations made by Thayer and Pipher suggest, there was not necessarily that much difference between the two companies' views. Julia Lovejoy, a Manhattan settler from the New England Emigrant Aid Company, saw only a slight difference between the two groups: "I happen to know well the spirit of this same Bro. Pipher toward New England Methodism, (especially if tinctured with what he contemptuously calls 'abolitionism') having lived the next door neighbor to him for a year; and, by the way, the term 'abolitionist,' in the minds of such men is associated with Garrisonianism and Abby Kellyism. No distinction is made, and it is never noticed that we entirely disclaim any connection with such radicalism."[12]

Despite the protestations made by Free-Staters, it is clear that Manhattan was dominated from the start by abolitionists — whether they would admit to that description or not. One proslavery correspondent opined in the *Squatter Sovereign* that some of "the vilest and meanest of the gang [of abolitionists]" could be found in Manhattan.[13] To be sure, Manhattan was founded specifically to help stop the spread of slavery in the United States, and it was certainly considered one of the sturdiest and most uncompromising of the Free-State outposts.

In addition to being Free-Staters, in terms of national political parties, Manhattan's founders were mostly Whigs and — after the birth of the Republican Party in 1854 — staunch Republicans. They stood opposed to all things the Democratic Party represented.[14] Yet these labels are profoundly misleading if thought of in modern terms. The antebellum Democrats were deeply conservative, generally approving of all things in America as they presently stood, including slavery. As the party of President Andrew Jackson, the Democrats favored a strong executive and argued that any action taken by the president was legal regardless of laws passed by Congress. They stood strongly in favor of a laissez-faire economy and states' rights, against taxes and public education, and found their base in the rural South. Democrats also argued that their "strict constructionist" reading of the U.S. Constitution did not provide a role for the federal government in matters as basic as banking or building roads. The Whigs and Republicans, on the other hand, argued in favor of an activist state, progressive causes, and a developed economy, and found their base in the growing cities of the North.[15] In sum, the antebellum Republicans and Democrats were in many ways the opposite of today's parties.

The New England Emigrant Aid Company's effort to establish Manhattan and other towns in Kansas Territory was massive — in all U.S. history perhaps the only larger migration undertaken to create a community of particular ideals was the Mormon migration to Utah. One Manhattan settler asserted, "It is not possible that any other state has ever been settled by so many who came not for Home or Business careers, but from a sense of Duty and Patriotism that included all races and both sexes."[16] Moreover, the beliefs carried to Manhattan at its founding were at the forefront of progressive thought in the mid-nineteenth century — questioning the prevailing views of a society that embraced and justified stereotypes of African American and female inferiority. Thus, in 1868 the *Manhattan Independent* — edited by an old Free-Stater — was moved to opine that "conservatism is the quintessence of evil. It is that and that alone which arrests the onward march towards perfection which is everywhere visible in the physical, intellectual and moral world."[17] Two years earlier, the newspaper similarly observed:

"We believe that there is no State in the Union, not excepting Massachusetts, in which a larger proportion of the people are thoroughly sound on upon every vital question now at issue in the nation, than the people of Kansas. We as a people are eminently radical."[18]

Yet, despite the town's roots in this radical movement, in the decades following Manhattan's founding, the town veered from this heritage and shifted into the rhythms of a quiet midwestern college town (today home to Kansas State University), characterized by political moderates. This shift in culture may be explained in part by the values of the town's Yankee founders themselves. Three principles underlay the founding of Manhattan: abolitionism, Protestantism, and public education. Abolitionism was of first importance; when the founders arrived, the fight over slavery was literally staining the Kansas prairies black with burned cabins and spilled blood. But with the complete destruction of slavery at the end of the American Civil War — just ten years after Manhattan's founding — this passion was drained from the town. With abolitionist zeal mooted, only silent pride in the Yankees' churches and schools was left to define Manhattan, and this started the town on a much quieter trajectory.[19] And while New England remained open to successive waves of progressive ideas (such as organized labor), the ideas carried by the Yankees to Manhattan stagnated and became fixed on religion and education — traits also present in the broader Middle American culture.

Tellingly, as the national Republican Party drifted toward conservatism over the coming decades — essentially switching identities with the Democrats of 150 years earlier — Manhattanites continued to vote Republican, electing Republicans to the State House of Representatives every single election, except for two, for 127 straight years, from statehood in 1861 to 1988. (The two elections during these decades when candidates were not elected on the Republican ticket were 1870, when Republican incumbent Edward Secrest ran for reelection as an Independent, and 1891, when a third-party candidate from the Farmers' Alliance Party was elected.) After Manhattan elected its first Democrat to the Kansas House in 1988, Republicans quickly retook the seat in 1990.[20] Clearly, Manhattan drifted toward conservatism over the decades. Recently, however, voting patterns have changed: in 2002 another Democrat was elected to one of Manhattan's two House seats, and in 2004 the town's second seat also went Democratic. All this being said, these voting trends are somewhat muddled by the fact that the ideology of Republican candidates in Kansas remained relatively progressive for a long time.[21]

This book covers Manhattan's history through 1894 — exactly four decades after the location was first inhabited by white settlers. The 1890s provided an appropriate end point for the book because the decade marked a distinct shift into a more modern era, and it also witnessed the eclipsing of Manhattan's original settlers, signified most clearly by the death in 1894 of leading Yankee settler Isaac Goodnow.[22] The information here is derived in significant part from letters and diaries maintained by the settlers themselves. Nineteenth-century writers often ignored conventional rules of spelling or grammar, and this history does not use "[sic]" for each error, instead presenting the documents largely as written.

The first forty years of Euro-American settlement in Manhattan can be roughly divided into five eras: the territorial era (1854–1861), the Civil War era (1861–1865), the postwar era (1866–1869), the transitional era (the 1870s), and the modernization era (1880–1894), by which time the town of Manhattan as it presently exists was starting to take shape.

During the territorial years, the settlers' first priority was simply the survival of the settlement, as many early towns in Kansas Territory failed in their struggle to exist.[23] For example, two nearby settlements established before Manhattan — Pawnee and Juniata — disappeared completely within a few years. But the site for Manhattan was carefully selected at a natural crossing point, and the colony was blessed with a citizenship that came to Kansas Territory for the purpose of building a Free-State settlement and was therefore unlikely — indeed unwilling — to abandon the site. Manhattan certainly faced the question of its viability in its first two years, but because of careful planning and plenty of good luck, by 1857 it had established amenities that other frontier settlements rarely offered, including a schoolhouse and a sawmill, which helped to ensure that it would not simply fade away.

During this earliest era of Manhattan's existence, Free-State interests reigned supreme. Additionally, thanks in part to the work of the settler Isaac Goodnow, education was also at the forefront in Manhattan: one of the territory's largest schoolhouses was built there in 1857 and a private college was chartered in Manhattan in 1858, which was converted into the state's first public college in 1863. However, as early as 1859 commercial interests in the settlement also began to assume importance, and the crusading spirit of the town's founders soon began to fade from the fore.

Subsequently, with the coming of the Civil War in 1861, saloons and criminal activity such as cattle rustling became widespread in Manhattan, and the town that was founded as a beacon of enlightenment for "the poor man of the South" nearly lost its moral compass just six years into its existence.[24] After the war, however, Manhattan quickly rebounded from these depths. With a vigorous religious revival and a majority New England populace, the town retained a distinctive Yankee character throughout the remainder of the 1860s.[25] The town's growth, which had stagnated during the Civil War era, was also revived in the postwar era when the railroad arrived in 1866.

The 1870s saw the start of a transition away from the New England roots of the town, with the Yankee population diluted by new arrivals and native births. Finally, the 1880s and 1890s saw a discernible change from progressive ideas to more conservative thought in Manhattan.

The modern town of Manhattan that sprung from these events today sprawls over fifteen square miles of rolling hills — only a third smaller in size compared to New York City's borough of the same name. Of course the population of the town that residents call "The Little Apple" — 52,000 as of 2010 — is in no way comparable to the 1.5 million residents in the borough of Manhattan.[26]

Manhattan's founders located their settlement in a broad valley in the Flint Hills, at the confluence of the Kansas River and the Big Blue River. The Kansas River (sometimes called the Kaw River) is the major east-west waterway in northern Kansas, and the Big Blue is its largest tributary.

The two rivers intersect between two high hills: Mount Prospect and Bluemont Hill (originally called Mont Blue or Blue Mont). Bluemont Hill is a steep 215-foot hill, which one early visitor described as "a bold prominence of singular beauty."[27] Lapping at the base of the hill, according to Charles Boynton's widely read 1854 guidebook, *A Journey through Kansas,* the waters of the Big Blue River ran "clear and beautiful, reminding one of the streams of New England."[28] (The natural surroundings of the town were altered in the early 1900s when massive floods shifted the intersection of the rivers more than a mile to the east, so that the Big Blue no longer flows alongside the base of Bluemont Hill or the downtown area.)[29] Explorer John C. Frémont, camping at the site with his guide Kit Carson on June 20, 1842, described the Big Blue River as "a clear and handsome stream, about one hundred and twenty feet wide, running, with a rapid current, through a well-timbered valley."[30] To the west is another large stream, called Wildcat Creek. Lying encircled by these waterways and hills was a sizable level and grassy floodplain — the spot where Manhattan would arise.

Beyond the flat floodplain at the rivers' junction, the surrounding area is all hilly uplands. Observing this, a visitor in 1856 wrote of Manhattan's setting: "Finely rolling prairies extend back of the town about four miles, where high bluffs surround all like a strong fortress."[31] Another early visitor, charmed by the scenery, similarly remarked that the spot "is surrounded on three sides by a high range of truncated hills or mounds, from which the view is splendid."[32]

In 1855 both the floodplain and the surrounding hills were covered with bluestem tallgrass, up to eight feet in height, mixed with an array of wildflowers including "acres of rose bushes."[33] Surveying the flowers, settler Josiah Pillsbury happily wrote to his sister that "there are a great number of them which Eastern people cultivate with the greatest care."[34] As for the grass, settler Isaac Goodnow later recalled, "I could tie the prairie grass, blue-stem, over my head while sitting upon my pony."[35] Although grass and flowers were plentiful, trees were very scarce; the plains and the tops of the hills were entirely barren of timber. The range of trees had been limited by natural prairie fires and years of planned burning by Native Americans, discouraging the growth of trees and encouraging the early growth of grasses to feed their ponies.[36] Still, small forests of oak, walnut, and cottonwood lined the rivers and were tucked into ravines between hills.[37]

The undulating hills themselves are composed of ancient bleached rocks and marine fossils; "limestones and shales distilled from the Permian seas that covered most of middle America off and on for fifty million years."[38] From this white rock comes the current name for the region: the Flint Hills. In most places only a thin soil covers this rock. Settlers quickly found this made farming difficult or impossible on top of the hills, although the river valleys were rich and highly productive.

Taking in the entire scene, an 1854 visitor wrote: "But oh!, to reach the summits of these elevations and allow the eye to sweep around in every direction and a richer, lovelier view seldom falls upon the eye. It must be seen to be comprehended or appreciated."[39] By all accounts, the river junction that Manhattan's settlers selected was indeed a scenic spot. In an 1883 book,

History of the State of Kansas, William Cutler wrote of the setting: "No such limited area in Kansas, has more of the combined works of nature and art to commend it than the township of Manhattan."[40]

Additionally, abundant wildlife roamed the area around Manhattan in the 1850s. Bears, coyotes, panthers, timber wolves, deer, otter, beaver, skunk, wildcats, wild turkey, bald eagles, game birds, and songbirds inhabited the hills and timber, while the flatter, short-grass plains leveling out seventy miles west of Manhattan were home to prairie dogs, wild horses, and awe-inspiring herds of millions of bison that stretched across the horizon.[41] The area's streams and rivers also teemed with fish.[42]

With natural features of such beauty and strategic value, it is unsurprising that long before European Americans settled in the spot Native Americans had made it their home.[43] For many decades before Manhattan was founded at the union of the Kansas and Big Blue rivers, the Kansa tribe of Native Americans — for whom the Kansas River is named — were based in a village at the spot. (The name of the tribe is also spelled "Konza," among dozens of other variations, and the tribe is also alternately called the Kaw.) The tribal village covered several acres on the eastern side of the mouth of the Big Blue River, on a neck of land between the rivers.[44]

The Kansa were only the most recent inhabitants of the area. The state has been continuously inhabited for at least 12,000 years, dating back to the era of mammoths and long-horned bison, and numerous villages and burial sites predating the Kansa, from the pre-Columbian "Smoky Hill" phase, have been found along Wildcat Creek.[45] However, the Kansa are the best-known native inhabitants because they lived in the area during the era of European American exploration.

The Kansa called their village Manyinkatuhuudje ("Blue Earth Village"), because it was at the mouth of a river that the tribe called the Great Blue Earth River — today officially named the Big Blue River. Blue Earth Village was the principal village for the Kansa tribe for about fifty years, from 1780 to 1830.[46] It was also the tribe's last freely chosen home before the U.S. government began carving the territory into reservations and establishing Native American "agencies" in the 1820s. At its peak, the rambling riverside village teemed with about 1,600 inhabitants — a population that Manhattan could not match until twenty-three years after it was founded.[47]

The Kansa tribe's move to Blue Earth Village around 1780 was likely facilitated by a massive epidemic of smallpox that ravaged Native Americans at that time, depopulating extensive swaths of land.[48] Before 1780 the tribe's principal village had been further east, near the junction of the Kansas River and Missouri River — the location of Kansas City today. When the Kansa moved their settlement to the mouth of the Big Blue River, it was about as close as the tribe was able to get on a permanent basis to the great herds of bison on the high plains in central and western Kansas without entering the territory of their traditional enemies, the Pawnees. (Even though the Kansa stayed to the east, in 1812 the Pawnees attacked Blue Earth Village, where the outnumbered Kansa achieved a stunning victory, killing many of the Pawnee's greatest warriors.)[49]

The Kansa followed a semi-sedentary lifestyle at Blue Earth Village. The tribe only occupied the settlement from mid-March to mid-May, and again from mid-August to mid-October. The other months were spent camped in bison-hide teepees on the vast western plains of Kansas hunting bison and elk (and dodging the Pawnee), because the large herds of bison integral to the Kansa lifestyle almost never ventured into the hilly country surrounding Blue Earth Village.

While in Blue Earth Village, the Kansa did not live in teepees: the housing there was composed of large circular or rectangular lodges. U.S. Army Major George Champlain Sibley visited the village in 1811 and observed that the domed lodges were "constructed of stout poles and saplings arranged in the form of an arbor and covered with skins, bark and mats; they are commodious and quite comfortable."[50] The interior walls were decorated with mats. The floors of the lodges were dug out to the depth of one to two feet below ground, and encircling the inside of the lodges were raised wooden platforms where the families stored skins, food, weapons, and other personal property. In August 1819 Blue Earth Village was visited by another U.S. expedition, which included the artist Samuel Seymour, who drew a detailed sketch of a war dance and the interior of a Kansa lodge. Seymour's party noted that inside the lodge "several medicine bags are carefully attached to the mats of the wall, these are cylindrical, and neatly bound up; several reeds are usually placed upon them, and a human scalp serves for the fringe and tassels."[51]

Major Sibley wrote that Blue Earth Village comprised 128 such lodges, bunched closely together: "The town is built without much regard to order; there are no regular streets or avenues. The lodges are erected pretty compactly together in crooked rows, allowing barely space sufficient to admit

*Kansa dog dance inside a lodge at Blue Earth Village. This sketch was
drawn by Samuel Seymour, a member of Stephen Long's exploring
party of 1819. It is the earliest surviving picture known to be drawn
in Kansas. (Courtesy of Kansas State Historical Society.)*

a man to pass between them. The avenues between these crooked rows are
kept in tolerable decent order and the village is on the whole rather neat
and cleanly."[52] While walking the paths between the lodges, yelping packs of
dogs would have weaved around the inhabitants' feet. In the land surrounding the village, the Kansa cultivated acres of maize, beans, melons, squash,
and pumpkins. Beyond the cropland, according to Sibley, "The prairie was
covered with their horses and mules."

The Kansa are of Siouan linguistic stock, and the tribe was closely associated with the Osage, its neighbors to the south. Yet the men of the tribe
had their own distinctive appearance: most of them plucked all the hair on
their arms, face, and head, except for a single lock of hair at the top and
back of their head, sometimes colored with vermilion or decorated with
an eagle feather. Like other semi-sedentary prairie tribes, they dressed in
breechcloth, leggings, and moccasins made from deerskins. In the warmer
months, the men were "generally naked with exception of the small [breech-
cloth] and sometimes a blanket thrown over their shoulders."[53] They decorated their ears with beads and other trinkets, and many had tattoos. The

women wore wraparound skirts, also made from deerskin, decorated with porcupine quills and beadwork.

The staples of the Kansa diet were buffalo meat, sweet boiled maize, and beans.[54] The 1819 party of explorers reported after sampling the food that "this mixture constituted an agreeable food; it was served up to us in large wooden bowls, which were placed on bison robes or mats, on the ground; as many of us as could conveniently eat from one bowl sat round it . . . and in common we partook of its contents by means of large spoons made of bison horn."[55] The men sometimes supplemented the bison meat by fishing or hunting deer and game birds around Blue Earth Village.

For entertainment, the Kansa enjoyed swimming in the two rivers flowing by their village or engaging in competitions such as gambling, horse racing, and wrestling. Part of their religion involved boys around the age of twelve or thirteen going on vision quests, at which time they went into the surrounding Flint Hills for several days without food and water. Upon death, the Kansa were interred in surrounding graves along with important mementos, and if the deceased was male, his best horse was killed and added to the gravesite.[56]

Although European American explorers occasionally visited Blue Earth Village, many early travelers regarded the Kansa as dangerous and unfriendly. Raiding their enemies was an important part of Kansa culture, and the tribe was said to cut out the hearts of their foes and burn them as an offering to the four winds. The Kansa's negative reputation with explorers was probably clinched when the tribe kidnapped French explorer Pierre Vial in 1792 while he was scouting a route between Santa Fe and St. Louis. Vial was threatened with death but was eventually released. When the American explorers Meriwether Lewis and William Clark passed near the mouth of the Kansas River in June 1804, they were informed that the Kansa "are a fierce & warlike people." When returning by the same route in 1806, Lewis and Clark encountered hunters who were nervous about tarrying at the mouth of the Kansas River for fear of the tribe. Similarly, in 1809 a member of the St. Louis Missouri Fur Company reported that "the Cansas have long been the terror of the neighboring Indians, their temerity is hardly credible. . . . They rob, murder and destroy when opportunity offers; fortunately for their neighbors, they are few in number."[57]

The Kansa were at the height of their influence while at Blue Earth Village. At that time, the Kansa controlled the northeastern part of the state

Chief Wom-pa-wa-rah (White Plume), leader of the Kansa at Blue Earth Village. This nineteenth-century lithograph is based on an earlier portrait by Charles Bird King, painted when White Plume visited President James Monroe in Washington, D.C., in 1821 as part of a Native American delegation. (Courtesy of Kansas State Historical Society.)

(along the Kansas River) and the allied Osage controlled the southeastern (along the Arkansas River), while the rival Pawnee exerted control in lands to the north and west of the Kansa. But beginning in the mid-1820s the United States initiated the forced resettlement of eastern Native American tribes out of white-dominated areas and into "Indian territory," in what would later become Kansas, Oklahoma, and Nebraska. To make room for this resettlement, the U.S. government concluded a treaty with the Kansa, dated June 3, 1825, wherein the tribe agreed to cede 20 million acres of land and settle within defined boundaries. The treaty was signed in St. Louis by superintendent of Indian Affairs William Clark and six Kansa leaders, including Chief Wom-pa-wa-rah ("White Plume").

On land ceded by the Kansa, in the far northeast corner of Kansas, the government soon situated the Iowa Nation, the Sauk and Fox from Missouri, and the Kickapoo — all of which retain reservations in the area. The Delaware, Potawatomi, and Shawnee were settled south of these tribes, along opposite banks of the Kansas River, while further west the Kansa were provided a large reservation for themselves centered on Blue Earth Village.[58] The 1825 Kansa treaty and the treaties relocating the other tribes indicated that the tribes would have this land permanently, and the United States planned a stable border between Indian territory and the state of Missouri.[59]

In fulfillment of one of the terms of the Kansa treaty, in 1827 the U.S. government established an agency for the tribe several miles east of Blue Earth Village, near the Wakarusa River. As soon as the agency was established, Chief White Plume and much of the Kansa tribe departed Blue Earth Village to settle nearer the agency. In 1830 the rest of the tribe abandoned Blue Earth Village, following three other chiefs: Kah-he-ga-wah-che-hah ("Hard Chief"), Kah-he-gah-wa-ti-an-gah ("Fool Chief"), and a man known as American Chief.

Although the Native Americans thought that they had their new lands permanently, by the mid-1840s Congress directed that the treaties be renegotiated, with an eye to opening the land for westward trails and white settlement. Accordingly, by a treaty dated January 14, 1846, the Kansa land was further reduced to a narrow stretch of land between the future towns of Manhattan and Topeka, for the first time opening the possibility of legal European American settlement at the junction of the Kansas River and Big Blue River.[60] In coming decades, the U.S. government would continue to move the Kansa again and again, eventually ordering the tribe completely

An 1841 drawing of the Kansa village, showing typical domed lodges, organized by Fool Chief near the Indian agency. (Courtesy of Kansas State Historical Society.)

out of their ancestral lands — which kept their name — and onto a reservation in what became the state of Oklahoma.

By 1854 the federal policy of marginalization and removal of Native Americans in present-day eastern Kansas was thoroughly accomplished, and the land was ready for white settlement. That autumn author Charles Boynton observed the emptiness of the land from a location in the Flint Hills:

> Now let the eye range round the circumference of this circle — one hundred and fifty miles, at the very least. See this plain around us — fifty miles, or more, across . . . we listen for the voices of human life. We start at the result. Not a single human dwelling can the eye detect in all the vast amphitheater; not even smoke curls up anywhere to tell of life; not a sound can be heard, beyond ourselves, that indicates the presence of man.[61]

Although the location was deserted, the site of old Blue Earth Village, together with outlying burying grounds, was obvious to Manhattan's white settlers when they arrived in 1854 and 1855, and was known by them as the Kaw City.[62] Because the Kansa lodges were dug into the ground, their foundations, together with many of the lodges' sod walls and poles, remained in place in 1854. Additionally, as early settler Amos Powers wrote, "Scattered about these ruins and grounds were corn cobs, beads, arrow heads, springs from steel traps, gun barrels, and very often was found good specimens of the famous red stone pipes that resembled marble — just the bowl; no stems."[63] But early Manhattanites made no real efforts toward preservation; in 1906 a longtime Manhattan resident wrote, "The many lodge circles that were once plainly to be seen in the fields are now fast disappearing under the leveling influence of the plow and the elements."[64] Today, the site of the old village for the tribe that gave the state of Kansas its name is located in eastern Manhattan. Much of the land is covered by an industrial park and vast concrete parking lots for shopping centers and car dealerships.[65]

In contrast to the steady settlement and cultivation of the land by Native Americans, the early European American presence in the land was far more intermittent, and their view of the land was far less positive. Before the Kansa moved to Blue Earth Village, the first European to set foot on the land that would become the state of Kansas was the Spanish conquistador Francisco Vasquez de Coronado. In 1541 — some eighty years before the *Mayflower* landed at Plymouth Harbor — Coronado traveled north from Mexico looking for Quivira, a mythical land of gold. In July he reached Kansas with thirty mounted Spanish soldiers. Historical evidence suggests that Coronado and his party traveled east up the Kansas River, past the current location of Salina, Kansas, stopping a few miles short of where Manhattan is now located.[66] At that point Coronado, seeing nothing but endless rolling prairie, gave up his search for the mythical land and turned back to the southwest. Soldiers traveling with Coronado apparently discarded their chain mail armor soon after, leaving it to be discovered centuries later in the fields of Kansas.

More than 260 years later, in July 1804, Lewis and Clark became the first recorded explorers from the United States to set foot in Kansas, during their exploratory trip to the Pacific Ocean. Others soon followed. In 1805 aging frontiersman Daniel Boone began taking regular hunting expeditions from his home in Missouri up the Kansas River in the direction of Manhattan's future site. The next year explorer Zebulon M. Pike (immortalized with Pike's Peak in Colorado) passed over the Great Plains on his way to the Rockies and concluded that much of the territory was nearly uninhabitable. In 1819–1820, mountaineer Stephen Long followed Pike's footsteps and labeled the area the "Great American Desert" on his published map of Kansas.

Pike's and Long's descriptions of the prairie as uninhabitable were widely accepted and helped influence the U.S. government to reserve the land between Missouri and the Rocky Mountains as territory for Native Americans from the 1820s to 1850s. Indeed, Pike observed that white settlers are "prone to rambling and extending themselves on the frontiers," but he predicted in 1811 that his "desert" would limit their spread "to the borders of the Missouri and Mississippi, while they leave the prairies incapable of cultivation to the wandering and uncivilized aborigines of the country." Nonetheless, U.S. citizens trickled slowly into the Indian territory that eventually became Kansas: the American Fur Company traded in Kansas, the Santa Fe Trail was established through Kansas in 1821, and in 1827 Fort Leavenworth was built on the Kansas side of the Missouri River—the first permanent white settlement in Kansas—to guard travelers on the nation's frontier. Finally, in the early 1840s, the Oregon Trail developed through Kansas as more and more Americans traveled into the West.

1854
"A MOST APPROPRIATE TOWN SITE"

On January 24, 1848, gold was discovered in the hills of northern California — the birth of the California Gold Rush. Nine days later, Mexico signed a treaty that transferred ownership of California to the United States, with no idea of the fortune it was losing. By 1849 word of easy money in the California hills had spread throughout the United States, and over the next two years 70,000 men beat a trail to California via the overland routes — the Santa Fe Trail and the Oregon/California Trail — taking them straight through the Native American lands that would become Kansas Territory.[1]

Following on the heels of this overland traffic came the first permanent settlement of U.S. citizens in the vicinity of what would become Manhattan. In 1853 the U.S. Army established Fort Riley eighteen miles west of the future location of Manhattan, largely to guard travelers on the westward trails.[2] In order to build and supply this new fort, the "Military Road" was established between Fort Leavenworth and the site of Fort Riley. (The U.S. Army had hoped to use steamboats to travel up the Kansas River to supply the new Fort Riley, but the army quickly discovered that the river was too shallow.) The trail generally followed the winding path of the Kansas River, and it was conceived as the main route into central Kansas and on to the Rocky Mountains.[3] As part of the road, the U.S. Army in 1853 assigned Samuel D. Dyer, a fifty-two-year-old Tennessee native, to run a U.S. government ferry across the Big Blue River, five miles north of the confluence with the Kansas River (Manhattan's future location) and one mile below an old river crossing known as "Rocky Ford."[4]

Other than Dyer, in 1853 virtually the only U.S. citizens living permanently on the lands that would become Kansas were religious missionaries

residing with Native Americans and U.S. soldiers stationed at Fort Leavenworth, Fort Scott, and Fort Riley.[5] But that would change as soon as the U.S.
government finished renegotiating Native American treaties — creating vast
tracts of empty land — and white "squatters" in the territory pushed hard to
open the land to legal settlement.

On May 30, 1854, the Kansas-Nebraska Act became law, creating the Territory of Kansas and officially opening it to settlement by American citizens.
The Kansas-Nebraska Act also effectively repealed the Missouri Compromise and opened the question of whether Kansas would be a slave state.
(The Missouri Compromise had prohibited slavery in any new territories
north of latitude 36°30'. Kansas Territory was north of this line, so slavery
would have been barred in the new territory under the Missouri Compromise.) Pursuant to the terms of the Kansas-Nebraska Act, settlers coming
to Kansas Territory would elect representatives to the first Territorial Legislature in 1855, which would in turn vote on whether Kansas would be a
slave state.[6] Ironically, this "popular sovereignty" provision in the act was
intended, in part, to hold together the unraveling Union. Instead, it helped
further split apart the North and South.

Predictably, in an effort to sway the slavery vote, in 1854 settlers began
rushing into Kansas Territory from states that strongly opposed slavery and
states that allowed slavery — mainly neighboring Missouri, home to 90,000
slaves.[7] The violent clashes that would follow were almost inevitable.

As settlers streamed into the newly created Kansas Territory, Samuel
Dyer, who operated the Military Road crossing on the Big Blue River, and
who had a near monopoly on traffic, smartly surmised that his crossing was
a prime location to start a settlement. Thus, in 1854 Dyer and his wife staked
out a "city" on the east bank of his river crossing, naming it Juniata.[8] (Writer
Horace Greeley later joked, "It takes three log houses to make a city in Kansas, but they begin *calling* it a city so soon as they have staked out the lots.")
Juniata, located about five miles north of where Manhattan now sits, was the
first non–Native American civilian settlement in the immediate area.

As traffic at the crossing increased, Dyer opened a small market in his
cabin. He and his wife also threw open the doors of their roomy log cabin
to serve as a boardinghouse. It was a welcoming spot in an otherwise deso-
late land, with four separate rooms, three big fireplaces, and accommodat-
ing hosts.[9] One early visitor appreciatively called it a "hospitable dwelling
where all travelers find a good home," and another raved it was "the best

and cheapest accommodations you can find in the Territory."[10] Supper was provided to guests at a large table together with the Dyer family. As one guest noted, "we sat down in the midst of the family, there being no alternative, unless we, or the family, should occupy the outside of the house."[11] A representative meal shared at the Dyer table was wild turkey and warm biscuits.[12]

In September 1854, a few months after Juniata was established, the Dyers were visited by a small party of travelers from Cincinnati led by the preacher Charles Boynton, who was researching a Kansas travel manual for Free-Staters, published the following year under the title *A Journey through Kansas*. In the book Boynton praised the Dyers' hospitality but also noted an incident where Samuel Dyer was unsettled by his wife's comment that he "used to say grace, before he came out here, but since we came to this place he has lost his manners." Boynton wrote, "The old man seemed to lose 'his manners' in another sense, after this frank confession of his wife. He was moody during the meal, and answered us rather gruffly, in some things."[13] After dinner, Boynton and his party were shown to their sleeping quarters and began to undress when Samuel Dyer "walked in with his pipe in his hand, a most capacious one, filled it, lighted it at the candle, and sat down as if he felt at home, in his own home, unmindful of the turning down and tucking up of bed-clothes, and the half undressed condition of his guests." Boynton's account continued:

> Something evidently was lying with great weight on his mind. He smoked with nervous energy, while it was clear that his conversation was only a skirmishing of outposts, a prelude to something which he had not yet got at. . . . Smoke now filled the room so that one of the party was absolutely "smoked out," and was obliged to seek the open air. I suggested to the old man that the tobacco had sickened him. It took him quite by surprise. It had not even occurred to him that anybody could dislike tobacco. As to the idea that his presence in our sleeping apartment was an intrusion, I saw that he could never be made to comprehend that, and what sort of a writ of ejectment could be served upon him was becoming a serious question, and though much amused, we were also not a little annoyed.[14]

In the end, Boynton coaxed Dyer, a physically imposing six-footer, into leaving the room by offering to pray with him, and the party was able to get some needed sleep. Dyer and his wife undoubtedly found their Christianity mollified a few weeks later on November 5, 1854, when the Reverend Charles Emerson Blood, a Congregational minister originally from New England, settled in Juniata with his wife Mary Coffin Blood and started preaching.[15]

Around the same time, the prospects for Dyer's settlement were boosted dramatically when the U.S. government constructed a grand 360-foot oak bridge over the Big Blue River there in October 1854 to replace the ferry service — the first significant fixed bridge anywhere in Kansas.[16] That same month Dyer hosted a meeting of all settlers on the Big Blue River, after which they released a series of resolutions that stated in part, "The Commercial, Natural and Geographical centre [of Kansas Territory] must certainly be on the Kansas River, near the mouth of the Big Blue . . . [and] we are deeply interested in building up a commercial point, somewhere in this vicinity, which appears to be the natural terminus for good Steam Boat navigation on the Kansas."[17] (The settlers were in fact correct that the junction with the Big Blue would prove to be the head of navigation on the Kansas River.)

As the Juniata settlement grew, it attracted a decisive proslavery element. The community's preacher, Rev. Charles Blood, was a solemn abolitionist who later wrote that he traveled to Kansas Territory "to fight the battles of freedom and save this beautiful country from the blighting curse of slavery," yet despite Blood's abolitionist influence, and despite the presence in Juniata of a handful of 1854 Free-State emigrants from New England, the settlement tilted proslavery.[18] Slaves could be seen following their masters down Juniata's dusty street. A resident named Chestina Allen recorded in her diary on March 18, 1855: "Booth Fox and his slave woman passed by to day. The poor creature had no covering for her head but picked up a cast off cap while in the neighborhood and went off running after her master and his ox team."[19] (Months later, Fox traded his slave for a stallion.)[20]

Dyer, an old Tennessean, was part of the proslavery component in Juniata. Manhattan settler Thomas Wells wrote in early 1856, "Mr. Dyer has turned strong pro slavery. . . . They have organized a church under pro slavery influence and intend to do all they can to bring slaves into Kansas and drive out the Yankees, 'for' they say 'they do not want Eastern men to rule the territory.'"[21] Dr. Samuel Whitehorn, a young doctor from Michigan who moved to Juniata in November 1854, later described Dyer as "a man of unusual kindness, and practical benevolence," even "generous to a fault," but also noted, "[he] was prejudiced by southern oratory, and political interpretations, from which source he drew his pro-slavery opinions."[22]

Later, after Manhattan was founded, Juniata for a time would act as a rival and counterweight to Manhattan's Free-State sentiment.[23] Yankee settler Thomas Wells noted "the society [near Juniata] is not such as I would choose it being mostly composed of western and Southern people, some of them very good neighbors in their way, and others pretty strongly tinctured with pro slavery notions, while the greater part of the settlers on the west side of the Blue are Eastern men."[24] Despite the differences, however, no major conflicts between the two settlements ever developed.

Dyer was not alone in the area for long. In the fall of 1854, a few months after Juniata was founded, George Shepard Park, a land speculator from Parkville, Missouri, established the first European American settlement within the borders of what would become Manhattan.[25] Park named his prospective village Polistra, derived from a Greek word (*polis*) referring to a city-state.[26]

George Park, a squat forty-three-year-old, was well accomplished and a prominent man in the region. The Vermont native was a veteran of the Texas War of Independence: he volunteered to serve under Col. James Fannin in 1836, after the Mexican Army and General Santa Anna crossed into Texas. In the signal event of his service, Park faced near certain death after Fannin surrendered his forces to the Mexican army after the Battle of Coleto. Days after the surrender, in an event known as the Goliad Massacre, Santa Anna ordered that hundreds of American prisoners, including Park, be shot while on a forced march. Park was one of fewer than 30 men to escape the massacre, while 342 were killed.[27]

After the war, Park invested shrewdly in land in Illinois and Missouri, and in 1844 he founded the town of Parkville, Missouri. By 1854 Parkville was thriving, and Park himself was editor of the town's newspaper, the Parkville *Industrial Luminary*. Park was also doing well financially by this time; his land speculation had paid off, and he was renowned as a man of "immense wealth."[28] A newspaper in Kansas Territory reported that he was "worth near half a million" at the time.[29] If accurate, this easily made Park one of the richest men on the frontier — although his wealth was almost completely tied up in land ownership.

Park selected the location for his new Polistra settlement while taking a trip up the Kansas River on the steamboat *Excel* in June 1854.[30] Following his trip, Park wrote of the future location of Manhattan: "We passed a large grove of timber on the right, and then passed a most appropriate town

*George S. Park, 1868. (Courtesy of Fishburn Archives,
Park University, Parkville, Missouri.)*

site — the first we saw for several miles. Here we saw Blue Hill, which is a prominent landmark overlooking the mouth of the Blue river. From this point upward the bluffs are higher and more abrupt, and the country back more elevated and broken."[31] Park also recorded that at the mouth of the Big Blue River he "saw a large eagle nest, out of which the old bird looked angrily at us, for intruding on its pre-emption; but she, too, must give way, with the red skins, to manifest destiny."[32] Concluding his report on the area, Park wrote, "We were pleased with its fine bottoms and long streak of timber; while, on the left, were conical bluffs and high prairie mounds, . . . contributing to the scenery a very romantic appearance."[33]

Park returned to the spot five months later in November 1854 and marked out Polistra. He also erected a log cabin on the site, with the aid of Rev. Charles Blood and Seth Child, another pioneer who had also recently settled nearby with his family.[34] The cabin was located near the junction of the Kansas River and Wildcat Creek and was the first building erected by European Americans within the borders of present-day Manhattan.[35] Park probably erected the cabin in the hope of securing a legal claim to the surrounding acreage under the federal Preemption Act of 1841, which allowed settlers to claim ownership of land if they lived on it for a certain period of time.

Although Park came to Kansas Territory from proslavery territory in western Missouri, his personal politics were not proslavery. He wrote in 1855 that he loved both the North and the South and favored "moderating the extremes . . . to promote the general good of the country."[36] Negotiating this moderate stance in the heated political environment of 1854–1855 was difficult, and months after he founded Polistra, in April 1855, a proslavery mob in Parkville wrecked Park's printing press for the *Industrial Luminary* and threw his type into the river because it believed he was a Free-Stater.[37] Park had intended to use his press to print a newspaper for Polistra beginning later that year, to be named the *Central American*.[38] Because of the actions of the Parkville mob, the *Central American* was never published. Whatever his politics, Park's true motive for establishing Polistra was almost certainly monetary, as part of his pattern of land speculation. In fact, he began advertising the sale of plots of land in Kansas Territory in his Parkville newspaper as soon as he erected his cabin.[39]

Meanwhile, the same month that Park built his cabin, November 1854, a second outpost within the borders of present-day Manhattan was also founded.[40] Named Canton, this colony was northeast of Polistra, several hundred feet up the Big Blue River, at the base of Bluemont Hill.[41] The Canton settlement was organized by Samuel D. Houston, a thirty-six-year-old strident abolitionist from Illinois.[42] (He was no relation to the general of similar name in the Texas War of Independence.) Houston was a tall, stout-framed frontiersman with black hair and dark eyes. As a speaker, Houston was described as dynamic but "oftimes crude in expression."[43] Most descriptively, one contemporary wrote, "His temperament is bilious, *decidedly*."[44] Despite his rough exterior, the *Lawrence Herald of Freedom* in 1857 described Houston as "a Free State man, against whom not a share of aspersion has ever been thrown. He is a devoted friend of Freedom in Kansas."[45]

Before establishing Canton, Houston had been in the area for almost a year, illegally squatting with his family on land north of the current borders of Manhattan and south of Juniata.[46] When Houston staked his original claim, in December 1853, the Kansas-Nebraska Act had not been enacted, so the land was still closed to white settlement. As a squatter, Houston likely raised the ire of the Native Americans who were being removed from the land. It is not surprising, therefore, that his family was reportedly harassed by Native Americans during this period.

After the passage of the Kansas-Nebraska Act in May 1854, Houston decided to organize his family and four other newly arriving settlers into a town company.[47] One of the members of Houston's new Canton Company was Judge Sanders W. Johnston, who had been dispatched to Kansas Territory by U.S. President Franklin Pierce to serve as one of three territorial judges.[48] The other three Canton Company members were J. M. Russell; Horace A. Wilcox, a Baptist clergyman from Connecticut; and Elisha Madison (E. M.) Thurston, the former secretary of the Maine Board of Education, who had come to Kansas Territory in hopes of improving his rapidly failing health. All three were New Englanders, and the latter two men were part of an organized group of settlers sent to Kansas by the New England Emigrant Aid Company in 1854.[49]

Johnston, Russell, Wilcox, and Thurston started the winter of 1854 in tents, until Russell built a dugout cabin — essentially a half-cave/half-cabin dwelling — at the base of Bluemont Hill.[50] Like Park, the men in the Canton Company hoped to preempt title to the surrounding land. When word spread during the winter of 1854–1855 that preemption might not be possible until the land was officially surveyed, Thurston complained in a letter to the *Industrial Luminary* in January 1855: "If those of us who have settled in

Samuel D. Houston, the fiery frontiersman, as he appeared later in life.
(Courtesy of Kansas State Historical Society.)

good faith on the unsurveyed lands have no rights that can be protected, the sooner that fault is known the better." Houston, meanwhile, left these four men to their primitive residences and, together with his wife and children, claimed another parcel of land west of Manhattan on Wildcat Creek. Here Houston erected a sturdy log cabin with no windows and a thick door to fend off feared attacks by Native Americans.[51]

Near the close of the year, in December 1854, George Park described the conditions at the mouth of the Big Blue River, writing, "Soft hands and soft heads are of no use, at present, in the country; money can't purchase comfort and convenience; even our august President Frank Pierce, were he here, would have to work or starve."[52] As winter set in, Park left his cabin in Polistra to pass the season in more developed regions of Texas and Missouri while the rest of the new emigrants settled in.[53] Through the winter of 1854, these scattered residents were the sole inhabitants of the land that would later become Manhattan.

3
WINTER 1854–1855
A NEW ENGLAND CRUSADE

Fifteen-hundred miles from Polistra and Canton, during the winter of 1854–1855, the town of Providence, Rhode Island, was experiencing "Kansas fever." Swept up into the excitement was Isaac Tichenor Goodnow, a thin, stern New England abolitionist who would prove to be the true lodestar of Manhattan's founding.[1] At the time, Goodnow was a forty-year-old lecturer and teacher of natural science at the Providence Conference Seminary, an academy in nearby East Greenwich, Rhode Island.[2] But he would soon leave behind that quiet life of letters to move to the frontier in support of the Free-State movement.

On December 5, 1854, Goodnow attended the first in a series of weekly Kansas meetings held in Providence's Franklin Hall, which featured a rousing speech by Eli Thayer, cofounder of the New England Emigrant Aid Company.[3] Thayer explained that the company had organized five groups of settlers who had traveled to Kansas Territory in 1854 (including E. M. Thurston and Horace Wilcox) and had founded the thriving Free-State village of Lawrence. He also said that the company planned to send hundreds more to Kansas Territory in the spring of 1855 and to found a second Free-State community — which would turn out to be Manhattan. Thayer's speech was followed the next week by a speech from Samuel C. Pomeroy, an agent for the company and a future two-term U.S. senator from Kansas, and two weeks later, on December 19, by the official formation of the Providence Kanzas League.[4]

The *Providence Freeman* newspaper later wrote of Thayer's speech: "We have seldom listened to a more effective speech on any subject."[5] Indeed, it was Thayer's speech and a one-and-a-half-hour private conversation that followed that ultimately convinced Goodnow to support the movement by immigrating to Kansas Territory.[6] It could not have been an easy decision: Goodnow was a true New England Yankee, born and raised in Vermont to parents whose families had emigrated from England to Massachusetts Colony. More important, Goodnow worried about the fragile health of his wife, Ellen; it was questionable whether she could handle the primitive conditions in Kansas Territory. In fact, after learning that the Goodnows were considering moving to Kansas, one worried friend wrote that he feared Ellen's "health is too feeble for a residence in a locality where she may be deprived of some of the items which might add to her comfort which could only be had in an older settlement—a new country is a new country and time is required to bring it into order."[7] Another friend was more direct in writing to Ellen:

> I do not want you to go—and I cannot see any *duty* in your going. You, my dear Mrs. Goodnow, will not be able to endure the hardship you will be called to bear, and you know you used to tell me that it was binding upon us to do all in our power to preserve life and health. But I suppose it is useless for *me* to say anything on this subject. You have, undoubtedly, decided the matter.[8]

Ultimately, the Goodnows decided that Isaac had a moral obligation to move to Kansas Territory to support the Free-State movement, and that Ellen would follow if it seemed prudent after Isaac developed a homestead in Kansas.[9] Isaac later wrote of his calling, "Believing that the rule of Slavery or of Freedom in the nation would be settled on the prairies of Kansas I felt impelled to throw myself into the scale, on the side of Freedom."[10] As Goodnow and many others saw it, this was the great good work that had fallen to New Englanders.

After reaching the decision to go, Isaac Goodnow promptly took a leading role in convincing other Yankees "of the right stamp" to settle in Kansas—giving speeches and writing letters and newspaper articles.[11] (Goodnow had an opinion about which settlers he preferred: he favored abolitionists and Methodists for the new settlement. He was not alone in desiring only a select group of immigrants; one future company settler named Samuel Wynn wrote to Goodnow: "There are two Irishmen (Catholics)

Isaac Goodnow in the 1850s, around the time he moved to Kansas Territory.
(Courtesy of Kansas State Historical Society.)

which want to go with us but we don't want them. One of them is going to Boston tomorrow to see if he can get some tickets. If you can prevent him from getting them we would feel very much obliged.")[12]

Goodnow first expressed his enthusiasm for emigration in a letter to a friend on December 16, 1854, writing: "I well understand the cry that Kansas *must & will be Free!* . . . There is only *one way* to have it, this is for every lover of Freedom with a strong will & the ability to start to make his arrangements with his best friends, or without them to go right on to the ground, and whatever he has of talent, money & influence, to use them *heartily* for Liberty!"[13] Goodnow also wrote newspaper articles extolling the virtues of Kansas and the New England Emigrant Aid Company, including a column published in the *East Greenwich Weekly Pendulum* on January 13, 1855, in which he declared, "Kansas is, and may be for years to come the great battle ground of Freedom and Slavery!" Goodnow continued: "While we talk, slave holders act. We have had enough of abstract, easy-chair speculations, it is now time for every man to show his principles by his works. . . . The *only* way to save the territory from the curse of human bondage, is for the men of puritan blood, the *practical Christians* of New England to rouse themselves, and emigrate by hundreds and thousands." Goodnow acknowledged in his column that emigrants "must be willing to endure hardship and privations," but he challenged his fellow Yankees by asking, "who would not make sacrifices in one of the most philanthropic enterprizes of this age?"

Quibbling with Goodnow's rhetoric, the *Providence Freeman* responded that Goodnow made a "very great and a very fatal mistake" in arguing that Kansas was the battleground, asserting instead that keeping New England strongly abolitionist was the key to fighting slavery.[14] Nevertheless, the paper opined, "We are glad to see so many intelligent and able bodied men interesting themselves in this movement." The *Providence Daily Tribune* was more enthusiastic, writing: "We cannot refuse encouragement to this spirit of emigration. . . . Our farmers are taking this Kansas fever. They are getting tired of this soils and rocks and frosts. Not a few of them — the very best of them — will go West in the spring. They are not the men our State can best spare; but their own circumstances will be improved by this change; and we offer no objection."[15]

Goodnow's decision to travel to Kansas Territory, and his newspaper articles on the subject, helped attract additional settlers to the cause.[16] One acquaintance wrote to Goodnow: "I am truly happy when I hear of men of

influence who are not only ready to write upon the subject but to act to go
on to the ground with companies of men and contest the battles of freedom.
Action is what is wanted."[17] Another friend wrote to Goodnow, "As I read
your article I thought of the crusaders in other days in seeking recruits for
the Holy Lands. This article shows that you have entered into the spirit of
the enterprise."[18] By January, Goodnow was besieged with letters containing
questions regarding immigration to Kansas and requests to join the company. One hopeful wrote to Goodnow: "I put myself down as one of the
right sort to go to Kansas. . . . I do not know but I have too exalted an opinion of the western land, but I think that's the land for me."[19]

Ultimately, many in New England found in Kansas immigration a cause
that was worth sacrificing for. Hundreds decided to join the movement, and
many sold their New England homes and the bulk of their possessions to
raise the necessary funds. Among those who decided to go was Isaac Goodnow's brother, William Eaton Goodnow. Hinting at the hazardous nature of
the decision to emigrate, William Goodnow renewed his life insurance and
acquired several guns in preparation for the move.[20]

The Yankees' fervor for moving to the frontier to fight slavery fell in line
with the ideals of the transcendentalist movement, which was then enjoying its full flowering in New England.[21] Personified by Henry Thoreau and
Ralph Waldo Emerson, transcendentalism was an intellectual movement
that emphasized nature, mysticism, and personal freedom, including abolitionism and women's rights. Thoreau had just published the most famous
transcendentalist work, *Walden*, in 1854. In 1855 Emerson would inspire
Walt Whitman to publish the first edition of his collection of poems, *Leaves
of Grass*. In the coming years, while the Yankee immigrants carried many
of their ideals to Kansas Territory, Emerson and Thoreau also became re-
motely involved in the events in Kansas through their support of the abolitionist firebrand John Brown.[22]

In addition to the mystical qualities of transcendentalism, there was also
a more frankly religious aspect to the Kansas immigration — something like
a crusade. As already noted, Goodnow hoped to create a strong and pure
New England Protestant community in Kansas Territory with settlers "of
the right stamp." Significantly in this context, in the 1850s, many of the progressive organizations that worked on issues such as abolitionism, public
education, and civil rights for women were religious at root, having sprung
from the Second Great Awakening of religion in the United States.[23] The

intellectual flowering that accompanied this movement has sometimes been termed the American Renaissance, and the settlement of Manhattan — an antislavery and educational stronghold — fits squarely into this tradition.[24]

The New England Emigrant Aid Company initiated its 1855 expeditions to Kansas Territory in Boston. The trip generally consisted of three stages: a four-day railroad trip from Boston to Alton, Illinois, just north of St. Louis; a seven- or eight-day trip by steamboat across the state of Missouri to Kansas City; and finally a wagon trip beyond the western border of the United States into Kansas Territory.[25]

The first departure of 1855 was scheduled for Tuesday, March 13.[26] However, dozens of Kansas immigrants, including Isaac Goodnow, had already gathered in Boston by the fifth of the month, so the company decided to send an advance team a week early, consisting of sixty-eight members.[27] As Goodnow explained to his wife in a letter on March 5, "A train of events, appropriately Providential, have presented themselves that have decided me to start tomorrow with a number of persons already to go & explore & fix on a location by the time the mass of our friends come on."[28]

Thus, on an unseasonably warm afternoon on March 6, 1855, Goodnow and the advance group boarded a smoky train in Boston, beginning the first leg of their journey, the "tedious and tiresome" rail trip to Alton.[29] Goodnow was one of two unofficial leaders of the group; the other was Luke Lincoln, who the year before had helped to settle Lawrence in Kansas Territory.[30] Goodnow carried with himself a letter of introduction to Samuel C. Pomeroy, the company's advance agent in Kansas City, which stated, "Mr. G is with us in heart and hand, in the glorious cause in which we are engaged, and will battle manfully for Liberty."[31] (The letter also punned, "This letter will introduce you to I. T. Goodnow, Esq., who not only is good now, but I trust will remain good thro' all time for freedom and justice.") Goodnow was promised that Pomeroy would help him to select a site for the town.[32]

One week after the advance team set out, the season's first regularly scheduled party of about 190 New England settlers left Boston on March 13.[33] The group's conductor, Dr. Charles Robinson, one of three principal agents for the New England Company, "knew the ropes" in Kansas and could answer questions.[34] The year before, Robinson had helped to organize Lawrence, and later he became the first governor of Kansas.[35] The *Boston Journal* reported that at their departure "a song was sung as the train was about to leave the station, and when at last it moved away, cheer upon cheer bade an adieu."[36]

Similar to Isaac Goodnow, many members of these first two parties were men traveling west alone to establish a homestead before being joined by wives and children.[37] Emigration also wrought more enduring separations: William Goodnow was permanently separated from his beloved wife, Harriet, who promised her mother "she would never come to Kansas to be scalped by Indians."[38] On the other hand, several full families also made the trip west together. Isaac Goodnow wrote of his fellow travelers: "Several families, with a 'smart sprinkling' of children were among them. To me this was not very pleasing, as I *felt* that they must pass through severe tribulations, perhaps beyond what they could endure."[39]

Among the families traveling with Goodnow was forty-three-year-old Rev. Charles Haseltine Lovejoy; his pregnant wife, Julia; and their three children. Before setting out, Reverend Lovejoy wrote to Goodnow: "We are not 'chicken-hearted' in this matter. . . . I have been an opposer to Slavery from my earliest recollections — have acted with Abolitionists from the first."[40] Another couple, Francis and Maria Abbott, were married on the morning of March 13 and then together boarded the train for Kansas Territory that afternoon. The Abbots were going to Kansas Territory to escape work in the cotton mills of Lowell, Massachusetts, and upon arrival in Kansas settled near Manhattan.[41]

Also included among the emigrants departing on March 13, 1855, was Thomas Clarke Wells, a sickly twenty-two-year-old former student of Goodnow's from Wakefield, Rhode Island. Wells was a prolific letter-writer, and his letters home provide valuable insight into the thoughts of Manhattan's New England settlers, beginning with Wells's initial trepidation about the venture, which many of his fellow settlers shared. (Several emigrants turned back to New England at various points on the journey.) The day before leaving, Wells wrote to his father: "I met James at the depot in Providence and he had found the tickets at the Express Office. I must say I had really hoped that he would not get them and that would furnish a reason for returning home. . . . I may yet see it best to return and not go at all, but if I do go I may not stay — or but a short time at any rate."[42] Wells closed his letter by reflecting on the unknown into which the emigrants were traveling: "I doubt not but that all will in the end be for the best though what the end may be I am sure I cannot now tell."[43]

After March 13, smaller parties of emigrants continued to depart weekly from Boston through the spring and summer. Relatively few settlers in these later groups ended up in Manhattan.[44]

At the start of their journey, the first trainloads of emigrants in 1855 had their spirits lifted by cheering crowds that occasionally appeared to show support as the trains passed through New England.[45] One passenger on the train that departed on March 13 reported, "At Fitchburg [Massachusetts] not less than one thousand of the citizens met us at the depot, and greeted us with songs and cheers that thrilled the heart of every Kanzas bound pioneer."[46] But beyond New England the emigrants no longer received cheering crowds, and they had little to do but futilely attempt to sleep or look at the passing scenery. Reverend Lovejoy observed, "Most of our company having never seen a prairie country before, were greatly delighted and at times perfectly captivated with the splendid scenery, although much of the country lies too flat to suit a New Englander."[47]

Travel by railroad in 1855 was not luxurious; it was smoky, loud, cramped, and marked by the "incessant motion" of lurching cars.[48] Julia Lovejoy described the train trip as "one continuous routine of 'jar and whistle.'"[49] The final stretch of railroad for the emigrants was the worst. One New England passenger observed, "the Chicago, Alton and St. Louis railroad is the worst road over which I have ever traveled . . . , if much worse I think every train would be thrown from the track."[50] Another 1855 traveler wrote of the same line, "At times you would feelingly imagine the cars had left the track and were running on the cross-ties; we passed that section in the night, and it was unsafe to be a 'nid, nid, nodding,' without having your neck in danger of breaking."[51]

Sleeping was nearly impossible during the train trip. Goodnow reported that the best night's sleep he received before reaching St. Louis was one and a half hours.[52] Three days into the railroad trip Wells wrote to his father: "I shall be glad when we get to Kanzas or somewhere where one can 'stretch his weary limbs' once more, for though I am not very tired, yet sleeping for three or four successive nights in the cars is not the most comfortable way of resting, especially when cramped up with two on a seat all night."[53]

When the emigrants reached Alton, Illinois, they switched from trains to steam-powered paddleboats for the short trip to St. Louis and then up the Missouri River to Kansas City.[54] Reverend Lovejoy wrote that his boat from Alton to St. Louis was filled with exhausted New England emigrants: "Some were napping with distended jaws in a remote corner . . . while others were sprawled at full length on the cabin floor, snoring lustily, having very little regard for the rules of etiquette or the annoyance of their neighbors."[55] After changing boats in St. Louis, Lovejoy and Goodnow's advance party headed west up the Missouri River on the steamboat *Kate Swinney*, which also carried a company of about one hundred U.S. troops, ninety-five horses, and "a splendid band."[56] The next group of emigrants left from St. Louis a week later aboard the steamer *Lonora*.[57]

The emigrants were given a choice of at least two classes of travel on the Missouri steamboats. Steamboats of the era offered stateroom or cabin reservations and a half-price deck passage. Along with Goodnow and others, the Lovejoy family paid ten dollars per person for the higher class on the *Kate Swinney*. Julia Lovejoy was quite pleased with the accommodations, writing, "If you can travel 500 miles for this 'wee bit' living in princely style, your every want anticipated by swiftfooted waiters, officers and crew, with clocklike regularity, moving in their appointed sphere of action, eager to answer all of your inquiries and show you every indulgence, why — in this matter — *we congratulate your good fortune!*"[58]

In sharp contrast to the Lovejoys' experience on the *Kate Swinney*, Thomas Wells reported that the larger group of deck passengers on the *Lonora* were crowded together at night on the floors and tabletops of the indoor common areas, with sickness infecting nearly everyone. One of Wells's shipmates wrote: "We were crowded in the most uncomfortable manner; and in consequence of unavoidable exposure in our sleeping arrangements, almost every person in our party took a violent cold, from which many have since suffered severely."[59] Wells noted, "I doubt not but that I should have felt better and stronger had I remained in a chair by the stove, as, indeed, I did one night."[60]

But even paying a premium fare could not spare passengers from suffering the inconvenience of running aground on sandbars in the Missouri River. Both the *Kate Swinney* and the *Lonora* grounded themselves numerous times between St. Louis and Kansas City due to low water and fog. Wells reported: "Every day, and sometimes several times a day we are delayed from half an hour to three or four hours on a sand bar. . . . [Yesterday] we had to [walk] five or six miles around to a point while the steamer worked her way across the bar."[61] New Englanders also complained about the muddy drinking water drawn from the Missouri River.[62] One passenger on the *Lonora* wrote that it was an "unavoidably tedious journey," and Wells summed it up by writing, "This steamboating up the Missouri, where the water is as low as it is now, in a crowded boat is just the meanest way of getting along that I ever tried."[63]

Although proslavery Missourians attempted to avoid patronizing boats that carried Northerners, the riverboats on the Missouri River often also carried slaves and sometimes confrontational slave owners — making concrete the issues that were at stake in Kansas Territory.[64] Isaiah Harris, an 1855 immigrant to Kansas on a later boat from St. Louis, wrote in his journal that he met a slave owner onboard who "showed me a negro girl perhaps 12 years old that he said he was as much attached to as if she was his own child, which was the first person I ever seen that a was a slave that I knew of."[65] Harris soon also found fifty slaves being transported by their owner on the deck of his steamboat: "There they were old & young, male & female, all going to make their Master & Mistress a comfortable living and secure what their own necessities required if they could get it or if Master and Mistress pleased to let them have it, and to raise more young ones for Master & Mistress to sell or for whatever."[66] The New Englanders on the *Lonora* also met proslavery Missourians during the trip upriver, and Wells's letters reveal that the Yankees suffered verbal harassment, though he opined, "I think there is more danger of being frightened than hurt by them."[67] Similarly, when the steamboats tied up at Missouri river towns along the way, they were also occasionally stormed by drunken and armed proslavery mobs, and passengers were threatened with death if they continued into Kansas.[68] This misbehavior was encouraged by the proslavery Kansas newspaper *Squatter Sovereign,* which provided advance notice of the arrival of the 1855 New England emigrants and darkly opined, "We hope the Quarantine Officers along the borders will forbid the unloading of that kind of Cargo."[69] The *Sovereign* added that a "horrible disease, and one followed by many deaths, we fear, may be the consequence if this mass of corruption, and worse than leprous loathsomeness, is permitted to land and traverse our beautiful country."[70]

Despite the possibility of confrontation, or perhaps because of it, Luke Lincoln organized a glee club of New Englanders on the *Kate Swinney* to sing songs of liberty. (Lincoln did not shy from confronting proslavery men. In June 1855 he inspired one proslavery advocate in Kansas to write, "I abhor and scorn this itinerant Abolition lecturer as I do the most loathsome worm that lives; and I shall ever think of him as I do of the venomous and hideous serpent.")[71] One song sung on such trips to Kansas Territory was "The Kanzas Emigrants," by Joseph Greenleaf Whittier (sung to the tune of "Auld Lang Syne"):

> We cross the prairie, as of old
>   The pilgrims crossed the sea,
> To make the West, as they the East,
>   The homestead of the free.
> The homestead of the free, my boys
>   The homestead of the free,
> To make the West, as they the East,
>   The homestead of the free.
>
> We go to rear a wall of men
>   On Freedom's Southern line,
> And plant beside the cotton tree
>   The rugged Northern pine!
>   The rugged northern pine, my boys . . .
>
> We're flowing from our native hills,
>   As our free rivers flow;
> The blessing of our mother-land
>   Is on us as we go.
>   Is on us as we go, my boys . . .
>
> We go to plant her common schools
>   On distant prairie swells,
> And give the Sabbaths of the wild
>   The music of her bells.
>   The music of her bells, my boys . . .

4

MARCH 1855
"DAMNED YANKEES" COME TO KANSAS

On March 18, 1855, twelve days after leaving Boston, on a sunny and piercingly cold day, Isaac Goodnow's boat arrived in Kansas City, six days ahead of the *Lonora*. The immigrants were expecting to arrive in a sizable city with warm spring weather.[1] "How different the facts," lamented Isaac Goodnow.[2] Winter had not yet released its grip on Kansas Territory, and after the steamboat was secured and the planks lowered, the passengers disembarked and found in Kansas City a small, "cheerless" village covered with snow.[3] The town was situated "upon a clay bluff, very steep, with one dirty street along near the landing."[4] One New Englander archly noted of its name, "It takes but a few buildings in this western world to make a city."[5] Another complained, "The place itself, the inhabitants and the morals, are of an indescribably repulsive and undesirable character."[6] The travelers were relieved to find their hotel was only "a few steps distant" from where the boat had docked.[7]

When the immigrants arrived, Kansas City was abuzz with news of proslavery Missourians flooding into Kansas Territory to vote in the election for the Territorial Legislature. The immigrants also probably learned for the first time that the date of the election would be March 30 — less than two weeks away.[8] Hoping to set up camp in Kansas before that date, Goodnow's party hurried to join the throngs buying wagons, horses, and oxen to carry them and their belongings west.[9] (As Goodnow observed before leaving New England, "[the election] is of the first importance as this legislature will have the power to legislate Slavery into, or out of the Territory.")[10]

On March 19, the day after arriving in Kansas City, Goodnow met with Samuel C. Pomeroy to discuss the location of the company's new town in

Kansas Territory. Missourians had already claimed most of the desirable property along the border in 1854, so the Free-Staters were forced to look deeper into Kansas. Anticipating that the Kansas River could serve as a highway into the new town, as well as provide drinking water and a power source, Pomeroy had scouted likely sites along the river earlier that month. In a late-night discussion with Goodnow, the two men determined that Goodnow would settle the new town either 125 miles up the Kansas River at the mouth of the Big Blue River (the eventual site of Manhattan) or a few miles farther west, at the junction of the Smoky Hill and Republican rivers.[11] They also decided that Goodnow and five other members of the party would go ahead as an exploring committee to make the final determination on the location, while other men in the company would follow with oxen teams and heavier provisions.[12] The five selected to travel with Goodnow were Luke Lincoln, Joseph Wintermute, C. N. Wilson, Nathaniel R. (N. R.) Wright, and Rev. Charles Lovejoy.[13] Lovejoy brought along his seventeen-year-old son, making the total number in the advance team seven.[14] Goodnow stayed up until 3 A.M. of March 20 finalizing preparations.

Later that morning, Goodnow's advance team lurched west out of Kansas City in a covered wagon, pulled by two horses, "loaded to its utmost capacity with tents, mattresses, provisions, &c."[15] Goodnow's team followed the Military Road connecting Fort Leavenworth and Fort Riley into Kansas Territory, and on the second day — which began with a snowstorm — reached the Free-State town of Lawrence.[16] Goodnow described Lawrence at the time as "a rude town of some 40 or 50 log and rough board cabins."[17] Lawrence was "crowded to overflowing," with people swarming into the territory for the election, so the primitive hotel and nearly every other warm place to stay was filled.[18] Goodnow only escaped the cold and snowy conditions that night by sleeping on the floor of the offices of a Free-State newspaper, the *Herald of Freedom,* as a courtesy from the editor.[19] The next night the men stayed in the settlement of Topeka, in even more primitive conditions, sleeping in a dugout on the banks of the Kansas River.[20]

On the afternoon of Saturday, March 24, 1855, after five days on the trail, suffering with cold and snow all along the route, Goodnow's advance group reached Juniata and the government bridge over the Big Blue River.[21] In approaching Juniata, Goodnow's party followed the route described by Boynton the prior fall in *A Journey through Kansas,* descending into a valley in the mostly treeless Flint Hills to find "a dark-blue line, stretching along the expanse, and looking like the coast in the far distance over water, show[ing] us that we were approaching the 'timber' that skirts the banks of the Big Blue, the largest and most beautiful tributary of the Kansas."[22] Nestled among the trees was Dyer's log cabin, a lodging "of somewhat more than the ordinary pretensions, three stories long, and one story high, around which was a paling fence, formed of split sticks, indicating that the march of civilization had begun."[23]

Without stopping at Dyer's cabin, Goodnow's team continued on over the bridge at Juniata, and at about two o'clock in the afternoon they reached the small cabin of Rev. Charles Blood, two miles past Dyer's crossing, where Reverend Blood and his wife, Mary, enthusiastically greeted the group.[24] That afternoon, Blood guided Goodnow's group around the area. They climbed Bluemont Hill, ascended an ancient Native American burial mound at the peak, and took in the view.[25] Goodnow was struck by the sight of the valley below where the Kansas and Big Blue rivers intersect; he wrote that it was "one of the most splendid views of natural scenery that my eyes ever rested upon."[26] Goodnow and his team watched the early spring sunset from atop the hill and then returned to Blood's cabin.

Although Isaac Goodnow later wrote that when he saw the valley he immediately felt that it would be the ideal site for the New England Emigrant Aid Company settlement, he actually agonized over the determination the entire next day. On Sunday, March 25, Goodnow spent a cold and rainy day brooding over the question in Reverend Blood's cabin. Goodnow wrote to his wife, Ellen, that day: "I am in a great quandary whether to settle here or *not*. It weighs upon my mind heavily!"[27] In his diary on that date Goodnow noted, "The responsibilities of my position almost press me down."[28] Anxiety over making this decision seems to have followed Goodnow for the entire trip; upon leaving Boston two weeks earlier he worried in a letter to Ellen that "much responsibility devolves upon me relative to selecting a location."[29] The site was certainly attractive, but Goodnow worried — as well he might — that there were not sufficient trees in the surrounding area to provide building material and fuel. "There's an abundance of Claims, and beautiful ones, here open to settlement, but there is a lack of timber," he wrote to his wife.[30] While the rest of the company awaited Goodnow's decision, Charles Lovejoy marked the Sabbath by preaching for the citizens of Juniata.[31] Meanwhile, Reverend Blood nudged Goodnow to select the site in order to surround himself with fellow Yankees.[32]

The next day, Monday, March 26, Goodnow finally decided to plant the company's new colony at the junction of the Blue and Kansas rivers. Having agonized over the determination, Goodnow now threw his wholehearted support behind the site, writing to a Rhode Island newspaper to praise it:

> At the South the Big Blue unites with the Kansas river, and between lies a beautiful plain 1½ miles square, gradually rising up to the high lands to the West between Blue Hill on the Big Blue, and a similar elevation on the Kansas, furnishing one of the finest city sites imaginable, with fine country claims around. God has done *his* part, now let man do *his*, and this paradise will soon rejoice and blossom as the rose.[33]

On the afternoon of the twenty-sixth, Goodnow, Lovejoy, N. R. Wright, and Joseph Wintermute went down to the valley and met with two of the settlers already on site, Seth Child and E. M. Thurston, to discuss their plans.[34] Goodnow's group was resolved to stake their claim between Polistra and Canton and consolidate them all into the company's town.[35]

Goodnow also sent word back to Kansas City—probably with C. N. Wilson—to tell those immigrants following behind to hurry to the camp to try to be present for the vote on March 30.[36] Goodnow wrote in a letter to his wife that he was anxious for the full company to come quickly in order to hold the land: "There is great danger that the Missourians will be on in Kansas to take up the location. A week's start here may decide the fate of one of the most beautiful settlements that your eye ever rested upon."[37]

Meanwhile, back in Kansas City, the *Lonora* had arrived around nine o'clock on the evening of March 24 with the first official party of New England settlers.[38] Goodnow left word before departing that he was headed "up the river toward Fort Riley"; so even before news could reach Kansas City that Goodnow had selected a final site, some of the New England company continued west out of Kansas City, up the Military Road, the next morning, Sunday, March 25.[39] The New Englanders realized that great haste was necessary to get to Goodnow's camp by March 30 to cast a vote for the first Territorial Legislature. Yet it was only the men who hastened into the territory, while most of the women and children who had made the trip from New England remained in Kansas City.[40] The women remained behind to allow the men time to build shelters in Kansas Territory, and also because they were ineligible to vote in the election; only men over the age of twenty-one with "pure unmixed white blood" could vote.[41] One Yankee woman later wrote of her husband and two sons who cast Free-State votes with Good-now in Juniata: "In getting the praise for these three votes all to myself, I will just say, if I had not come to Kan. they would not. Can a woman do any better bound by the wretched laws men made?"[42]

Freed from the need to travel, Julia Lovejoy watched as parties of New England men prepared for the trip. Observing a party of usually prim and proper New Englanders leaving to follow Goodnow into Kansas Territory, she wrote: "The company, some of whom were clergymen, presented a very unique and ludicrous appearance when fully equipped for their journey. Some with oil-cloth hats and overcoats, and long boots drawn over their pants, to protect them from the mud, each armed with his rifle or revolver, for game, not for fear of the Indians or Missourians."[43]

Remarkably, the New England immigrants were only a small part of the influx into Kansas Territory in those last days before the election. From her Kansas City vantage point, Julia Lovejoy wrote: "It would seem almost incredible to all, save an eye witness of the fact, of the hosts whose name is 'legion' that have been emptied from the boats on to the shores of Kanzas during our stay here [in Kansas City], and still they come! Thousands upon thousands, from almost every State in the Union, arrive here, and many go to Westport and Parkville, without stopping here."[44]

Having already suffered discomforts large and small in reaching Kansas City, the New England men now found that travel *into* Kansas Territory was the most primitive part of the trip. Trails into the territory — where they even existed — were uneven, rutted and rocky, and the only way across rivers and streams was by ford or unstable ferryboat.[45] One immigrant observed with vexation, "The road through the country is simply an Indian trail, meandering like the curves and bends of a river."[46] Wagon wheels broke on the treacherous ground. John Mails, a Pennsylvanian pioneer who settled in Manhattan, shattered a wagon wheel during his trip into the territory; but, demonstrating frontier resourcefulness, with "a bushy sapling placed under the wagon he made the rest of the journey on three wheels."[47]

For his part, Thomas Wells headed west out of Kansas City on foot with a group of seven other New Englanders on March 26, a cold and blustery day.[48] Wells estimated that his group covered twenty miles the first day.[49] The next day Wells's group walked the remaining thirty miles to Lawrence. (Another New Englander walking the same route later in the year quipped, "This is a glorious Country to try 'men's soles.'")[50] Traveling with Wells's party on the second day was "a large party of Missourians, number about 200, who were going to Lawrence to vote and a pretty rough looking set they were, some on horseback, some in covered wagons, and others on foot, all hardy, sunburnt, frontier men, and all well armed with guns, revolvers and bowie knives."[51] As they traveled, the Missourians threatened Wells and his fellow settlers: "When they learned that we were from the East we had the pleasure of being called 'damned Yankees,' etc., but they did not succeed in frightening us or in driving us back, though they assured us that they could fire some twenty shots each, and that they had a six pounder [cannon] with them."[52] Such proslavery men from Missouri were soon labeled "Border Ruffians" by Free-Staters in Kansas Territory. A visiting writer from the *New York Tribune* later derisively described Border Ruffians as being of "yellow complexion, hairy faced, with a dirty flannel shirt, red or blue, or green, a pair of commonplace, but dark-colored pants, tucked into an uncertain altitude by a leather belt, in which a dirty-handled bowie-knife is stuck, rather ostentatiously, an eye slightly whiskey-red, and teeth the color of a walnut."[53] "Any one could tell a pro-slavery man as soon as he saw him," asserted Manhattan settler William Mackey.[54]

Up the river in Polistra and Canton, the inhabitants were facing their own troubles in the lead-up to the election. At some point during the winter, George Park's log cabin in Polistra had been broken into and claimed by Abraham Martin, a proslavery Virginian.[55] Meanwhile, the erstwhile owner of the cabin, George Park, was still back in Parkville, Missouri.[56] When Goodnow and his party set up camp on March 27, Martin happened to be away from the cabin, and the Yankees pointedly pitched their tent within 500 feet of the cabin, to neutralize Martin's claim.[57] On March 29 Martin returned and ordered Goodnow's group off the land.[58] They refused to leave. Tension mounted.

By the next day, when the vote for the Territorial Legislature was held, a total of thirteen eligible voters from the New England Company were in Goodnow's camp.[59] The Yankees' encampment fell within the "Blue River Precinct" of the Tenth Election District, whose polling place was the Dyer cabin in Juniata.[60] The men in Goodnow's camp arose early on March 30 and headed north to Dyer's crossing to vote.

The contest for the Territorial House of Representatives in the Tenth District was between the ardent Free-Stater Samuel D. Houston, who had founded Canton, and Russell Garrett, the proslavery candidate and

an "acculturated" Wyandot Indian.[61] Running for the Territorial Council (equivalent to the Senate) were Free-Stater Martin F. Conway and John
Donaldson, the proslavery choice.[62]

On Election Day 1855 thirteen to fifteen armed men, described by local
Free-Staters as "fierce, ignorant partisans" from Missouri, arrived at Dyer's
cabin, "boldly and defiantly swore they were, and intended to remain citizens
of the county, and voted [for the proslavery candidates]."[63] One Free-State
voter in the district later complained about these outsiders in the *Herald
of Freedom*: "Must the settler in Kansas always be treated thus shamefully?
Will the Missourians continue to interfere with our elections? Will not the
general government protect the purity of the ballot-box in this Territory?"[64]
Notably, many of the "Missourians" who showed up at the polls that day in
1855 shared a long history with the candidate Russell Garrett. Garrett had
earlier been part of a little-known chapter in Kansas history: a failed effort
by Native Americans to establish an independent government in the territory from 1851 to 1853, before the land was opened to white settlers.[65] Several
of the outsiders who showed up that day were proslavery Wyandots who
had worked on this project with Garrett and had come to Juniata to cast
votes for him.[66] The Wyandots were not local residents, and thus were im-
proper voters, but the Native Americans may have been motivated less by
proslavery beliefs than by the more universal incentive of helping their good
friend get elected.

After the final votes were cast in Juniata, the three precinct judges retired
behind a closed door at Dyer's cabin to debate whether any voters should be
disqualified as nonresidents (none were) and to tally the votes. Meanwhile,
several men who waited at Dyer's crossing to hear the results passed the time
by getting drunk.[67] (The New Englanders returned soberly to their camp after voting for the Free-State candidates.) By the time the votes were being
counted, there was a drunken, raucous scene at the cabin — a fairly typical
occurrence at all-male antebellum election sites — best reflected by the Juniata resident who tried (unsuccessfully) to open the solid wood door the
judges were behind by taking a full running start at it and head-butting it.[68]

When the votes were finally tallied, it was announced that Houston prevailed at Dyer's cabin by a 43–21 count in the contest for the house of representatives, and that Free-Stater Martin F. Conway took the vote 42–27 in the
election for council. Because other locations in the sparsely settled western
regions also voted on the same candidates, it was not yet clear that Houston

and Conway had won the election, although, in the end, both would prevail by comfortable margins.[69] (Nevertheless, the *Squatter Sovereign* later sulkily claimed that "that contemptible puppy, M. F. Conway," lost the election, and it objected to him taking office: "We can't stand that certainly. D — d if we do!")[70]

Isaac Goodnow's tremendous efforts had proven worthwhile, as the thirteen votes from the New Englanders at Dyer's crossing rather perfectly offset the votes of the Wyandots and Missourians who had shown up to support Garrett, and helped to provide an uncontestable winning margin for the Free-State candidates at the site.

Meanwhile, after the local election results were announced, two opportunistic proslavery citizens of Juniata — probably including Abraham Martin, the man who had occupied Park's cabin — convinced the visiting Missourians and Wyandots that Goodnow was a claim-jumper and recruited them to drive Goodnow's group away. Likely fueled by a combination of alcohol and frustration over the election, these Border Ruffians stormed Goodnow's camp that afternoon on horseback and on foot, "howling defiance and rage, and declaring their intention to drive off the Yankees."[71] One of the Missourians fired a musket at Goodnow's tent, fortunately missing Luke Lincoln, who was napping inside.[72] After that near miss, Goodnow managed to calm the mob and a discussion ensued. Goodnow finally resolved the matter by consenting to move off Park's disputed claim and over to the Canton claim the following day, ending the confrontation.[73] (The incident is illustrative of the general willingness of Southerners to use force in Kansas and the abolitionists' preference for "Christ-like" nonviolence.)[74] In all events, agreeing to temporarily cede Park's claim certainly mattered little to the Yankees in comparison to their triumph at the local polls that day.

Despite the Free-State victory in the election at Dyer's cabin, the results were vastly different throughout the rest of the territory. Due in large part to an influx of Border Ruffians throughout Kansas, the vote was a complete disaster for Free-Staters: Houston and Conway were the *only* Free-Staters in the entire territory elected to the thirty-nine-man Territorial Legislature. As a letter-writer in the *Chicago Daily Tribune* later described it, Free-Staters "were outvoted at every precinct excepting alone Manhattan, whose distance from Missouri saved it from the human vermin."[75]

The day after the election, Goodnow moved the company's camp over to Canton, as he had promised the Missourians, and immediately turned to consolidating Canton, Polistra, and the still-arriving New England immigrants into one settlement, eventually to become Manhattan.[76] Goodnow wrote, "We hope to make it a N.E. [New England] Settlement of the right sort with the blessings of the Lord."[77] For his personal claim, Goodnow on April 2 purchased from a land speculator fifty acres of land west of the proposed town, on Wildcat Creek, where Samuel Houston was his neighbor.[78]

On the afternoon of April 3, 1855, Goodnow organized a meeting of all Free-State settlers, where they agreed to consolidate the claims and establish a town — which they named Boston — and a town company to run it.[79] At seven o'clock that evening, the settlers convened at N. R. Wright's tent and agreed on the borders for the official town site. At the same time, a committee was selected to draft a constitution for the Boston Town Association (BTA). Selected for the task were three men from the New England Company — Goodnow, Wright, and George W. Lockwood — and two men from the Canton Company — Wilcox and Thurston.

Over the next two days, Thurston, who was a lawyer by trade, took the lead in drafting the constitution, which the other committee members readily approved. Then, at two o'clock in the afternoon on April 6, 1855, the full group of Free-Staters reconvened at Wright's tent to ratify the charter. At the meeting, chaired by Samuel D. Houston, the constitution for the BTA was signed by twenty-four founders, including recent New England immigrants and earlier settlers from the area, such as Houston, Thurston, and Wilcox.[80] Another signatory was Rev. Charles Blood, who had decided to relocate with his wife, Mary, to the new town.[81] Given the background and crusading goals of the founders, it is striking that neither religion nor abolitionism was mentioned in the town charter; instead, it was an entirely secular document covering solely procedural matters.

At the same meeting where the BTA constitution was adopted, the signers also selected twelve additional men who were absent from the meeting to be honorary constitutional "proprietors," including Seth Child, Martin F. Conway, and J. M. Russell.[82] (George Park, founder of Polistra, was not included.) Within the next few days, a self-serving and enthusiastic announcement of Boston's founding was supplied to the *Lawrence Herald of Freedom,* which described the BTA's founders as "men of intelligence, enterprise, moral worth, and good pockets."[83]

Following the creation of the BTA, it immediately organized six committees to tackle various projects for the town. The six committees reveal the

immediate priorities of the founders: (1) establishing mills to grind grain
and cut wood, (2) creating ferries across the rivers, (3) building a warehouse
and steamboat landing, (4) securing timber for city usage, (5) surveying city
lots, and (6) obtaining ownership of land for the town site under federal
preemption laws. In a first step toward "preempting" the town site, on April
19, 1855, the Boston Town Association purchased the rights to the claims
asserted by George S. Park and the Canton Company, including both Park's
and J. M. Russell's cabins.[84] BTA settlers were then assigned specific plots
within Boston's proposed borders on which to homestead, with the goal of
cooperatively securing legal title to all of the town's land.

In this way, the initial governance of Boston came in the form of central-
ized planning performed by members of private corporations. Democracy
was absent at the town's founding — the only way to have a say in its governance was to hold a share in the BTA or the New England Emigrant Aid
Company. The arrangement echoed the control exerted by the early Puri-
tans in Massachusetts and may have reflected Goodnow's express desire to
create "a N.E. Settlement of the right sort," composed of settlers "of the right
stamp."

In any event, while the town's organization was quickly falling into place,
actual citizens were still fairly scarce. Many New England immigrants, even
from the season's first two parties, did not end up following Goodnow all
the way west to the company's newest and most distant settlement. Several
stopped along the way in Lawrence or helped settle Topeka, which developed into another important Free-State town between Lawrence and Boston.[85] Thus, the wagon delivering Isaac Goodnow's trunks from Kansas City
made it no farther than Topeka, and as a result his possessions were left
outside on the streets of Topeka for weeks. Moreover, some settlers who did
manage the trip to Boston did not stay long. For example, Joseph Wintermute, one of the first New Englanders at the site, returned back East immediately after casting a Free-State vote on Election Day, and N. R. Wright
followed a few days later.[86] Goodnow wrote in his diary in April that he
"had to spend much time almost every day in encouraging the young men
& keep[ing] them from going home."[87] Another Boston settler noted with
obvious contempt in a letter to New England in June, "There has, it is true,
been many chicken-hearted, unstable & unfit men returned from this Territory."[88] By the end of April 1855, only about fifty of the Emigrant Aid Company's immigrants had settled permanently in or near Boston, including the

young letter-writer Thomas Wells and Isaac Goodnow's brother William.[89] Isaac Goodnow optimistically spun the situation, writing that month, "The distance from the borders, 130 miles, and the journey has been so trying, owing to the dust, wind, and scarcity of provisions and fodder, that we get the wheat, while the chaff of emigration blows away, or does not reach us."[90]

On April 18, 1855, George S. Park delivered a speech to the Boston Town Association suggesting the establishment of an agricultural college in the town — the germ of the idea for the future Kansas State University.[91] Around the same time, Abraham Martin, the proslavery man who had jumped Park's claim, lost interest in remaining in Park's cabin and decided to return home to Virginia. (It is unclear whether Park spoke with Martin while he was in Boston.) Because Park himself had already returned in haste to Parkville by the time Martin finalized his decision to leave, the BTA stepped in and readily agreed to purchase the much-disputed Polistra claim for $150.[92]

A week later, when Isaac Goodnow took a two-horse wagon to Kansas City on April 26 to retrieve his sick brother-in-law Joseph Denison and family, he also brought along the former claim-jumper Martin to the riverboat docks in Kansas City.[93] Goodnow later wrote: "In our camping out we slept side by side and parted good friends. I do not know of another case of the kind in Kansas, settled without a fight."[94] Indeed, the annals of Kansas Territory history reveal few such disputes settled in amicable fashion.

After delivering Martin to Kansas City, Goodnow traveled to nearby Parkville on April 30 to visit Colonel Park.[95] There Goodnow received $100 from Park to partially reimburse the buyout of Martin, and Goodnow learned that Park would soon be temporarily relocating from Parkville "to save his life from a Pro-Slavery mob."[96] In fact, sixteen days earlier, while Park was on his way to deliver his speech to the BTA advocating for a college, a mob in Parkville had tossed Park's boxes of type for his newspaper, the *Industrial Luminary*, into the Missouri River "with three hearty cheers."[97] The mob, calling itself the Kansas League, covered the type in a white sheet that said "Boston Aid" before throwing it in the river.[98] The mob then issued a proclamation, declaring Park a "traitor" and stating that the mob would "meet here again on this day in three weeks, and if we find G. S. Park or [coeditor] W. J. Patterson in this town then, or any subsequent time, we will throw them in the Missouri River, and if they go to Kansas we pledge our honor as men, to follow and hang them wherever we can take them."[99]

The proslavery *Squatter Sovereign* had been advocating for action against Park for some time — the paper wrote on March 6, 1855: "The Parkville Luminary is ripe in Abolitionism. The harvest is near at hand when all such fruit in Missouri will be plucked!" — and the newspaper rejoiced after the attack on the press, writing, "We look upon the destruction of the Abolition printing office in Parkville, Mo., as necessary for the security of the lives of the citizens in that neighborhood, the protection of their property, and the well-being of the Slave-holding population."[100] On the other side of the issue, Samuel C. Pomeroy wrote to Park to encourage him to revive the newspaper in Parkville: "I can raise you 1,000 new subscribers. One more sack will be worth to you $10,000. There is a good time coming this side of heaven."[101]

On April 23, 1855, Park issued his first public response, publishing a defiant letter to Parkville and to the mob that had destroyed his paper:

> With regard to leaving this community, I would do so cheerfully as soon as I could dispose of my interests here, were I satisfied that a further residence was not agreeable; but to leave the grave of my wife, the home I have toiled years to establish and improve, and many interests interwoven with the growth and prosperity of the country, and flee for no offence like a base culprit — I cannot! I would rather prefer death at my own home. . . . Our press has been thrown into the Missouri river. I may be buried there too. An humble individual is in the power of hundreds of armed men; but his death will not destroy the freedom of the AMERICAN PRESS![102]

Despite Park's rhetoric, the *Luminary* was not revived and he soon departed the town for one of his Illinois properties. Over the next several years, Park bounced around his various landholdings, including frequent stays in Parkville.[103] But having played the role of founder and visionary in Manhattan's history — he was the first European American to build a structure in the future Manhattan and the first to propose a college for the town — Park soon faded from its story. Park's last connection to Manhattan was serving as a trustee for a private Methodist school that was chartered in the town in 1858 (Blue Mont Central College).[104] Moreover, Park apparently left a sour impression with the town's founders — he had received more BTA shares than any other individual based on a promise to bring his printing press to town and to build a block of businesses, and he failed to do either of these things.[105]

After Isaac Goodnow met with the shaken Park in Parkville on April 30, 1855, he returned with his wagon to Kansas City to pick up his ailing brother-in-law Joseph Denison and his family, to carry them on to Boston, Kansas Territory. Denison and his family had originally stopped in Kansas City because their son Charles took ill with pneumonia on March 24, the day they arrived in Kansas City on the steamboat *Lonora*.[106] While waiting out the illness in a Kansas City hotel, the situation grew worse six days later when Joseph also caught pneumonia, and then worse again on April 6, when young Charles died of the illness.[107] Because Joseph was confined to his room at the time, he was not even able to attend his son's funeral.[108] Joseph's wife, Sarah, recalled in a letter to her sister later that month that "the night Charley died Joseph was sickest and I returned after laying Charley away ... to watch [Joseph], not a little fearing I might be called to a greater loss."[109] Joseph soon, however, began to recover his health, and despite the death of their son, the Denisons resolved to continue their journey into Kansas Territory. On April 19, Denison wrote, "We are all very deeply afflicted and tired but are not discouraged."[110] By the time Isaac Goodnow arrived in Kansas City at the end of the month, Joseph was healthy enough to travel. Goodnow and the Denisons left Kansas City on May 1, 1855, and headed to Boston, Kansas Territory, taking seven days to make the trip.

Meanwhile, around the same time in Boston, Kansas Territory, Rev. Charles Lovejoy was setting out on foot in the opposite direction to retrieve his pregnant wife and two young daughters from Kansas City, as he had just received word that they were in trouble. Indeed, Julia Lovejoy had grown desperate in her efforts over the past month to get herself and her two daughters out of Kansas City, which by then had grown crowded with immigrants too sick to continue into Kansas. The hallway of her Kansas City hotel was lined with men who were sick, dying, or already dead.[111] When Julia Lovejoy learned that the first boats of the season were heading west up the Kansas River in mid-April, she immediately booked passage for herself and her girls, who were also now wracked with illness, "to escape from that place of sickness, and death, for I feared every one of us would die, if we remained there."[112] But to her great despair, their boat traveled only four miles before it stuck fast on a sandbar. On April 25, Julia took her sick children off the boat and sent a message of distress to her husband while the other passengers continued west on foot.[113] This was the message that soon alerted the Reverend Lovejoy to his family's plight.

Julia Lovejoy, eloquent author of letters about life on the frontier,
circa 1861. (Courtesy of Kansas State Historical Society.)

Julia Lovejoy waited several days in dilapidated cabins near the stranded boat while her younger daughter Edith continued to grow sicker, until she finally commissioned a teamster's wagon to carry her and her daughters to Lawrence.[114] The Lovejoy women were approaching Lawrence on May 3 when they saw Reverend Lovejoy walking up the road to meet them from the other direction. Julia wrote, "We simultaneously, uttered a cry, and the next moment, we were sobbing in each other's arms."[115] Yet the reunion did not bring lasting joy: the next day Edith Lovejoy succumbed to pneumonia, dying in Lawrence on May 4, 1855, four days short of her sixth birthday.[116] The Reverend James Griffing, an early circuit preacher in Kansas Territory, encountered the Lovejoys in Lawrence after Edith's death and wrote that the family was deeply stricken. "The grim monster had been there and, just one hour before I came, had snatched away a most lovely little daughter of six years."[117] The necessity of continuing west to Boston made the awful situation even worse for Julia Lovejoy. She wrote: "In a few hours from the time we saw the cold clods heaped upon our darling, we were obliged by the forces of circumstances, to tear ourselves from the grave of our loved one, and continue on our journey of nearly 90 miles, scattering our tears along the road, as we turned our eyes across the prairies that stretched away toward her grave."[118]

Her later writings make it clear that Julia Lovejoy did not soon recover from this loss; five years later she recalled that the scenery she first found in Manhattan presented "a panorama of beauty as is seldom seen from any standpoint," but also noted, "We could never fully appreciate its beauty; for our heart in those days was so surcharged with sorrow that we neither asked nor desired that any earthly gratification of the eye, ear, or palate, should for a moment make us forget."[119]

5

SPRING 1855
BECOMING MANHATTAN

When Isaac Goodnow and the other settlers established Boston, Kansas Territory, in April 1855, it was literally on the U.S. frontier. Even though the small settlement was located in the eastern part of Kansas Territory, there was little to be found west of Boston but Fort Riley and vast plains stretching to the Rockies, the bison hunting grounds for Native American tribes.[1] To the south of Boston were camps of Osage traders and, beyond that, Indian territory extending south to the border of Texas.[2]

When the Territorial Legislature established thirty-three original counties in Kansas Territory in August 1855, Boston's county — named Riley County — was on the westernmost edge of organized lands. Vividly demonstrating its frontier location, Riley County originally had attached to it for administrative purposes all land stretching west from its border across Kansas Territory, deep into present-day Colorado. In 1855, when Kansas Territorial Governor Andrew H. Reeder appointed Seth Child to a brief term as county Sheriff, the position theoretically covered land stretching almost to the Rocky Mountains.[3]

Although the U.S. government had removed most native tribes from eastern Kansas, Native Americans yet remained in frontier areas such as Boston. One settler observed in 1855 that "various tribes of roving Indians are scattered about us."[4] In one typical story, Yankee settler Josiah Pillsbury recorded in July 1855 that when 500 mounted Native Americans passed near his cabin on the way to a hunt, "some five or six rode down to our cabin, but did not come in — talked and laughed and looked in at the windows."[5] That same summer, Samuel Dyer's daughter Sarah wrote of a more anxious encounter at the family's cabin in Juniata with a band of Otoe warriors who first appeared in the distance as a terrible cloud of dust:

> We got the field glass and discovered that [the dust cloud] was caused by hundreds of Indians, all warriors. My father sent down the hill and got some men who were getting out bridge timber, and with our own family, all got in the house, hunted up all the firearms, axes, hatchets, and everything that could be used to defend ourselves, and waited for their attack. Well on they came and when they got there they discovered a large grindstone and went to grinding their knives and tomahawks. We thought our time had come and I remember feeling my head, wondering how soon I would be scalped.[6]

The tension was defused when an English-speaker from the tribe approached the Dyers's cabin and informed the inhabitants that they meant no harm. The tribe was going down to fight the Comanches, and they wanted Samuel Dyer and all of the other men to come out and smoke "the pipe of peace." Sarah Dyer continued: "There were about 300 warriors I think, but anyway they looked pretty scary, painted red and with red blankets. In about six weeks they came back but the brave warriors were over half gone. One poor fellow had been shot with an arrow and four Indians were carrying him on a rude stretcher made of rough poles. Father and Doctor Whitehorn dressed his wound."[7]

Far out on this Kansas prairie, at the farthest reach of white settlement — at the "ends of the earth," as some eastern friends joked — the frontier village of Boston and its environs had grown to a population exceeding sixty settlers by the middle of the first spring in the valley.[8]

In April 1855 the town's pioneers were hard at work building their settlement. Isaac Goodnow observed that month that "this is a country that will *try* men & show what they are made of."[9] Boston's pioneers were working so intently in those early days and weeks that they rarely took the time to shave or wash. Goodnow wrote to his wife in April: "We need women here very much. We shave & wash but little. My N.E. friends would hardly know me!"[10] In addition to being dirty and unkempt, Goodnow was probably even a bit stronger smelling than other settlers, because his possessions were still stranded in Topeka and he was unable to change clothes for a month. "My old gray pantaloons & overalls, old coat & overcoat I have worn most of the time since I left Kansas City."[11] For a man raised on the Methodist maxim that "cleanliness is next to godliness," the grubby conditions would only have added to the foreignness of the frontier. Goodnow's trunks, after remaining untended for a month in the Topeka weather, were finally picked up and delivered to him by a friend returning from Kansas City in late April.[12] Food was equally inelegant in those first days on site; Rev. Charles Lovejoy wrote, "Our living was mostly [corn] mush & molasses."[13]

The first structure in the colony built by 1855 settlers — the third overall after the cabins built the prior winter by Park and Russell — was a rickety cabin hastily put up in April by Lovejoy and his son (before the family's womenfolk arrived) near the junction of the rivers.[14] After Julia Lovejoy arrived from Kansas City, she described it as "a floorless cabin, built of logs, the crevices filled with sticks and mud, the roof covered with 'shakes' split from logs, resembling your Eastern clapboards, in a rough state. These answer a good purpose in a fair day, but woe to the beds and everything else when the rain falls heavily."[15]

Despite the relentless hard work, with springtime's beautiful weather and rapidly growing crops, many were enthused by the experience.[16] One settler later recalled, "No one that has not experienced the sensation of being the very first inhabitants of a hitherto unsettled country can be made to realize the exhilarating effect."[17] Isaac Goodnow, too, noted the invigorating effect of the settlement experience: "Though I have been confined to the shade, the school-room, for the last eighteen years, I find myself a match, in hardship and endurance, for the strongest most robust men."[18] He also joked, "My friends are as astonished at this as I am myself."[19]

Julia Lovejoy also extolled the exhilarating effect of the settlers' experience, attributing it to the climate, and cited the case of E. M. Thurston, who, when he had come to Kansas in 1854 was "in the last stages of consumption, given over by his physicians to die, [and] as a last resort came to Kanzas, has lived here through the winter, and now is so well he labors constantly, and at night wraps a buffalo robe about him, and throws himself on the open prairie, with no covering but the canopy of heaven."[20] Thomas Wells, who had also been quite sickly before coming to the frontier, likewise believed that his health was improved by the Kansas climate. In June 1855, he wrote: "Everyone says that I look much better than when I came here. Indeed, I *know* that I am better, am not sick at all now. The country agrees with me well."[21]

By May, Julia Lovejoy reported that the fruits of the settlers' hard work were becoming evident: "Frames and cabins are going up all around to se-cure this city property, whilst for miles around farm claims have been taken, and five, ten, and so on acres planted, and every thing is growing rapidly."[22] The same month William Goodnow gushed, "It is a charming site for a city & I think it is destined to be one of the largest in this Territory."[23] The Boston Town Association helped the forward momentum by erecting a river land-ing and a temporary warehouse.

Although Boston, Kansas Territory, was quiet and industrious in the two months following the March 1855 vote, the rest of the territory began to boil over the disputed election results. Free-Staters complained that the mass influx of proslavery Border Ruffians had fraudulently influenced the out-come of the election. In response, Territorial Governor Andrew H. Reeder invalidated the results from five districts where citizens alleged voter fraud (not including Boston's precinct). A special election was then held in those locations on May 22, 1855, to elect replacements. Proslavery voters protested by boycotting in most locations. Predictably, eight of the eleven delegates elected in the special election were Free-Staters, with three proslavery del-egates reelected in Leavenworth. Together with Houston and Conway, the eight new Free-State delegates brought the total number of Free-Staters to ten out of thirty-nine in the Territorial Legislature. Although Boston was relatively isolated from this dispute, the entire mess was soon to arrive in its backyard.

In June 1855 the population instantly doubled in and around Boston when a group of seventy-five settlers arrived on a 144-ton paddlewheel steamboat named the *Hartford*.[24] The group was part of the Cincinnati and Kansas Land Company, which planned to establish a town in Kansas Territory and name it Manhattan. Unfortunately, surviving evidence provides no record of why they chose the name Manhattan, although it certainly had some-thing to do with the fact that the name was reportedly selected by one of the leaders of the company, Andrew J. Mead, who was born in New York City on the island of Manhattan.[25]

The *Cincinnati Enquirer* described the company as "an association of gentlemen comprising some of our worthiest citizens."[26] One of its leaders, Judge John Pipher, wrote in turn, "We are not rich, yet we are sober and industrious, and hope we have energy and perseverance enough to eventually build up a thriving town and an important business place."[27] Many of the members of the Cincinnati company were infused with the strong Free-State interests present in Cincinnati, which had already led Cincinnatian Charles Boynton to travel to Kansas in 1854 and write *A Journey through Kansas.*[28]

A good deal of planning went into the company's venture before they set out for Kansas, but it is not clear when plans for the Cincinnati and Kansas Land Company venture were originally proposed. The company apparently was not officially formed until articles of association were signed on April 25, 1855, the day before the group boarded its boat to Kansas.[29] But prior to that, in mid-April 1855, the principals were already actively seeking to purchase a riverboat for the trip. On April 20, 1855, the *Daily Cincinnati Gazette* announced that the company had purchased a steamboat, the *Louisville,* and planned to set out within the week to establish a town "near Fort Riley, to be called Manhattan."[30] (This was the first time, it should be remarked, that the name of Manhattan, Kansas, appears in print.) The deal to purchase the *Louisville* promptly fell through, but the company's leaders immediately found a replacement steamboat to purchase: the *Hartford.*[31] On April 22, 1855, the *Cincinnati Daily Enquirer* began running daily advertisements for the *Hartford's* trip to Kansas, writing on the morning of the twenty-fourth, "This is the first and best opportunity that has or will offer for adventurers to seek the new country about which so much is said."[32] The following morning, another advertisement for the trip in the *Daily Enquirer* added Manhattan to the list of destinations for the *Hartford,* even though, of course, no settlement by that name yet existed in Kansas Territory.[33]

After a delay for late-arriving passengers, the *Hartford* set out for Kansas on the evening of April 26, 1855, leaving from a dusty landing at the base of Cincinnati's Main Street on an overcast and warm night.[34] The steamship was loaded with travelers and tons of cargo: parts for prefabricated buildings, a printing press, a steam engine, a small gristmill, cooking stoves, seeds and agricultural implements, personal effects, and 153 barrels of whiskey.[35] The *Cincinnati Daily Enquirer* reported the next morning: "The Hartford left last evening for Kansas, *literally* crowded. We know there will be a good time on board."[36]

Decades later, one passenger, Amanda Arnold — a girl of seventeen at the time of the trip — recalled some good moments: "There were a variety of entertainments on board ship. It might be a prayer meeting one evening and a dance another."[37] Yet the trip was not consistently enjoyable. Delay piled upon delay as the *Hartford* traveled down the Ohio River to the Mississippi River, west from St. Louis on the Missouri River to Kansas City, and then finally up the Kansas River. For religiously inclined passengers, the extended time on the steamboat presented challenges to their routines. For example, Isaiah Harris, an immigrant on another boat from Cincinnati to Kansas Territory, complained about a Sunday service: "Here was the Minister Preaching and all the machinery of the boat at work as hard as fire & water could generate steam to propel it and there were the deck hands with a wood boat lashed along side at work as hard as any other day of the week, so it hardly appeared there could be a *Real* Worship present in all this confusion."[38] Far more tragically, seven passengers on the boat reportedly died of cholera during the trip and were buried along the riverbanks.[39] No matter how settlers made the journey, getting to Kansas Territory in 1855 was not easy.

The *Hartford* arrived in St. Louis on May 1, 1855. The town's *Missouri Democrat* announced the next day, "The Hartford, recently purchased for the Kansas river trade, arrived yesterday morning with some freight and several families and their plunder."[40] Two days later, the boat steamed away from St. Louis and up the Missouri River.[41] The *Hartford* was fortunate that it was not detained longer in St. Louis. Many boats were being held there by riverboat captains seeking to keep a monopoly on Missouri River trade.[42] Other vessels were quarantined in St. Louis as a precaution against cholera, a common practice during outbreaks. Cholera was the most dreaded disease in the Western world at the time — literally sending people fleeing from locations where it appeared — and because its causes remained a complete mystery in 1855, the only treatments were quarantining and unproven elixirs. (Treatments advertised in contemporary newspapers included "Dally's and Connell's Magic Pain Extractor" and "McLean's Strengthening Cordial and Blood Purifier.")

Following the departure from St. Louis on May 3, the pace of travel slowed significantly: the steamer did not arrive in Kansas City until two o'clock in the afternoon on May 11.[43] The creeping pace across Missouri was caused by low water on the Missouri River and questionable piloting.[44] Taunts and threats from Missourians during this leg of the trip also added to the *Hartford* passengers' misery; the atmosphere in Missouri had poisoned further since the disputed election in Kansas Territory on March 30. Many Free-State immigrants would soon avoid Missouri completely.[45]

Unfortunately for the Cincinnati company, the water was even lower on the Kansas River, so that once the *Hartford* reached Kansas City, Missouri, the boat and its passengers were forced to tie up outside the town from May 12 to May 20, waiting for the river to rise.[46] For some time it looked uncertain whether the *Hartford* would ever make it into Kansas Territory, and several passengers abandoned the boat to take wagons into Kansas.[47] Those who remained on the steamboat were charged one dollar a day rent. Meanwhile, proslavery newspapers attempted to inflame passions by reporting that the *Hartford*'s passengers were "all anti-slavery."[48] By the time the boat was able to leave Kansas City, the remaining passengers were more than ready to depart. One passenger groused after leaving: "Kansas City, Missouri, is the worst enemy that Kansas Territory has. There you will get no encouragement from any one."[49]

Luckily, on May 20, 1855, the water level rose enough for the *Hartford* to resume its journey.[50] By one o'clock the next afternoon the steamer was docked at the far friendlier Free-State town of Lawrence.[51] From Lawrence, the Cincinnati and Kansas Land Company planned to steam farther into Kansas Territory, beyond the Boston settlement, to the headwaters of the Kansas River at the junction of the Smoky Hill and Republican rivers. In fact, a small forward group from the company, including Judge Pipher and Andrew J. Mead, was already at the head of the Kansas River, staking out a town and awaiting the arrival of the *Hartford*.[52] But the boat would never reach that location.

Although the *Hartford* unloaded a sizable amount of goods in St. Louis, a Lawrence newspaper described the boat as still "heavily loaded with passengers and freight."[53] This was a bad omen on the low river. Not surprisingly, only a few miles past Lawrence the paddleboat snagged on a sandbar.[54] It took one day for the craft to shake loose from this bar, and then it spent the next nine days moving slowly up the Kansas River, repeating the cumbersome process of grounding and working loose from obstructions. On June 1, 1855, the *Hartford* again ran aground, half a mile below Boston. It eventually shook loose but then stuck fast on June 3, just past the mouth of the Big Blue River, where the boat was destined to remain high and dry for a month.[55] One *Hartford* passenger wrote a letter to Cincinnati at this time observing it was "not our destination" but almost certainly "the end of our journey."[56]

Sensing an opportunity, the Boston Town Association acted quickly, voting on June 2 "that members of the Cincinnati and Kanzas Land Company be invited to come up from the boat and hold a consultation with us in reference to locating at this place."[57] During these consultations, the BTA offered the Cincinnati company the southern half of its town site as incentive to settle there. The BTA also agreed to a power-sharing arrangement and consented to rename their settlement Manhattan if the *Hartford* passengers joined.[58] Any desire for exclusive New England control over the settlement at this point was overcome by the recognition that the little village needed actual settlers.

The *Hartford* passengers had rejected invitations to join other settlements along the Kansas River, including Lawrence, Topeka, and Lecompton.[59] But when Pipher and Mead ventured down from the intended settlement site to the stranded boat, the Cincinnati group took a hard look at the low river and their dwindling supplies of food and whiskey and promptly agreed to join the Bostonians.[60] On June 4, 1855, the leaders of the Cincinnati and Boston companies signed a letter of agreement. Then on June 29, the BTA was reorganized as the Manhattan Town Association, and a new constitution officially established the town of Manhattan where Boston had stood.[61]

Although it was not their intended destination, the Cincinnati settlers were happy with their new home. One *Hartford* passenger, William Hoon, raved that the location had "all that is necessary to make a large town." In a letter to the *Daily Cincinnati Gazette* he wrote: "The site selected is on a most beautiful one for a city. It is on the point of the Big Blue and Kansas rivers. We have good landings on both sides of us." Hoon continued: "We have, also, in the neighborhood plenty of good farming land. And then, again, we have the best water to drink—both spring and river water. The water of the Big Blue is clear as crystal."[62]

As promised, the town's land, as well as responsibility for its governance, was divided equally between the two private corporations.[63] The two groups also informally divided spheres of interest in the new town: the New Englanders focused on matters of public education and morality, while the Cincinnati transplants concentrated on developing commerce. With different visions for the community, the two groups disputed many issues, reaching into nearly every aspect of life in early Manhattan. One resident later observed that early Manhattanites "were divided into cliques, the leaders of which gave to the pleasant task of thwarting each other's schemes the time and energy that should have been devoted to laboring for the general weal."[64] Nonetheless, the town ultimately thrived. As Goodnow later rhapsodized,

Share certificate for Manhattan Town Association, issued to
George S. Park. (Courtesy of Kansas State Historical Society.)

"The union of the two companies, of the East and of the West, produced a grand practical combination, the best kind of business compound to make the right kind of a town to live in and to educate our children."[65]

Immediately after the reorganization, Goodnow reported enthusiastically to a Rhode Island newspaper: "Our city Manhattan, changed from Boston, is growing. We have united with a fine energetic company from Cincinnati."[66] By the end of June many of the ten prefabricated buildings that the *Hartford* carried to Manhattan were already assembled.[67] The frontiersman Samuel D. Houston, who had been almost alone on the prairie with his wife, Tabitha, and his family just a year and a half earlier, wrote that the addition of the *Hartford* settlers and their houses "gave the place, in a short time, the appearance of a small village at the Junction of the Blue and the Kansas rivers. And the town seemed to be established."[68] As for the name change for Polistra/Canton/Boston/Manhattan, one Juniata resident observed in June 1855, "The City of many names . . . is now permanently named Manhattan."[69]

BLEEDING KANSAS
"TYRANNY IS NOW IN THE ASCENDANT"

Kansas Territory was soon to be embroiled in violent clashes between proslavery and antislavery zealots, earning it the nickname "Bleeding Kansas." As Abraham Lincoln would observe of the territory in August 1855, "It was conceived in violence, is maintained in violence, and is being executed in violence."

But not all of the violence in the territory during this era was related solely to slavery—some confrontations arose from claim-jumping or disputes over property lines. Confusing the issue further, parties sometimes claimed that property fights were actually about slavery. It appears that this was the case in a well-publicized incident involving a proslavery settler in Manhattan named William J. Osborn. Although the fight was originally about land, Osborn tried to rally support by claiming he was being persecuted for proslavery beliefs, and with the nation's eyes already drawn to Kansas Territory, the Osborn affair became a small national story and an early marker on the way to Bleeding Kansas. The incident also made the name Manhattan synonymous with the antislavery movement, even before the new name of the settlement was officially adopted.

The episode began on June 4, 1855, when the Boston Town Association negotiated a transfer of land formerly belonging to J. M. Russell to the Cincinnati company, as part of Boston's grant of half the town site.[1] Russell, an original member of the old Canton Company, apparently left town immediately afterward.[2] The following day, while the Cincinnati men were elsewhere assembling the frames of their prefabricated buildings, William Osborn rode his horse down from Juniata and occupied Russell's dugout cabin.[3] After Osborn was discovered emptying out the cabin, Luke Lincoln and members of the Cincinnati group forcefully drove him from the area.[4]

Ten days later, on June 15, 1855, the proslavery *Leavenworth Herald* carried a sensational story, subsequently reprinted in papers nationwide, with details of the incident, stating, "We can truly say that we never listened to the recital of a more gross and infernal outrage, than was recently perpetrated on a Mr. Wm. J. Osborn, by a gang of Cincinnati Abolitionists, known as the MANHATTAN TOWN COMPANY."[5] The *Herald* reported that on June 5, the Cincinnati group "armed with guns, pistols and clubs" ordered Osborn off the claim, "on account of his being a strong advocate and zealous supporter of the institution of Slavery."[6] When Osborn refused to leave, he was reportedly "violently seized, and taken by force on board the steamboat *Hartford*. . . . There he was abused, derided at, and offered every revolting insult that the base, cowardly and infamous villains could think of."[7]

Osborn was released from the boat after a few hours. He promptly left Boston, stopping on his way out of town for dinner at the cabin of his acquaintance Isaac Hascall.[8] Hascall subsequently told the townspeople that during this dinner Osborn had threatened the safety of the *Hartford* and its captain, David Millard.[9] That night, Osborn slept outside of town at the cabin of Russell Garrett, the losing proslavery legislative candidate. Meanwhile, at some point that night Russell's old cabin in Manhattan mysteriously burned down. Two days later, on June 7, Osborn returned to the *Hartford* — either "with the view of holding some conversation with the leader of this company relative to his case," or for the more sinister purpose of burning the boat.[10] Whatever his true intentions, upon Osborn's return the Manhattan group again detained Osborn and accused him of "having threatened to destroy their boat *Hartford*." The group then took Osborn to Isaac Hascall's cabin to see if Hascall would reconfirm that Osborn had made threatening statements about the boat.[11] When Hascall refused to comply, the townspeople released Osborn, the Leavenworth newspaper reported, but not before "his horse was taken possession of, rode around at [high speed], beaten and otherwise maltreated in the most inhuman manner."[12]

With an eye to the recent election, the *Leavenworth Herald* also added that "the notorious S. D. Houston, the Abolition (would-be) Representative of the Pawnee District, is President of this infernal company, and that their infamous conduct had met with his most unqualified sanction."[13] In closing the story, the *Herald* issued a call for action against Manhattan: "Let meetings be held and forces raised for the purpose of replacing [Osborn] in the possession of his claim. Let the vile, dishonest and infamous abolitionists be made to know that they are not, as yet, or never will be, masters of the virgin soil of Kansas. Let justice be done in this case, though the Heavens should fall."[14]

Osborn followed up with a letter to the editor that provided additional incendiary detail. He wrote that he had informed the Cincinnati company on June 5 that "ere I would give up one jot of my rights to such a set of menials as they were, I would let my blood drench the soil. . . . I told them they were a set of Abolitionists and paupers; the veriest slaves of designing men; that I did see before me a crowd of villains and cut-throats — the foul scum of prisons and brothels, come merely to deprive me of my rights."[15] Providing an alternate (and far less colorful) narrative, Judge John Pipher explained in a letter to a Free-State newspaper that Osborn had simply jumped the Cincinnati company's claim, and "as agent of the Cincinnati Company, I was bound to protect their interests, and in doing so I have done no more than my duty."[16] Chiming in on the dispute, the *Cincinnati Enquirer* opined, "Under all the circumstances, as related to us, Osborn was treated with uncommon forbearance."[17]

Meanwhile, some in the southern press seized on the affair as evidence of mistreatment of proslavery settlers in Kansas Territory. In Richmond, Virginia — the heart of the antebellum South — the *Daily Dispatch* described it as an "outrage" and wrote that Osborn's treatment "shows the justice of the cry of persecution" from Southerners in Kansas.[18] The *Daily Picayune* of New Orleans called it a "gross offence" and argued that the proslavery side in Kansas deserved greater respect, noting that the Osborn affair was equivalent to "the stories of pro-slavery outrage which the Eastern papers have been filled with, and have used for inflaming a sectional animosity towards the whole South, the fruits of which we see in the discords which convulse the whole land, and threaten so many dangers to the peace and continuance of the Union."[19] Looking more broadly at the events in Kansas Territory from a southern perspective, the *Picayune* also asserted: "There is a pro-slavery and an anti-slavery party in Kansas, and unhappily they represent opinions actually within the Territory less than they do interests and passions without. . . . New England Abolitionists make Kansas a field for crusade against Southern institutions and choose to open there a campaign against the constitutional rights and domestic peace of the South."[20]

Back in Manhattan, in light of the proslavery call for revenge against the town's "vile, dishonest and infamous abolitionists," Pipher later recalled, "it was feared that serious trouble might ensue."[21] Yet little followed from the event except a brief personal confrontation between Osborn and Luke Lincoln in Leavenworth in June 1855.[22]

Very soon after the Osborn affair, Osborn's friend Hascall was also forcibly driven from his Manhattan property in another heated dispute — one of several early claim-jumping quarrels in Manhattan.[23] Hascall had originally settled in the area in 1854, greeted Samuel C. Pomeroy when he scouted the location before Goodnow's arrival, and was even selected as a "proprietor" of the old Boston Town Association.[24] But he ran afoul of the New England leaders when he built a cabin on land that the BTA had assigned to William Goodnow for homesteading in May 1855.[25] Although William Goodnow was lodging with the Denison family at the time and had done nothing to establish his claim, on June 11 Hascall was "tried" and condemned as a claim-jumper by Manhattanites.[26] The next day, Hascall's cabin was torn down, but he still refused to leave the land. Finally, on June 23, 1855, a mob of about thirty men gathered to drive Hascall from the property. Isaac Goodnow wrote in his diary on that date: "Shouldered my gun & went to town to drive Haskell from Wm.'s claim."[27] Judge John Pipher, who had piercing eyes and a visage that commanded respect, rode ahead of the mob yelling at Hascall: "Run, run for your life, for I cannot answer for what my men might do."[28] Hascall got the message and set out on foot across the prairie at full speed, reportedly losing a shoe in his fright.[29] Notably, Hascall's claim to the land was later established in court, and the town eventually paid him compensation.[30]

A year later, in 1856, Hascall testified about the attacks both on himself and Osborn before the congressional Special Committee Appointed to Investigate the Troubles in Kansas. In his testimony, Hascall noted, "One of the Cincinnati company stated that they intended to regulate matters in that part of the country, and if a man settled there he would have to come under their regulations."[31] Hascall's statement probably refers to Pipher and his "Manhattan Invincibles," a magnificently named company of armed locals that Pipher formed on January 22, 1856, "for the purpose of protecting each other in our natural, political and personal rights."[32] Isaac Goodnow later wrote of Pipher's efforts with admiration: "In all our contests with town-jumpers and border-ruffians, [Pipher] had the tact to come out ahead and without any bloodshed. . . . Really, we did not know then how we could have got along without the Judge."[33]

In order to fully understand the context in which Manhattan developed, it is necessary to briefly provide an overview of the chaos raging throughout Kansas Territory in 1855 and 1856 before returning again to Manhattan's situation in the summer of 1855.

In April 1855, following a spirited lobbying campaign by several villages in Kansas Territory, Territorial Governor Reeder decided to establish the territorial capital at Pawnee, a small settlement that he helped to create ten miles west of Manhattan.[34] This was where the delegates elected in the disputed March and May elections would convene — as a result, the "bad feelings . . . grand row and smash up" expected to accompany the legislators was coming to Manhattan's backyard.[35] Many Free-Staters labeled it the "Bogus Legislature" and continued to claim that the proslavery majority was elected only because of voter fraud. Manhattanites preferred to call it the "Missouri Legislature." As Thomas Wells explained, "The truth is many of the members were Missourians, elected by fraud and mob force."[36] Isaac Goodnow wrote that it was "a body of usurpers & looked upon as such by the Citizens of Kansas."[37]

The first session of the Kansas Territorial Legislature was scheduled to begin on July 2, 1855, and by late June the (overwhelmingly proslavery) delegates began to assemble in nearby Pawnee.[38] Of the gathering, Julia Lovejoy observed, "A more reckless set, stirred up to deeds of daring by the fumes of the brandy bottle, never probably met for like purposes."[39] Manhattan settler Amos Powers concurred that the legislators "looked as if they had always had a plenty of 'O-be-joyful."[40] In Manhattan itself, confrontation was feared due to the proximity of Pawnee and threats of revenge for the Osborn affair. Julia Lovejoy wrote that Manhattanites expected "trouble if not 'hard fighting' in our quiet community at the opening of the Legislature, in Pawnee, a few miles from here, as some of the 'viler sort,' had threatened to 'exterminate every abolitionist here, and demolish their houses' and I can assure you, every man, not excepting our good peace-loving minister, WAS PREPARED FOR THEM!"[41] In order to stand ready for any attack, on June 27–28, the townspeople gathered "to take measures to guard against an invasion by Missourians."[42]

On June 30, two days before the legislature convened, the Free-State council delegate for Manhattan, Martin Conway, resigned his seat in protest of the election irregularities. Conway wrote, "Instead of recognizing this as the Legislature of Kansas, and participating in its proceedings as such, I utterly repudiate and reprobate it, as derogatory to the respectability of popular government, and insulting to the virtue and intelligence of the age."[43] After Conway's resignation, the proslavery candidate he had defeated, John Donaldson, was sworn in to take his position.

Finally, on Monday, July 2, 1855, the first contentious session opened. When the thirty-nine-man legislature convened, Manhattan's remaining abolitionist delegate, Samuel Houston, found few allies; his Free-State viewpoint was vastly overshadowed by the thirty-strong proslavery faction. Then the legislature, in one of its first votes, unseated all eight of the Free-State delegates elected in the special election ordered by Governor Reeder in May, rendering Houston completely, totally alone in the antislavery camp. Houston dissented from the decision to remove the other Free-Staters, writing, "I cannot agree that this body has the right to go behind the decision of the Governor, who, by virtue of his office, is the organizing Federal arm of the General Government."[44] Houston's protest was ignored, and all of the other Free-Staters were unseated.

Following the removal of the Free-Staters, the legislature worked directly through the week, not stopping to acknowledge the Fourth of July holiday. (Nearby, in what would become a significant early tradition, Manhattan celebrated its first Independence Day with a picnic and speeches outside town, "in beautiful woods beside a beautiful spring of water.")[45] Having unseated all but one Free-State delegate, the legislature next passed a bill to depart Pawnee and move the territorial capital to Shawnee Mission, on the Missouri border. Governor Reeder vetoed the bill, but the proslavery members had a veto-proof majority, and on Friday, July 6, the fifth workday of the session, the legislature overrode the veto. Already on July 5, legislators had begun abandoning Pawnee.[46] The legislature thus relegated dusty Pawnee to the dubious distinction of being the shortest-lived capital in U.S. history.[47] The move also cost Governor Reeder a great deal of money since he was heavily invested in Pawnee. (The *Boston Post* later mocked Reeder with a poem that included the lines: "The legislature, he approved / From Pawnee to Shawnee removed. . . . The governor swore like all tarnation / That they had spoilt his speculation.")[48] In the fall U.S. Secretary of War Jefferson Davis ordered that the borders of Fort Riley be expanded to encompass

LIBERTY, THE FAIR MAID OF KANSAS—IN THE HANDS OF THE "BORDER RUFFIANS".

*Political cartoon from the 1850s illustrating Kansans suffering outrages
at the hands of Border Ruffians. The Border Ruffians pictured here include
U.S. President Franklin Pierce (center), at whose feet "Liberty, The Fair
Maid of Kansas," is kneeling. (Courtesy of Kansas State Historical Society.)*

Pawnee, and the settlement dwindled to nothingness. Only the shell of the
capitol building remained at the site.

With the bustle of the legislature gone, Manhattan was again left a remote frontier settlement. Imminent threat of attack also passed. Indeed,
Manhattan suffered no violence during the short legislative session in Pawnee. Julia Lovejoy would exult after the legislature departed, "Notwithstand-
ing the blustering and threats of the half-drunk pro-slavery party, not one
solitary revolver was fired at any free-soil man or one bowie-knife aimed at
one defenceless head."[49] The change in the capital's location probably saved
Manhattan much misery during the coming years, as the focus of the fight
between Free-Staters and the proslavery faction shifted away from Pawnee
and back to the eastern border of Kansas Territory.

When the Territorial Legislature reconvened in Shawnee Mission on July
16, 1855, it immediately began passing laws that would codify the establishment of slavery in Kansas. Manhattanite Samuel Houston delayed in going
to Shawnee Mission — he faced the prospect of a long trip to rejoin a body
that was eviscerating his Free-State views. So, on the first day at the new

location another legislator crowed: "Mr. *Houston,* the free soil Abolitionist member from Pawnee, has not yet arrived, and as he is the only *'black sheep'* in the fold, it is supposed he will resist the *acts* of this Legislature. A fine time is coming when these fellows, whose valor is now oozing out at their finger ends, will be put to the test, and made to . . . take the punishment due to criminals and offenders of the laws of the country."[50] When Houston did ultimately set out from Manhattan, Goodnow wrote with resignation, "S. D. Houston, one of nature's noblemen, has gone down to do what he *may,* to expose the chicanery of the Slavery Propagandists."[51] Only days after arriving at Shawnee Mission, on July 22, Houston realized, however, that there was nothing he could do by himself to thwart the proslavery legislation, and he resigned his seat in the Territorial Legislature in disgust. Houston published an explanation for his resignation, decrying the actions of the legislature as "unreasonable and unconstitutional and which must, if not checked, precipitate this Territory into a state of complete anarchy."[52] In writing his history of Kansas, future governor Charles Robinson later wrote that Houston's resignation was "regarded as [a] most able and conclusive" denunciation of the legislature.[53]

Among the laws the Territorial Legislature passed during this session were those making it a felony to criticize the institution of slavery and imposing two to five years of hard labor upon anyone possessing any abolitionist publication, ten years of hard labor for helping a slave to escape, and the death penalty for inciting a slave revolt.[54] It's worth noting that slaves were a not inconsiderable presence in Kansas Territory at the time. A February 1855 census revealed that the territory was home to 192 slaves out of a total population of 8,601.[55]

Manhattanite Thomas Wells expressed the defiant reaction of many Free-Staters to the legislature's embrace of slavery in a letter to his family in August 1855: "The people will not trouble themselves to obey any laws passed by such a sham Legislature."[56] Isaac Goodnow similarly wrote in a letter to Rhode Island: "Our Missouri-Kansas legislators are doing their best to render themselves ridiculous, and to excite the indignation of every friend of liberty. Their laws will be for the most part a dead letter. Already the people of the territory have repudiated them!"[57] Goodnow also issued a plea for more emigrants from New England: "Though Tyranny is now in the ascendant, Freedom will triumph, if her sons do their duty. . . . N.E. men have a heavy responsibility & while the battle is doubtful, should not hesitate."[58]

A letter from Julia Lovejoy written during the same month took an even more martial tone: "Scenes have been enacted in this Territory, within a few months past, and lawless ruffianism, perpetrated on peaceable, unoffending citizens, sufficient to rouse the spirit of '76, in the breast of every freeman; and it is aroused." She continued: "Military companies are forming, and though we may be accounted feeble in regard to numerical strength, compared with the hordes that may flock here from Missouri, the 'battle is not always to the strong,' and truth and justice, will eventually triumph. 'Kanzas must be free' though blood may be shed, and hundreds fall victims to the bloody moloch of slavery."[59]

Free-Staters began to stir into action in August, when an assembly of men from around the territory met at Lawrence and resolved not to obey the laws of the Territorial Legislature, nor to pay taxes to the territorial government.[60] Members of the convention included Isaac Goodnow, Luke Lincoln, and John Brown Jr., the eldest son of abolitionist zealot John Brown. A written address from Samuel Houston—the only popularly elected Free-Stater to have held office in Kansas—was read to the assembly, which concluded, "Your work will be done when slavery's dark belt of hell no longer encircles a single hill or valley of Kansas."[61] A month later, many of the same Free-Staters met again and determined to grab the initiative by drafting a constitution for Kansas that would bar slavery.[62] In October 1855—the same month that John Brown arrived in Kansas Territory—the Free-Staters reassembled in Topeka and drew up a constitution that prohibited slavery (and that also would have barred free African Americans from settling in Kansas) in defiance of the elected legislature.[63] After this point, the debate over slavery in Kansas Territory devolved into open violence, making the earlier Osborn misadventure in Manhattan look positively quaint in retrospect.

On October 25, 1855, a proslavery settler killed Free-Stater Samuel Collins in Doniphan, Kansas.[64] A month later, on November 21, another proslavery settler killed Free-Stater Charles W. Dow south of Lawrence.[65] Although Dow was actually killed over a land dispute (as in the Osborn affair), those arguing over slavery latched onto his murder and it led to a series of escalating reprisals.[66] As a result of events stemming directly from Dow's murder, by early December over 1,000 proslavery men were camped south of Lawrence, threatening attack.[67] On December 8, 1855, Chestina Allen, a New England immigrant living in Juniata, reported: "A circular was received from Lawrence asking aid from our Freesoilers to protect them in their

Notice for Free-State mass meetings in the fall of 1855.
(Courtesy of Kansas State Historical Society.)

rights as citizens. . . . A Collision is expected in Lawrence."[68] Two days later Isaac Goodnow wrote that "Missourians are threatening Lawrence with fire & war."[69] Several volunteers from Manhattan marched to defend Lawrence, joining John Brown and other Free-Staters from across the territory. Goodnow later wrote of those who went to defend Lawrence, "The spirit of 76 was thoroughly up & our army really wished for the assault."[70] In the end, however, the situation was defused without violence and both groups peacefully dispersed, ending the tense standoff now known by the overblown name of the "Wakarusa War."[71]

On January 15, 1856, an election was held for a shadow Free-State government under the constitution the Free-Staters drafted in Topeka the previous October. In the balloting, Dr. Charles Robinson was elected governor.[72] Nine days after the election, U.S. President Franklin Pierce gave a lengthy address that fiercely condemned as rebellious the Free-Staters' attempt to form their own government. President Pierce said, in part: "In fact what has been done is of revolutionary character. It is avowedly so in motive and in aim as respects the local law of the Territory. It will become treasonable insurrection if it reach the length of organized resistance by force to the fundamental or any other Federal law and to the authority of the General Government."

The Pierce administration was clearly siding with the proslavery government, despite allegations of voting fraud in March 1855. Abolitionist Horace Greeley, editor of the New-York Tribune, the most influential paper in the United States, observed, "The Border Ruffians have been raised entirely off their feet by Pierce's extraordinary Messages, which they regard as a complete endorsement of all their past outrages and an incitement to persevere in their diabolical work."[73] Despite the president's speech, from March 4 to March 19, 1856, the shadow Free-State government convened in Topeka. But, for defying President Pierce, a grand jury responded by ordering the arrest of several leaders in Topeka.[74]

The Free-Staters still held out hope that they might receive support from the federal government when the U.S. House of Representatives sent a three-man congressional investigating committee to Kansas Territory in April to look into voting irregularities. On April 4, 1856, William Goodnow wrote that the committee had arrived in the territory and predicted that "the facts of the numerous frauds at the polls by the Missourians will soon be made known in substantial proof."[75] While in Kansas Territory, the congressional committee took testimony from numerous settlers on both sides of the question of whether the Missourians' actions constituted election fraud. Upon completion, the majority report strongly favored the Free-Staters' point of view. It was highly critical of Missourians and concluded that if the election in March 1855 had been limited to "actual settlers" it would have elected a Free-State legislature.[76] The report also stated that the legislature actually seated "was an illegally constituted body, and had no power to pass valid laws."[77] Nonetheless, Free-Staters were once again disappointed by the outcome, as the U.S. House of Representatives ultimately took no steps to unseat the Territorial Legislature elected in March 1855.

Thomas Wells, who had returned to the East Coast to pass the winter of 1855–1856, wrote to his family upon returning to Kansas Territory in April 1856: "There has been more trouble in Kansas this winter than I had supposed; the wrongs of the free state people have not been exaggerated in the papers. . . . For a long time no one could go to or from Kansas City without having his baggage searched, and even now the Missourians frequently break open heavy trunks or boxes to search for Sharps rifles of which they stand in great fear."[78] At the start of the same month, John Brown Jr. also wrote from Kansas: "The question here is, shall we be freemen or Slaves?" Brown explained: "The South is arming and sending in her men, the North is doing the same thing, it is now decreed and certain that the 'Slave power' must desist from its aggressive acts upon the settlers of Kansas or if they do not, the war-cry heard upon the plains will reverberate not only through the hemp and tobacco fields of Missouri, but through the 'Rice swamps,' the cotton and sugar plantations of the Sunny South."[79]

On April 23, 1856, Lawrence's proslavery sheriff Samuel Jones was shot and wounded while attempting to arrest some Free-State leaders in Lawrence. Tension again escalated. On May 5, another Free-State settler, named John Stewart, was fatally shot. Three other Free-Staters went to investigate the shooting, and one of those, Charles Lenhart, was also shot and killed.[80]

On May 11, 1856, federal marshal I. B. Donaldson declared the residents of Lawrence to be in defiance of the grand jury subpoena for harboring members of the Free-State government. The town's residents fully expected Sheriff Jones to use this order as a pretext to seek vengeance for his shooting, so Lawrence again summoned help from other Free-State towns. After receiving notice of these affairs, William Goodnow wrote that Manhattan was "prepar[ing] for war! war!! war!!!"[81] Although it was a very busy time for farmers, many Free-Staters, including thirty-five men from Manhattan,

A cartoonist's view of the federal government forcing slavery on Kansas Territory in the 1850s. (Cartoon by John L. Magee. Courtesy of the Kansas State Historical Society.)

again gathered whatever arms they could find and marched to defend Lawrence.[82] William Goodnow noted, "It is a very bad time in calling them away now from their much needed labors — but they leave their plows in the field & grain unplanted to assist the needy as our fathers of the revolution did."[83] As the Manhattan contingent marched east up the dusty trails from Manhattan to Topeka, they also lobbied vigorously to recruit Free-State reinforcements along the way.[84] But when the Manhattanites reached Topeka, they received news that there would be no fight in Lawrence, so after lingering a while they turned back. Thomas Wells was among the Manhattanites who had marched to help defend Lawrence, and he explained in a letter that "as we could not afford to remain a long time at Topeka for nothing we returned home, but the Missourians were permitted to remain where they were committing every kind of outrage upon the free state people."[85]

Sheriff Jones patiently waited for the furor to pass and the reinforcements to disburse, and then on May 21 he marched on Lawrence with several hundred men. The posse was authorized to make arrests and eliminate resistance, but under cover of enforcing the federal subpoena the mob also illegally ransacked and burned several buildings, including private residences, and destroyed the equipment of the *Lawrence Herald of Freedom* — though without killing or seriously injuring anyone.[86] Afterward, a delighted Sheriff Jones declared: "This is the happiest moment of my life. I determined to make the fanatics bow before me in the dust, and kiss the territorial laws; and I have done it — by G-d I have done it."[87]

Still the violence spread. The day after the sack of Lawrence, on May 22, 1856, U.S. Congressman Preston Brooks from South Carolina viciously attacked Senator Charles Sumner of Massachusetts in the Senate chamber. The assault was in retaliation for a speech given by Sumner entitled "The Crime Against Kansas," which criticized proslavery senators for supporting violence in Kansas Territory. Brooks beat Senator Sumner with a gold-headed cane until he was bloody and unconscious.[88] Sumner's injuries were so severe that he was unable to return to duty in the Senate for three years, and Massachusetts left the seat empty to illustrate southern violence.

The Free-Staters hung fire until this point; as already noted, they preferred a nonviolent approach. (This approach was taken to absurd extremes by Manhattan settler Andrew Scammon, who once defended himself from violent threats from Border Ruffians by warning them that he possessed a copy of the Massachusetts Constitution — a "weapon of warfare more formidable to slavery than rifles.")[89] But two days after the attack on Senator Sumner, on the night of May 24, 1856, abolitionist John Brown and seven other men hacked five proslavery men to death with broadswords along Pottawatomie Creek in Kansas Territory.[90] A week later, on June 2, John Brown took the future Confederate Colonel Henry C. Pate and twenty-two other proslavery soldiers prisoner at the "Battle of Black Jack."[91] The fighting was heating up.[92]

On June 21, 1856, Manhattanite Thomas Wells wrote a long letter to his brother, reflecting on the violence unleashed in Kansas Territory: "We *have had* pretty hard times in our territory since we have been here. The 'border ruffians' accompanied by a large number of Southerners have been over here with the intention of either driving the Yankees home or making them submit to the laws of the *bogus legislature, neither* of which they have been able to do." Elsewhere in the territory, Wells reported that the Border Ruffians had been "committing all sorts of depredations, stealing cattle, robbing private houses, and searching, and taking whatever they wished from, every wagon or individual that attempted to pass by them, and they killed several men and took others prisoner."[93] Wells maintained hope, however, that Manhattan could remain relatively unscathed: "As yet all is peaceable where we are, but we know not how long it will remain so, yet it seems that the present state of things cannot last long or if it does there will be civil war between the whole North and South and then we shall be as well off here as elsewhere." He concluded: "We can but hope however that these troubles will soon ease, and we trust that Christians in the east will unite their prayers with ours to the great Ruler of the Universe for a return of peace and prosperity to this part of the country and for the removal from our midst of that great evil which has caused such disturbances — American Slavery."[94]

On July 4, 1856, three squadrons of federal troops broke up another scheduled meeting of the Free-State legislature in Topeka.[95] John Brown marched his men to Topeka to defend the meeting, but he decided not to oppose the federal troops and remained outside town.[96]

In August thousands of proslavery Southerners formed into loosely organized armies and marched into Kansas.[97] In Manhattan, Thomas Wells recorded that month that "a party of armed Southerners" marched on a campaign of intimidation up the Blue River past Manhattan, but "without doing any damage that I have heard of."[98] Chestina Allen in Juniata described the group as a large party of Georgians who were intending "to camp and hunt Free states men," although she too reported no local casualties from the mob.[99] Almost certainly the citizens of Manhattan were spared from violence due to their proximity to Fort Riley. Elsewhere, at the same time, Kansans saw "the dogs of war let loose, and armed men, thronging the streets of Lawrence and Topeka."[100] According to one breathless report, "the roads were literally strewn with dead bodies."[101] Though only fifty-six people actually died during the entire Bleeding Kansas era, the immediacy of civil war — not knowing whether neighbors might turn against you — understandably made it appear far deadlier and terrifying for the participants.[102]

Finally, on August 30, 1856, John Brown and several of his followers engaged 300 proslavery soldiers in the "Battle of Osawatomie." Echoing the colonists' attack on the British during their march from Concord to Lexington in 1775, John Brown's men fired from the wilderness as the proslavery soldiers marched down the road to Osawatomie. Brown's men were eventually routed by the numerically superior troops, but casualties were heavy for the proslavery men, and the attack cemented Brown's exalted reputation among abolitionists.[103]

By the end of the summer, the sustained violence had apparently worn out both sides, and an uneasy quiet settled over Bleeding Kansas for several months. Tensions were further eased by the departure of John Brown from Kansas Territory and the arrival of a more effective and impartial territorial governor, John Geary.[104] But at the same time, the Free-Staters were dealt two disheartening blows when Democrat James Buchanan was elected U.S. president in November and the U.S. Supreme Court issued the *Dred Scott* decision in December. Buchanan, who defeated Republican John C. Frémont (the first presidential candidate from the new party), had no sympathy for the Free-Staters and no intention of intervening in Kansas. Goodnow lamented his election as "a National calamity & especially a calamity for poor Kansas!"[105] Indeed, in Buchanan's inaugural address, he condemned the abolitionist movement generally and the Free-State movement in Kansas specifically, stating, "whilst it has been productive of no positive good to any human being it has been the prolific source of great evils to the master, to the slave, and to the whole country." The *Dred Scott* decision, for its part, held that Congress did not have the power to exclude slavery from any of the country's territories, including Kansas, and that all African Americans were not -- and never could be — U.S. citizens. Interpreting the language in the Declaration of Independence that states "all men are created equal," the Supreme Court wrote, "it is too clear for dispute, that the enslaved African race were not intended to be included."[106]

7
THE WEARYING WORK OF FRONTIER LIFE

Against a backdrop of terror and violence, Manhattan's settlers toiled in 1855 and 1856 to carve a model community from the wilderness. Fortunately, two factors allowed Manhattan to remain relatively untouched by the violence that took place elsewhere in Bleeding Kansas. The first was Manhattan's location: it was both far from the Missouri border (125 miles) and near to the U.S. troops at Fort Riley. The second was Manhattan's largely homogenous Free-State population, or as Samuel D. Houston put it at the time, "the absence of disturbing elements in our midst."[1] Isaac Goodnow noted this good fortune in July 1855: "As to Missouri fire-eaters and wickedness, we see but little of them. We are so far off from the border that we are not troubled with them."[2] Likewise, Thomas Wells wrote the following year, "We are enjoying a time of comparative peace and quiet, though the Missourians, Georgians, etc seem to hold a grudge against Manhattan and threaten to destroy the town."[3]

The peace provided Manhattan a unique opportunity to grow and prosper during the early, chaotic years of Kansas Territory. But building civilization on the wild and sparsely settled frontier was astonishingly hard, even if Bleeding Kansas violence did not visit Manhattan directly. And Manhattan's founders took on a heavier burden than merely surviving in this atmosphere. As Eli Thayer wrote in his book *Kansas Crusade,* the New England Emigrant Aid Company expected the communities it founded to be beacons of enlightenment to guide the southern masses; their emigrants were "to go to the prairies of Kansas and show the superiority of free-labor civilization; to go with all our free-labor trophies: churches and schools, printing presses, steam-engines, and mills; and in a peaceful contest convince every poor man from the South of the superiority of free labor."[4]

. Nevertheless, basic needs such as shelter and food took precedence over Eli Thayer's "trophies" in the summer of 1855. Much of the work that year was mundane and backbreaking. In June 1855 Isaac Goodnow observed that the settlement of Manhattan required "men not afraid of hard work, willing to rough it!"[5] Another exhausted new arrival wrote that settlers "must have the determination to bear all, and more if necessary."[6] Manhattan's settlers spent a good deal of the spring and summer seasons clearing land so that crops could be planted. Isaac Goodnow wrote in July, "In the spring [the prairies] were covered with weeds, some eight feet high, and shrubs and brush and logs, but fire and the axe and grub hoe prepared the way for the plough."[7] After clearing the land, it had to be plowed, and this "sod busting" was also no easy task: accumulated grass roots made the dirt nearly hard as rock.[8] Once the fields were plowed, the most common crop planted by Manhattan settlers was corn, although they also planted small sections of wheat.[9] The Yankees also planted small vegetable gardens and fruit trees, hoping to provide themselves with favorite foods from back home.

Hard work in the fields quickly paid off: by the first of July, green corn, peas, squash, and beans were already available.[10] Grapes were planted on the sides of the hills and, together with "luscious" wild grapes and raspberries, provided enough fruit that first season to make jellies and preserves.[11] (Children growing up in the early years of the town enjoyed going "graping" in the hills and along the banks of the Kansas River, where "vines clambered up trees and bushes creating beautiful arbors.")[12]

The settlers supplemented their young crops with abundant game and fish found in the area. The bounty prompted Julia Lovejoy to list the available game in May 1855, when she reported seeing "wild geese, turkeys, ducks, prairie hens, and deer; but they don't always stop long enough for a ball to hit them." She also added, "The rivers are full of fish of the finest flavor I ever tasted, similar to the Eastern trout, but a richer treat for the table. They are called catfish, and some of them weigh over 50 lbs., and sometimes twice that amount."[13]

At the same time, those who could find the time were also constructing cabins. Julia Lovejoy wrote that summer, "The sound of the hammer is heard on every hand."[14] Building these cabins was a labor-intensive project that required chopping down trees, hauling logs (often from some distance away), and sawing timber — simply to prepare the raw materials for construction.

The shortage of trees in the area significantly complicated the process, as Isaac Goodnow had worried before selecting the site. The limited choice of trees also forced the pioneers to build with less-than-ideal twisted tree trunks, resulting in large gaps in the walls. As Goodnow noted of his cabin in a letter to his wife: "The little Cabin in which I write is built of logs plastered outside with mud. . . . The cabin has no windows, as light can come in *through* the door! & the *chinks!*"[15] Many settlers found themselves hard-pressed that summer of 1855 to find the time to clear land, plant crops, hunt game, *and* build their cabins. For example, George Lee elected to build a cabin, but by the time he completed the walls, "our oxen had strayed away & our provisions gave out," requiring an emergency trip to Juniata just to get something to eat.[16] Accordingly, the prefabricated houses carried from Cincinnati on the *Hartford* — called "balloon houses" — were a tremendous blessing for the Manhattanites.[17] Just as important, the quality of the prefabricated buildings was better than the log cabins, so that the Lovejoy family happily replaced its original primitive cabin with one of the *Hartford*'s houses during the summer of 1855.[18]

Others resolved to make do with less permanent housing arrangements, such as tents, dugouts, or lean-tos. Indeed, Julia Lovejoy reported that there were nine *Hartford* cabins erected in Manhattan's city limits at the end of July 1855 but "25 or more 'habitations' of one kind or another."[19] The Cincinnati settlers also relied on the grounded *Hartford* as a temporary shelter throughout the summer.[20] Thomas Wells, like many others, passed the summer in a little canvas tent that he had carried from Rhode Island, reporting: "If I should tell you how we live here you would think we had rather a hard time — you could not bear it, — 'twould kill you, etc., but I like it very well especially in pleasant weather; 'tis not quite so pleasant when it storms."[21]

Many settlers early on even made do with no shelter at all. One of the pioneers who arrived on the *Hartford* commented that anyone coming to Manhattan "must not think hard if he sleeps on the wide prairie, with nothing above him but the blue heavens. It will not injure his health, I'll guarantee."[22] Julia Lovejoy likewise observed: "Men (and even ladies too) . . . can . . . sleep in the open air, on the prairies, in the ox-wagons, or wherever night

A family in Ellsworth County, Kansas, in front of their log cabin,
demonstrating the questionable quality of homes that early settlers were able
to build without sawmills. (Courtesy of Kansas State Historical Society.)

overtakes them, and suffer no inconvenience. I mean delicate ladies, who have been bred to effeminacy and accustomed the luxuries of a home, where wealth abounded."[23] Thomas Wells also noted: "The cooking is all done over the fire out of doors, something as yould cook at a picnic in the east. We set our table under a large oak tree and under it's shade we sit and talk or read when we have nothing else to do."[24] Another Manhattan settler later recalled the astonishing freedom of these experiences: "We were in a new world, as it were living a new life, a life as free as the air we breathe . . . un-hampered by the conventionalities of the so called civilized life." Neverthe-less, the settler continued, "While this was extremely romantic it was not always comfortable."[25]

Understandably, the pioneers certainly preferred having *some* sort of shelter. The wife of immigrant George Lee wrote that it was a particularly "sorry day" for her when one of her fellow settlers departed for Topeka in the spring of 1855, because he took with him the tent they had been sharing.[26] As a practical matter, exposed settlers were troubled by thunderstorms, small pernicious pests such as chiggers, and more deadly beasts like wolves and snakes. Francis Abbot later wrote, "In those days coyotes, wolves and other wild animals were a great deal more plentiful."[27] Likewise, Julia Lovejoy unhappily recalled, "Our nervous system received such a shock, partly real and half imaginative, from the 'serpent tribe' and the repeated 'calls' of the natives of this country."[28]

Succinctly summing up the settlers' experience, Julia Lovejoy wrote in August 1855, "Drones that cannot work hard or live on coarse fare, or sleep in cabins, with or without a bed, or on the open prairie need not come here."[29] Yet, despite the rough conditions and the pioneers' seemingly endless tasks, the first summer in Manhattan was not entirely unpleasant. Settlers in Manhattan often made social visits to each other. Community celebrations also provided an opportunity for the scattered settlers to gather — exchanging gossip, humorous anecdotes, home remedies, and news about crops, weather, and natural predators. The first opportunity for the pioneers to congregate was Independence Day 1855. On that day, a picnic at Wildcat Creek featuring public speakers brought together most of the settlers in the area.[30] New England abolitionists had recently claimed the Fourth of July — with its emphasis on liberty — as a major opportunity to criticize slavery, so it is not too surprising that the holiday became the largest annual gathering in Manhattan's early years. In addition to the first Fourth of July celebration, Thomas Wells wrote of a wedding later that summer, revealing that a fine feast could be prepared even on the frontier: "We had a wedding here last week out of doors! . . . A long table was set under the trees, loaded with cake of various kinds, tarts made from native grapes, which by the way are much smaller than the wild grapes of the east, custards, preserves, etc., while at a side table was roast pork, mutton and chicken in abundance."[31]

The pioneers also combined work with socializing, pitching in to help their neighbors whenever possible, particularly when a fellow settler was sick or injured. Settler Amos Powers later reminisced that people "can scarcely realize what the words 'good neighbors' meant in those pioneer days."[32] Manhattan's settlers helped each other to erect cabins, cooked for each other, and served as caregivers during times of sickness.[33] One New England immigrant observed, "In the simplicity of nature, in a new country, there is a mutual dependence between all, which is not realized at home."[34]

As the summer progressed, women began arriving in Manhattan to join their husbands and sons.[35] Among them was Ellen Goodnow, who joined her husband, Isaac, in Manhattan in July 1855.[36] Ellen Goodnow had set out from Boston on June 19, with a company of fifteen Emigrant Aid Company travelers, and met her husband in Lawrence on July 3.[37] For Ellen and Isaac, the months apart had been difficult. During his trip west, on March 24, Ellen wrote to him: "I feel you are sacrificing so much in being away from every privilege, and comfort of civilized life [and] I do feel it quite a self denial not to be with you. . . . I hope God will watch between us, and help us."[38] After arriving in Kansas, Isaac wrote to Ellen on April 8, "It is rather lonesome here without you." Two weeks later, Isaac was far more expansive, writing: "This living away from *one's wife* is poor miserable business *any way! Lonesome!* I daily feel the want of your presence & society."[39]

On deciding to join her husband in Kansas Territory that summer, Ellen wrote, "One thing I do believe I should not stand acquitted in the great day, had I not been willing to join my husband in laboring for the freedom of this territory."[40] Happily, it would also turn out that Ellen's friends' dire predictions that her health would fail in Kansas were groundless. To the contrary, moving to the frontier seemed to reinvigorate Ellen, as it had for several others. Upon arrival, she faced down typically primitive frontier conditions. When she arrived at her husband's cabin she found it measured a meager 10 feet by 12 feet inside, and "the carpet was freshly mown hay on the ground."[41] But the situation seemed to provide Ellen with a rejuvenating sense of purpose; two weeks after arriving she asserted, "God had reserved [Kansas] for his chosen people; it is too good for bondage, or for the oppressors rod ever to be raised over it."[42] By 1863 Isaac Goodnow reported to his mother: "Ellen is getting to be quite a healthful woman."[43] Ellen Goodnow lived in a house west of Manhattan for most of the next forty-five years, and she passed away there on April 23, 1900.

Nevertheless, the health dangers of the frontier were certainly not imaginary. In late July 1855, in the sickly heat of summer, a major outbreak of cholera struck in nearby Fort Riley. By the time it ended, there were 137 deaths — about a third of all men at the fort — including the commanding officer, Major Edmund A. Ogden.[44] News of the epidemic spread slowly at first, but on August 3 Isaac Goodnow noted in his diary, "Cholera raging at the Fort."[45] On August 6, Goodnow recorded that people were abandoning the fort, and two days later Thomas Wells noted in a letter: "The cholera has been raging terribly at Fort Reiley. . . . Some forty five or fifty persons died there last week."[46] Manhattanite Amos Powers had an intimate view of the outbreak while working in a civilian construction crew at the fort, and he later wrote of the full horror of the circumstances: "The men for a while died at the rate of twenty a day. I saw one young fellow lying near the sawmill dying in terrible agony. In a few hours his skin turned yellow and shrunken. . . . Major Ogden kept us well ones at work until he himself died [on August 3], then everything stopped. The Fort was deserted."[47] The state of affairs appeared most desperate after the fort's physician literally abandoned his post and fled the area, along with about 150 other deserters, following Major Ogden's death.[48] An even worse calamity was averted only when Dr. Samuel Whitehorn of Juniata heroically hastened to the fort to treat the sick men. (Dr. Whitehorn's youthful appearance raised doubts about whether he was actually a doctor until he produced a copy of his diploma and testimonials from Juniata.)[49] Although the outbreak never reached Manhattan, the village's residents looked on with dread at the events taking place upriver.

Immigration to Manhattan continued to be slow into the fall of 1855.[50] Nonetheless, by early October Manhattan acquired its first commercial operation — a small market opened by two Cincinnati settlers, Ira Taylor and Thomas Platt.[51] The two merchants arrived in Manhattan with a stock of goods, probably transported on the *Hartford*. Among other items, the store sold clothing, whiskey, dry goods, and foods such as bacon and flour.[52] Many New Englanders were not entirely happy about the presence of the town's first store, however, because it stocked liquor. Isaac Goodnow disgustedly wrote of Taylor, "I consider the influence of a Rumseller deleterious to any place."[53] Similarly, the *Lawrence Herald of Freedom* later complained, "There is but one drawback to this upper country (Manhattan and vicinity), that is, they sell and drink too much whiskey."[54]

Despite the backbreaking work of its settlers, as the year progressed, Manhattan's pioneers began to worry that the settlement was not growing sufficiently quickly. When Ellen Goodnow arrived in Manhattan in July 1855, she could not hide her disappointment: "Owing to not getting sawmills going as they would like to . . . , there are not so many buildings in the city as I had anticipated."[55] To help spur development, the Manhattan Town

Association voted at a meeting on June 29, 1855, to distribute ten shares to any stockholder who would build a structure worth $250 within the next sixteen months.[56] The offer was soon also extended to nonshareholders. Yet progress remained slow.

As autumn deepened, the need to improve the makeshift living arrangements in Manhattan became more pressing. Because the previous winter had been mild in Kansas Territory, and the Kansas summer was hotter than in New England, several Yankees were misled and "supposed that a tent or a rude cabin would be sufficient shelter" for the Kansas winter.[57] This was not true. Although Kansas is a hot state — temperatures in Manhattan have soared over ninety-five degrees every month between March and October — it is also very cold — subfreezing temperatures have been recorded in the state every month of the year.[58] In October 1855, temperatures plunged dramatically, and what settler Amos Powers later simply called "the cold winter" began.[59]

As Ellen Goodnow had observed, part of the reason that there were so few buildings in Manhattan was the absence of a sawmill to cut logs and limestone, which would have greatly eased cabin construction. The New England Emigrant Aid Company had in fact promised to provide a mill for Manhattan, and Isaac Goodnow wrote to ask for it just days after his arrival on site, but the company failed to fulfill this obligation for months on end.[60] Exasperated, on October 9, 1855, the Manhattan Town Association sent Rev. Charles Lovejoy to meet with the New England Company agent Samuel C. Pomeroy in Lawrence "and urge the matter forward as fast as possible."[61] Finally, in November the company delivered a steam-powered, thirty-horsepower sawmill to Manhattan.[62] Upon hearing that the mill was coming, Goodnow exuberantly wrote in his diary, "Hurrah! Hurrah!"[63] Describing the importance of the mill, Goodnow asserted years later that "the arrival of the Emigrant Aid mill from Lawrence, drawn by twenty yoke of oxen, was a greater event to us than that of the Union Pacific Railroad [in 1866]."[64]

Pomeroy supervised the erection of the mill, which was installed on land bordering the Big Blue River.[65] The townspeople also set up a small grindstone at the mill — the first grindstone in the territory outside of military outposts and missions.[66] However, because the sawmill was not operable until December, it came too late in the season to have much impact on the miserable housing situation.[67] Manhattan's settlers therefore entered their first winter in Kansas with a primitive housing stock; their cabins were incredibly drafty and absurdly small.[68] The wooden walls lacked plaster to stop the winds, and the cabins also lacked floors, being built directly on the cold, damp earth. Thomas Wells, who acquired a split-log cabin in October 1855, described it as principally an enclosure for his tent and campfire:

> We have just moved into a house, that is a pile of logs with a roof on top of them. The spaces between the logs are not filled up yet, but we have a tent cloth, wagon cover, quilts comforters, etc hung up around the sides to keep off the wind for the present, and have, also a tent set up inside of the house; we have no chimney but build our fires on the ground in one corner of the house . . . and old mother earth serves us for a floor. But this is a great improvement on "camping out" as we have done.[69]

One Manhattan settler observed of the cabins that "the snow, rain and wind found ready access, and were unwelcome visitors in every household."[70] Amos Powers wrote that during one snowstorm in 1855 six inches of snow accumulated inside his cabin: "I built a big fire in the fireplace. Soon the snow began melting around the children's heads. The oldest girl was the only one who was frosted. Her face and hands swelled up like puff balls. The mud on the floor was several inches deep, so we brought in more 'prairie feathers' [straw] and spread over it."[71] Another Manhattan settler wrote back East in 1856, "Our house is quite comfortable or more so than any in this region, and yet you would almost as soon think of moving into a barn, in the east, as of moving into an unfinished house like this."[72]

Additionally, because the settlers were limited in what they could transport across the country, the small, drafty cabins contained few domestic comforts. Settler George Lee's wife recalled, "We spent the first summer [1855] having neither stove, chairs, table or floor in our cabin."[73] Bed frames were sometimes made of forked sticks, driven into the dirt floors, with "poles laid across these and securely fastened to a log in the house."[74] One nearby resident recalled an improvised bed in 1855 made out of planks covered with cut grass, which was made to hold several families: "We arranged it so that one lady could go to bed on one end, the husband next, then another husband, then his wife, and so on."[75] "O how I sighed for a comfortable home, in N.E. again," wrote Julia Lovejoy.[76]

Left with few other options, some frigid immigrants, such as Thomas Wells and C. N. Wilson, returned to New England to pass the winter season.

As Isaac Goodnow understatedly observed, "such cold weather is rather discouraging to new settlers in their open cabins."[77] Those remaining in Manhattan in their tents or rude unfinished cabins suffered during the winter of 1855–1856. On January 26, 1856, Goodnow wrote from his own tiny, drafty log cabin: "We are having a trying winter. I feel very grateful that I am so comfortably provided for. But fear that many emigrants are not so well off."[78] The cold did, however, provide Goodnow with the cheering thought that "such weather must frighten off slaveholders & their servants."[79]

Although shelter was a serious problem, no deaths from exposure were recorded. Moreover, thankfully, the settlers were sufficiently provisioned with food, so at the very least starvation was not an issue that winter. Indeed, just as winter was settling in, the men of Manhattan supplemented the village's stores of food by going on a "meat trip" with members of the Kansa and Potawatomi tribes to hunt bison on the plains west of the settlement. Isaac Goodnow later wrote of the trip: "It was all very good business so long as we kept clear of the warlike Cheyennes. The Kaw and Pottawatomie Indians, always ready for war in their hunting expeditions, usually kept the hostile Indians at a distance."[80] As with the Kansa who lived there before them, the winter bison hunt would become an annual event for Manhattanites, drawing teams of men onto the western plains.[81]

Isaac Goodnow later wrote that the exposed living conditions, difficult travel, and wearying work were enough to permanently drive many New Englanders back to the United States before the first year was out, but he would not be discouraged: "Half the company . . . stopped by the way or became discouraged from the hardships and returned, not having counted the cost to begin with. Even of those who reached us, probably one-half left us the first season. It required special effort to drive off homesickness. I told them that I had come to Kansas to help make it a free State, and should remain till that was accomplished, if they *all* left."[82]

1856
WAITING OUT THE VIOLENCE

When 1856 dawned, white settlers had been at the junction of the Kansas and Big Blue rivers for a year and a half. The pioneers felt that they had done well in establishing the colony, particularly considering they "labored under every disadvantage for want of lumber, roads, etc."[1] Yet the frozen outpost remained extremely primitive. Despite receiving ten prefabricated buildings from Cincinnati, Manhattan still had only eighteen to twenty total buildings in January 1856.[2] Moreover, none of the settlement's cabins were built of anything more permanent than wood or sod brick, many residents lived in tents, and the community itself offered no amenities other than a sawmill (operating under a temporary shelter) and one water well.[3] There were probably fewer than one hundred settlers living within the borders of Manhattan, although the population of farmers immediately outside the town's borders likely counted an additional one hundred.

The settlement also faced the serious challenge of having the more established village of Juniata only five miles north. Juniata was estimated by one settler in 1855 to be home to "about fifty families."[4] Although this was probably an overestimate of its population, Juniata was certainly better situated than Manhattan — it benefited from receiving the bulk of the overland east-west traffic because it was on the Military Road, and it boasted the only bridge over the Big Blue River. Tellingly, Manhattan residents were forced to trek to Juniata to collect their mail, at least until Manhattan's first post office opened in the autumn.[5]

But early in the new year fortune smiled on Manhattan: as a result of runoff from heavy snows and "an unusual quantity of ice," on February 26,

1856, a flood of water and ice washed away Juniata's invaluable bridge over the Big Blue River.[6] Seizing the opportunity, the very next day Cincinnati company leader John Pipher hurried to Fort Riley to ask the army to build a replacement bridge in Manhattan.[7] The army declined to build a new bridge in either Manhattan or Juniata, and both towns moved quickly to respond to the changed situation. In Juniata, Dyer promptly established a new ferry at his crossing by March 18, 1856.[8] But the natural disaster spelled the beginning of the end for his settlement, because travel through Manhattan cut a few miles off the trip west, and from that point forward river crossings increasingly took place in Manhattan.

By April 1856 Manhattan residents had instituted their own ferry across the Big Blue River, near the base of Bluemont Hill, and were marking out a new road leading to their crossing.[9] One of the early ferrymen was Amos Powers, a sardonic twenty-six-year-old settler originally from Kentucky.[10] He operated both a small ferryboat and a larger seventy-foot boat, capable of carrying teams of horses, each of which was maneuvered by pole and a cable running from shore to shore.[11] The cost for an individual to cross the ferry on foot was ten cents, a rider paid fifteen cents, a horse and carriage cost twenty-five cents, and a large wagon with a team of horses or oxen was charged seventy-five cents.[12] Powers occasionally poled the ferryboat down to the Kansas River and used it for crossings on that river as well.[13] On April 20, 1856, with arrangements for the Blue ferry finalized, the Manhattan Town Association turned to the task of also establishing a permanent ferry across the Kansas River with an even more southerly trail.[14] The ferry across the Kansas River, near the present base of Yuma Street, would be up and running by the end of the year.[15] Significantly, on May 21, 1856, three months after the failure of the Juniata bridge, the U.S. Army started sending its teams across the Big Blue River on the Manhattan ferry instead of the Juniata ferry.[16] Manhattan had stolen Juniata's lifeblood.

That same month, Manhattanites approved publication of a map of the town that boldly showed a fully established community. The map, initially commissioned in July 1855, showed a town that could accommodate tens of thousands, despite the fact only one hundred or so were living in the little village when it was drawn. As one settler cracked, "The town plat was laid out by an imaginary survey into nine thousand imaginary lots, with the necessary streets, avenues, public squares, markets, parks, etc., needful for a city of such imposing magnitude — on paper."[17]

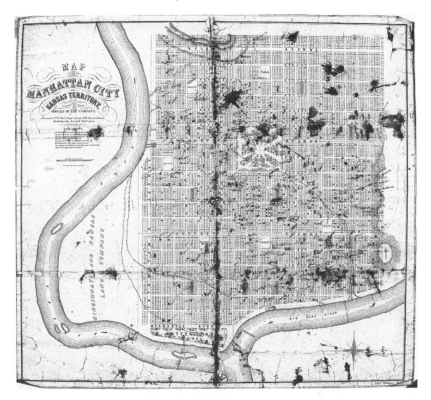

An 1856 map of Manhattan commissioned by the Manhattan Town Association. Only a few scattered cabins actually existed when it was printed, but the map set forth the grid and street names for the future town. (Courtesy of Kansas State Historical Society.

The map showed the town laid out on a grid, with each street named. The principal street, which headed west from the conjunction of the rivers, was laid out wide enough to accommodate horse teams turning around, giving Manhattan the broad main street common in many old Kansas towns. It was originally called Main Street, but it was renamed Poyntz Avenue on the map in honor of Col. John Poyntz, an Ohioan who had helped finance the purchase of the *Hartford* but probably never set foot in Manhattan.[18] The first cross street, on the banks of the Kansas River, was named Wyandotte Avenue. Above Wyandotte Avenue cross streets were generally numbered, starting with First Street.[19] The map also showed a forty-five-acre park in the center of the proposed town (which now exists and is named City Park);

a smaller park at the junction of the two rivers to be named Battery Park (which was never fully developed); and public squares throughout, as in a New England village (most of which are currently used for some public purpose). The Manhattan Town Association approved the map on May 31, 1856, and quickly had it published.[20] In this way, most of the street names and the grid at the core of present-day Manhattan were centrally planned. The idea for the map may have come from the concept of the preplanned utopian communities tried in the United States during the prior two decades, or it may simply have been an advertisement to attract settlers.[21]

As the spring of 1856 progressed, more businesses began to crop up in the town. To accommodate travelers on Manhattan's new ferry, Andrew Mead, one of the leaders of the Cincinnati company, enlarged one of the prefabricated buildings brought on the *Hartford* and converted it into the town's first hotel, built on the southern side of Poyntz Avenue by the Kansas River crossing.[22] Meanwhile, to receive and hold goods arriving with the new traffic, William Goodnow, who had been a merchant in Maine, built a small stone warehouse — the first stone structure in the town.[23] Also, early in 1856 two new markets opened in Manhattan. The first was opened by the industrious William Goodnow, who began selling provisions out of his log cabin on Leavenworth Street, including flour, meat, candied apples, sugar, tea, and molasses.[24] Shortly afterward, John Pipher and George Miller, from the Cincinnati company, opened a far more substantial general store on Poyntz Avenue, on the southwest corner of Third Street.[25] Pipher's shop on Poyntz quickly became the "center of attraction" for the small settlement, serving as host for public meetings and dominating the commercial trade in the town's first years.[26]

At the time, operating a store anywhere in Kansas Territory was a fairly risky proposition because of the very real chance that partisans from either side of the Bleeding Kansas violence would plunder it for supplies.[27] In fact, William Goodnow had at least one shipment raided, complaining in a letter in May 1856 that a "load of goods [was] overhauled & damaged by a party of Southerners."[28] Unfortunately for Manhattanites, the difficulties faced by the merchants in moving stock long distances by wagon through uncertain territory were reflected in higher prices; as Pipher noted, "we are so far from the States that the expense of procuring food & clothing is very great."[29] Even so, the merchants' problems were not universally appreciated; nearby settler Josiah Pillsbury wrote to his brother that "they are such a set of cutthroats there [in Manhattan] that the people are ready to go anywhere to trade with an honest man."[30]

At the same time, the town's cabins were slowly also being improved. In April, newly arrived settler John Kimball wrote to tell his family that he had built a ten-foot-square cabin, "not as warm as your barn, but . . . better than some of the folks had here last winter." Kimball also noted that his fellow Manhattanites "are fixing up now what they did not have time to do last fall."[31] Most notable among the new and improved residences in the colony was a limestone house, being built west of town by C. N. Wilson in May 1856 — the first residence constructed of stone in the area and today the oldest structure inside Manhattan's expanded borders.[32] That same month, Thomas Wells wrote that Manhattan proper had grown to "not more than twenty five [buildings] . . . including two stores, and one very good saw-mill with grist-mill attached which work very well. Quite a number of homes are going up very soon, some of them will be built of stone, and another saw mill is going up within two miles of the 'city.'"[33] Plans were also forming to build limestone churches, although for now religious services were still held "out of doors under the trees, in tents, in cabins."[34]

The town was also receiving a fresh infusion of Free-State immigrants. In May 1856 William Goodnow boasted: "Emigrants are arriving now almost every day from the Eastern & Western states & our Territory is filling up with Free State people. You need not fear, I think, as to slavery ever being established here."[35] The month of May in fact saw the arrival of several settlers who would later play significant roles in the town's development. First to arrive, on May 1, 1856, were two enterprising Free-State brothers from Virginia, Uriah and George Washington Higinbotham, who originally homesteaded in Eureka Valley, southwest of Manhattan.[36] The Higinbothams — approvingly described by one contemporary as "hustlers" — immediately established a freight line to transport goods from Leavenworth to Fort Riley. Three years later, in January 1859, they purchased a store on Poyntz Avenue to sell their goods directly.[37] George W. Higinbotham also opened the first bank in Manhattan in December 1866, at Poyntz Avenue and Third Street, and later served two terms as Manhattan's mayor.[38]

Next to arrive, a few days later in May 1856, was Washington Marlatt, a young man from Indiana.[39] Marlatt was an interesting character. Proud, outspoken, and highly combustible, he once described himself as full of "brass."[40] Others described him when upset as having "the resolution and

Purcell and Higinbotham storefront at Poyntz Avenue and Third Street, 1860s. The store was opened by John Pipher in 1856 and was one of the first buildings in Manhattan. (Courtesy of Kansas State Historical Society.)

demeanor of a lion and the roaring of tempest," and in his letters he de-
nounced certain of his fellow Manhattan settlers as "asses," "rascals," and
"loafers."[41] Yet, because he was a devout Methodist, the testy Marlatt was
able to ingratiate himself into Isaac Goodnow's circle and to play a significant role in helping Goodnow establish a school in Manhattan in 1858 (Blue
Mont Central College). Marlatt also served as a county commissioner and,
after Blue Mont College opened in 1860, as a teacher and principal of the
preparatory department at the college.

Manhattan's first full spring also saw tremendous growth in settlers' crops
and their stock of animals. William Goodnow noted on May 4, 1856, "We
are now having frequent showers of rain, and the grass is green and nice &
cattle have good feed & the cows give lots of milk."[42] Later that month he
observed, "Vegetation is coming along fast, and our prospects fair for a good
crop."[43] The settlers were fortunate to be blessed with good weather, because
many were inexperienced farmers making rookie mistakes along the way.
For example, Isaac Goodnow, a teacher by trade, planted a field of corn in
1856 that simply did not come up, so he plowed it under and tried again.[44]
That same year Thomas Wells, a former clerk, wrote, "I did not get my field
fenced and the stray cattle have harvested considerable of my corn for me
which is not very pleasant."[45] Settler Francis Abbott, who had worked in the
cotton mills in Massachusetts, recounted yet another mishap: "The first fall
I was here I had, by hiring help, gotten up a fine lot of hay for my oxen and
cows. In trying to burn around the stacks to protect against prairie fire, I lost
control and burned them all."[46] Wells later summed up his experiences: "You
know I was a perfectly *green* hand at farming when I came here and have had
to learn everything by experience; sometimes such knowledge has cost me
considerable."[47] The bumbling farmer-settlers of Manhattan did, however,
have one unique advantage in plying their new trade: the proximity of a
ready market for surplus crops and livestock in the U.S. Army at Fort Riley.[48]
Historically, most Americans arriving in the hinterlands had to wait years
before they had the opportunity to sell produce — until a consistent market
developed nearby or reliable transportation arrived. In the meantime, frontier farms grew only what they could personally use.[49] But Manhattanites
began selling their produce to the fort almost immediately.

The first five months of 1856 saw a great deal of growth and bustling activity in Manhattan. But in late May, following the sacking of Lawrence,

John Brown's massacre on Pottawatomie Creek, and a shocking increase in violence in Kansas, Manhattan's forward momentum abruptly stalled. Violence raged at such a level that summer that when the U.S. Army marched through Manhattan's streets on its way to Topeka to break up the Free-State legislature, it left behind twenty blue-clad soldiers stationed in Manhattan, including a sentinel stationed at the top of Bluemont Hill to watch for the approach of belligerent armies.[50] While gazing out at the army sentinel from her cabin that July, Julia Lovejoy despaired in her diary: "Almost every week sombody falls by the hand of violence, and I know not that any place is secure. The Free State men, are shot by pro-slavery villains, as beasts of prey."[51] The U.S. troops soon decamped from Manhattan but returned again briefly the next month after a squad of proslavery Georgians marched through the town on a campaign of intimidation.[52]

At the same time, it also became far more hazardous for Free-State immigrants to travel to Manhattan. Settlers destined for the town had their wagons ransacked by proslavery mobs to make sure they did not carry guns.[53] An overexcited William Goodnow complained from Manhattan, "Peaceable emigrants and men of legitimate business passing through pro-slavery localities . . . are stopped and the most insulting language is used especially if they are free state men, & they [are] robbed of their personal property and some for refusing to surrender their most valuable articles are shot down in cold blood!"[54]

During that bloody summer, William Goodnow wrote often to his wife, Harriet, back in Maine, explaining he felt morally obligated to be on the front lines and angrily questioning why more New Englanders were not in Kansas Territory. In May he wrote to his separated wife, "I appreciate your feelings for me & feel much for your loneliness, and I hope & trust that we may yet enjoy each others society much, but above all these considerations I feel that duty to God, and myself, and my fellow men requires my labors here for the present." In the same letter, he also pleaded, "We *now* need and should *have* thousands of men from the free states to aid us & help drive from this territory the last border ruffian that has presumed to invade our beautiful Territory."[55] Later that summer, he despairingly asked, "How many more lives will be sacrificed in Kansas before the Eastern & Northern people will show themselves to be *men* & deny themselves of the comforts of home & come here and place themselves where they can do the most good to the cause of Humanity?"[56] Manhattanites were now feeling isolated and under siege.

The distress of the Free-State settlers in Kansas Territory that summer was not unrecognized. For example, the *Cincinnati Daily Gazette* wrote in June, "Our brethren there, worn out and exhausted by the trials of the last few months, must give way before this army of fresh invaders, and abandon their homes, unless speedily strengthened in numbers and supplied with provisions."[57] Not surprisingly, however, only a few very dedicated immigrants arrived in Manhattan in the second half of 1856, while others already in Kansas were driven away by the violence, so that the population within the town's borders remained essentially steady during the remainder of the year at around 150.[58] In September 1856, Thomas Wells recorded the downtrodden condition of the town, writing that violence "cuts off in a great measure communication with the states ... [and] it prevents settle[r]s from coming among us, and filling up the country thereby putting [off] for a year or two at least, the growth of our cities and villages, and it tends greatly to discourage the settlers that are here from building churches or school houses, engaging extensively in any business or, indeed, making any improvements."[59]

Nonetheless, 1856 proved to be an extremely important year for Manhattan's future. In addition to gaining the Military Road and related traffic at the start of the year, in November Manhattan acquired title to the land within its putative boundaries, by purchasing two Wyandot "floats" from Samuel C. Pomeroy in Kansas City.[60] These floats were ownership rights to parcels of 640 acres of land that the U.S. government had granted to thirty-five members of the Wyandot tribe, which could be sold and located on any land west of the Mississippi River.[61] After the floats came on the market in 1855, the Manhattan Town Association asked Pomeroy to purchase two of them as the easiest, quickest way to establish good title and to end the festering problem of claim-jumping within the town's boundaries.[62] After the Manhattan Town Association purchased the floats from Pomeroy in 1856, it and the Cincinnati company suddenly held title to 1,280 acres — the core of the city of Manhattan. Although minor disputes over title would continue until 1886, acquiring ownership of the land was an extremely important step forward for the young village.[63]

Near the close of the difficult year, Territorial Governor Geary and a traveling party camped across the Kansas River from Manhattan as part of a tour of the territory. While Geary was encamped south of town, a group of Manhattanites took a boat across the river and invited the governor to give an address to the weary citizens. Geary's traveling secretary recorded that "a congregation had assembled at [Manhattan] to hear preaching done by the Rev. Charles E. Blood, who learning of the approach of the governor, adjourned the meeting and with other gentlemen, crossed the river in a small boat to invite him over to Manhattan to address the citizens in his stead."[64] Reverend Blood told Geary "that the obligations of religion could not be properly discharged unless peace and order were preserved, and he assured his excellency that a few words of advice and encouragement from him at that particular period would be of more service than any sermon he could utter."[65] Accepting the invitation, Geary then delivered a speech that was well received by the assembled citizens of Manhattan, who particularly welcomed his promise to do justice for the territory's Free-State settlers.[66] When the governor's party struck camp, his secretary offered a favorable impression of Manhattan: "The town is located in a valley of great fertility, and contains about one hundred and fifty inhabitants, who are generally moral, intelligent and industrious."[67]

Despite the year's tremendous difficulties, in his diary on December 5, 1856, Isaac Goodnow proclaimed: "The friends of Freedom do not yet give up Kansas to slavery. A hard battle is to be fought yet." Thomas Wells confirmed that the settlers remained committed to the cause: "Sometimes we think the future looks dark, but generally we keep up good courage and hope for better times at all events we (I mean our free state settlers) are determined to 'stick to the ship until we know she is lost' and whether we remain in Kansas or not we will do all we can, to prevent slavery from coming hither."[68]

1857
A TOWN BUILT FROM STONE

In January 1857 the future of the settlement called Manhattan still remained uncertain. The town was not yet incorporated, and the few buildings that existed were generally flimsy assemblages of logs or shingles. The primitive buildings resulted in another hard winter for many Manhattanites.[1] However, as Isaac Goodnow observed that spring, the town's settlers had done admirably well to reach this stage: "With all the labors coexistent with pioneer life & the troubles of coming out of our Kansas troubles, they have had hard work to build them the rudest kinds of houses, furnish food & clothing sufficient to keep soul & body together."[2]

Certainly the town's pioneers could be forgiven for not progressing further during the turbulent second half of 1856. But now, with the lessening of Bleeding Kansas violence, 1857 was predicted to be a breakthrough year. Thomas Wells wrote on February 1, "During the coming year we expect to have good schools established and churches built."[3] Although there were unexpected setbacks, the town's advances during 1857 more than met expectations: the year saw the official incorporation of the town of Manhattan, the town's first election, the erection of stone buildings in significant numbers, and the development of full-scale commerce.

The year began promisingly when regional stagecoach service began in March, providing a weekly connection to Topeka. But disaster struck soon afterward, when the village's first major fire occurred on April 21, 1857. The fire burned three buildings to the ground on Poyntz Avenue, including two of the earliest businesses in the town: Ira Taylor's store and the Cincinnati hotel.[4] All of the contents of the buildings were destroyed, including the trunks of several new immigrants staying at the hotel, where "guests barely escap[ed] with their lives."[5] Ellen Goodnow, a teetotaler, pointedly claimed that the fire was caused when "one of the men went to bed drunk and left a candle burning in a wooden candlestick."[6]

Andrew Mead was unbowed by the loss of his hotel, writing, "before the smoke from the embers had disappeared plans were being formed for the construction of a stone hotel building on the same site."[7] Two days after the fire, the Manhattan Town Association generated competing plans to build a hotel, forming the Bluemont Hotel Company.[8] However, while Mead had the resources and experience that allowed him to quickly rebuild his hotel, the MTA enterprise lacked direction and the Bluemont Hotel project was abandoned partway through construction, with the building later converted into a flouring mill.[9] Meanwhile, Ira Taylor, the owner of the market that had burned, decided to open a saloon to focus more directly on selling liquor instead of reopening a general store.[10]

Soon after the fire, another scare struck the town when a traveler staying at Charles Barnes's boardinghouse on Poyntz Avenue developed smallpox in May 1857.[11] The stricken visitor was quarantined and no further outbreak of the disease followed.[12] Nevertheless, although smallpox was not nearly as terrifying as cholera for white settlers in the 1850s — a vaccination for the disease was already in wide use — the appearance of the disease in Manhattan caused a brief fright.

Despite these setbacks early in the year, Manhattan's population had already begun to grow again after the long pause in the second half of 1856. A local census in March 1857 showed 358 people living in the vicinity of Manhattan, between the Big Blue River and Wildcat Creek.[13] That number continued to swell throughout the year, with many of the new arrivals coming from New England. Ellen Goodnow observed on April 17, 1857, "It is becoming thickly settled all about us with the right stamp of New England people."[14] Thomas Wells also boasted that spring, "Our citizens generally will compare *favorably* with those of *any* New England town, I do not care where you find it."[15] One notable arrival in April 1857 was James Humphrey, a twenty-four-year-old Englishman by way of Massachusetts. Over the next several years, Humphrey held a variety of positions in Manhattan, including mayor, treasurer, marshal, city attorney, editor of the newspaper, and district judge.[16] Arriving the next month, also under the auspices of the New England Emigrant Aid Company, was the blacksmith Samuel Williston, along with his family, including five-year-old Samuel Wendell Williston, who would later become a prominent scientist. Decades later, the younger Williston's account of the final leg of the trip was published in the book *Fossils and Flies*. He wrote that his family "remained a few days [in Leavenworth] in a very small hotel while my father bought a wagon and yoke of oxen and such provisions and household things as were indispensable, and we started on the slow and tedious drive of 115 miles to Manhattan through a country but very sparsely settled. For the most part we children rode in the covered wagon, while my father and cousin walked and drove the oxen." Williston also clearly recalled: "My mother was very homesick on the way. I can remember how long and bitterly she cried. One could not blame her. She now realized for the first time in this wilderness what she was leaving behind, perhaps forever."[17]

Not surprisingly, Manhattan's status as a small outpost in a vast wilderness shocked and dismayed Mrs. Williston and other women newly arrived from the East. The move to Kansas Territory for these women meant shedding middle-class comforts and abruptly acquiring direct responsibility for new tasks such as managing farm animals, making clothing, and converting rude log cabins into livable spaces.[18] As one settler sarcastically observed, "If your wife and daughter could consent to live for a time in a cabin *sixteen feet square,* and do without a thousand luxuries and many necessities which you enjoy in New-York, you could live very well."[19] Women lost much of their social support moving to the frontier, often staying home alone, great distances from neighbors, while their husbands toiled in the fields. For the Yankee women, the harsh reality of frontier life perhaps also seemed a step backward from the new women's rights movement, which had sprung to life at the Seneca Falls Convention in 1848. Bluntly summing it up, Ellen Goodnow wrote in 1857 that for many women newly arrived in Manhattan, "Kansas was a prison."[20] Even ten years later, when activist Susan B. Anthony visited Kansas, she observed that "twenty-five years hence it will be delightful to live in this beautiful State, but now, alas, its women especially see hard times, and there is no poetry in their lives."

In contrast to the distress of some new arrivals like the Willistons, many of the earliest settlers, who had witnessed firsthand Manhattan's development from an open prairie in 1855, derived considerable comfort and pride from the progress their small settlement had already made. In July 1857 Thomas Wells boasted that "houses are springing up like mushrooms, and it will soon be quite a town."[21] Moreover, several of the new buildings built that year were constructed of stone, providing a more permanent and "substantial" appearance to the settlement.[22] A. F. Grow, a settler who arrived in 1857, noted Manhattan was "not . . . so large; but certainly prosperous for its size."[23] The first stone house built inside the borders of Manhattan was constructed in 1857 by Sheriff David A. Butterfield at 307 Osage Street.[24] (It was demolished in 1964.)[25] Construction of a limestone Methodist church on Poyntz Avenue also began that year. The town was finally developing into something more than a motley collection of tents and log cabins.

The stone used for the buildings was limestone from local quarries. Limestone quickly became a principal building stock in Manhattan, and visitors soon observed that this yielded an entirely unexpected benefit from the lack of trees: "The scarcity of timber is a blessed thing for Kansas. It secures buildings of brick and stone instead of log shanties and frame shells."[26]

One other stone building erected in 1857 was a schoolhouse, built on land donated by the Cincinnati company on Poyntz Avenue. (Schooling in Manhattan before 1857 consisted of private lessons taught in the homes of Mary Blood and Elenora Strong.)[27] The schoolhouse was built west of Manhattan's boundary, beyond the hog pens that lined the town, at what would become Ninth Street, so that the school would not block the construction of any new business houses.[28] In fact, the schoolhouse did not crowd the business core; instead, parents were soon complaining that it was too far from town.[29]

Plans for the school had been in place since 1856, and funds for the schoolhouse were raised locally from "almost everybody" in Manhattan — fund-raising events included town socials and a speech by the Reverend I. S. Kalloch.[30] By February 1857 the Manhattanites had also appointed an agent in Boston to raise funds for the school and a library in Manhattan. The Boston agent was author and entrepreneur James Redpath, who created a certain measure of John Brown's national fame by covering Brown's exploits in Kansas Territory in the eastern press. Only a few months earlier, Redpath had visited Kansas and was a guest in John Brown's secret campsite. All told, the efforts in Manhattan were truly remarkable during an era when the modern educational system did not yet exist and was still decades away from taking shape.[31]

While work was under way on the schoolhouse, a group of townspeople also rented a room in the Manhattan Town Association's office at the foot of Poyntz Avenue in March 1857 to host a school session.[32] For their teacher, the group hired Amanda Arnold, a nineteen-year-old who had arrived on the *Hartford* two years earlier.[33]

Work on the schoolhouse moved quickly in 1857, and construction of the building was substantially completed early in the summer, at which time classes were reconvened there.[34] The two-story limestone school, which came to be called the Avenue School, was described after it opened as "the best and most expensive school-house in Kansas," and it may in fact have been the first schoolhouse in the territory built of stone.[35] One visitor commented that the building "would do honor to almost any place."[36] But the building's interior was very primitive. Both floors were used as one-room classrooms — although only the upper floor was used originally — and the ground floor always remained unimproved with roughly plastered walls and an exposed pine ceiling.[37] To help start the school, James Redpath and other Boston donors sent to Manhattan a large dry-goods box filled with "old, second-hand and tattered books."[38] Importantly for the little settlement, the schoolhouse also served as a community center, hosting public meetings, festivals, and religious services.[39]

The stone buildings erected in Manhattan in 1857 largely reflected the priorities of the New England settlers: homes, schools, and churches. In this way, Manhattan was distinguished from its nearest neighbor of comparable size, Junction City, which was settled at the junction of the Smoky Hill and Republican rivers in 1857. James Humphrey, who lived for years in both communities, later observed that "two different ideas underlaid the founding of Manhattan and Junction City." He explained: "In the case of Manhattan the original scheme comprehended a finished community; schools, churches, college, libraries and literary societies all existed in embryo, ready to be launched forth at the earliest opportunity. In Junction City a town-site was platted, hotel and saloon started, and the rest was expected to follow by a process of natural evolution. . . . Manhattan bore the image and superscription of New England — Junction City of the frontier."[40]

Specifically, it did not escape notice that the schoolhouse was "almost the first (stone) building erected in the village."[41] Because New England had a proud history of public schools, while Southerners rejected common schools on the basis of higher taxes, Manhattan settlers proudly acknowledged that their school followed from the "New England instincts" of the town's founders.[42] Notably, an emphasis on education has remained a defining characteristic of the town: when KU professor James Shortridge classified each town in Kansas under their principal emphasis in his 2004 book *Cities on the Plains,* he listed Manhattan under "Education."[43]

On May 30, 1857, the town of Manhattan was officially incorporated. The first local elections — for mayor and city council — were held the same day. The private corporations that had governed the town quietly ceded control, and for the first time Manhattan was governed by a democratic government.[44] As if to underscore the new democracy, the town marshal was assigned to ring a bell to call all citizens to Saturday council meetings, just as was traditionally done for New England town meetings.[45]

The first mayor elected for the tiny little village was Andrew Mead, from the *Hartford* company. Mead was a thirty-eight-year-old native of New York City. He was described by contemporaries as highly sociable, with a "graceful ease in society, and worldly tact and skill."[46] A traveling correspondent for the *Leavenworth Daily Times* later observed of Mead, "Socially he is one of the most amiable, pleasant and intelligent gentlemen whom I have ever met."[47] Yet Mead was also relentless in his goal of developing commerce in Manhattan, particularly on the southern side of Poyntz Avenue, which was controlled by the Cincinnati settlers and where Mead owned a great deal of property.[48] And Mead was politically savvy; one fellow merchant noted that he was "a student of New York City politics," and he rarely lost a political battle.[49] (The second mayor of Manhattan, E. M. Thurston, elected in May 1858, was Mead's opposite in many ways. Thurston was a "scholarly" New England immigrant.[50] However, Thurston was likewise not politically naive; he had been elected to the Free-State government in Topeka in 1856, and before immigrating to Kansas Territory he served as secretary of the Maine State Board of Education.)

As 1857 progressed, a significant number of commercial enterprises also began to flourish in the newly incorporated town for the first time. In December 1856 Isaac Goodnow had complained in his diary that there was "not a shoemaker this side of Lawrence! With the population, & the time of settlement of this region it seems almost incredible that we have no shoemaker, Harness maker, nor watch repairer. Manhattan has not now even a blacksmith!"[51] But by August 1857 Manhattan offered two blacksmiths, a tailor's shop, a cabinet shop, a liquor store, one carriage shop, one tin shop, and "various other mechanical trades."[52] Construction of stone hotels was

The Manhattan House hotel, located at the foot of Poyntz Avenue, opened by Manhattan's jovial mayor Andrew Mead. (Courtesy of the Riley County Historical Society.)

also well under way in August, with the Manhattan House rapidly nearing completion.[53] The eastern end of Poyntz Avenue, where the two rivers converged and the river landing was located, was quickly becoming established as the town's commercial hub. Commerce for the town's new merchants was boosted by consistent traffic to and from Fort Riley and by occasional transcontinental travelers such as teams of drovers taking cattle to California.[54]

In August 1857 a traveling correspondent for the *New York Times* visited Manhattan and described it as "a flourishing town containing about 40 houses."[55] A Manhattan resident similarly estimated that same month that there were fifty buildings in town — double the number that had existed the prior summer.[56] The next month a correspondent for the *Lawrence Herald of Freedom* wrote: "They have five stores in the place, and the sixth is now being erected, of stone. A two-story stone school-house, 25 by 40, will be completed in time for a winter school. There are also several stone dwellings in process of erection. Mr. G[oodnow] estimates that there are seventy-five buildings either completed or in the process of completion on the town site."[57] Growth continued throughout the fall. Indeed, as settler A. F. Grow later noted, "The fall of 1857 being favorable, and the winter following open and pleasant, building went on nearly all winter."[58] In October Wells wrote: "The country is continually filling up and cabins and houses are going up all the time. Manhattan *'city'* has got to be considerable of a place."[59]

Few physical confrontations occurred in Bleeding Kansas in 1857, but the year was not uneventful politically. The first and most widely significant event was the election of the second Territorial Legislature, in voting held on October 5. Writing before the election, Thomas Wells characterized the "great question" at issue as no less than "whether the people of Kansas shall rule Kansas or not."[60] Goodnow informed the Lawrence newspaper that Manhattanites "will do their best to carry the election by all honorable means."[61] Free-Staters desperately hoped to avoid a repeat of the disastrous vote of March 1855, and a group of men in Manhattan led by Albert Griffin was appointed to guard the local ballot boxes.[62] As fortune would have it, by this time demographics throughout Kansas Territory had shifted to the point where Free-Staters were easily elected to a clear majority of seats in the legislature, including the election of Andrew Mead from Manhattan.[63] Wells called it a "perfect triumph to the free state party."[64] In the wake of the victory, he wrote, "So now I hope the question is settled that we shall have a free state, and there will be no more trouble."[65]

But later that same month, proslavery advocates in Kansas Territory struck back with a blow for their side, drafting an official state constitution at a convention in Lecompton that would permit slavery in Kansas.[66] The Lecompton Constitution was the second proposed for the territory, after the unsanctioned Topeka Constitution drafted by the Free-Staters two years earlier. Manhattan's county (Riley County) sent two delegates to the Lecompton convention: John S. Randolph and Claiborne R. Mobley.[67] Like many of the Lecompton delegates impaneled by the first Territorial Legislature — a proslavery body — Mobley was a proslavery man; he later fought for the Confederacy during the Civil War.[68] Unsurprisingly, the constitution drafted by these delegates allowed slavery. After the constitution was drafted, a special election was held on December 21, 1857, putting the proslavery provision (but not the entire constitution) before the voters of Kansas Territory. Because the electorate was denied the chance to reject the constitution as a whole, Free-Staters boycotted the vote. As a result — predictably — the vote favored the proslavery provision. That was not, however, the last word on the issue; further events would take place in 1858, including two more votes on the Lecompton Constitution. Although the Free-Staters were making clear gains, toward the end of 1857 Goodnow was moved to write in his diary that "politics look unsettled yet."[69] Goodnow also added the next day, "The cause is critical — more so than an outsider would imagine."[70]

At the local level, Manhattan closed the year by attaining an important political distinction. By December 1857 the newly incorporated town of Manhattan was on its way to being established as the county seat in Riley County. When the county was originally organized in 1855, the legislature had named Pawnee as the county seat, but when Pawnee was wiped out and swallowed up by Fort Riley later that year, the issue was reopened and put to a countywide vote during the election of October 5, 1857.

The effort to establish Manhattan as the seat of Riley County was not without drama. The vote in October 1857 resulted in the new village of Ogden being named county seat by a margin of 193–162.[71] (Ogden was sort of a reconstituted version of Pawnee. One settler observed that it "caught the debris of Pawnee when that ill-fated town was swept from its moorings.")[72] But Manhattanites strongly suspected that Ogden's victory was secured by election fraud. Acting quickly, Manhattan immediately appointed a local committee of three — Judge John Pipher, William M. Snow, and Elliot Taylor — to investigate. Pipher and Snow began by seeking to enlist the help of Territorial Governor Robert Walker, who had recently visited Manhattan, but they received no relief from the governor.[73] Next, because the county officers holding the tally sheet of voters refused to release it to the Manhattanites for review, Judge Pipher summoned Ogden resident Lemuel Knapp to Manhattan to give sworn testimony about the voting rolls.[74] The severe Pipher somehow compelled Knapp to testify that fifty-nine ineligible voters — minors and soldiers — had voted for Ogden and that Manhattan was thus the true victor in the election.[75]

Yet, even having solicited testimony of election fraud, this was not the end of the issue. On December 10, 1857, when Sheriff David Butterfield sought to secure the county's books and records for transport from Ogden to Manhattan, the county clerk in Ogden refused to turn them over. Two days later, the clerk resigned and Manhattan physician John Winter Robinson assumed the position. Upon resigning, the former clerk finally delivered the county's official papers to county commissioner Amory Hunting, but Hunting was promptly ambushed by six men who took the papers back.[76] Finally, on December 14, Sheriff Butterfield was dispatched with a posse to retrieve the documents by force, and Manhattan at last acquired the county books.[77] Manhattan hosted its first county commissioners' meeting on December 21, 1857.[78]

Shortly thereafter, Manhattan's delegates introduced a bill in the Territorial Legislature in January to formalize Manhattan's status as county seat. As soon as the citizens of Ogden learned of the bill, they hastened to the capital to defend their interests, still hoping to bring the county seat to Ogden.[79] But the Ogdenites were too late. On January 30, 1858, the new governor, James Denver, signed a bill that officially named Manhattan as county seat and imposed a fine on any county officer who refused to move his offices or papers to Manhattan.

Even as it ascended to be the seat of local government, Manhattan remained on the American frontier, and the townspeople's early accounts are filled with stories of interaction with the native inhabitants of the region: bison and Native Americans. In one of the most spectacular encounters with bison, a herd "in formidable numbers" stormed off the plains and into the northern valley of the Big Blue in 1857.[80] But incursions like this near Manhattan were otherwise unknown, and the town's settlers generally had to travel seventy miles west to the plains in order to find the shaggy beasts, which they regularly did on hunting expeditions.[81] Thomas Wells wrote the following account of one such expedition in December 1859: "We were away from home four days and a half. . . . We did not kill any buffalo or even shoot at any, though we saw a plenty of them, and they are the most *ugly looking creatures* that ever I saw. The main herd had gone south, and those that we saw were all old fellows, and hardly worth killing."[82] Wells wrote that the hunt ended when a sudden cold front blew in: "The last night we were out it snowed quite hard nearly all night, the wind north and very cold; we managed to keep very comfortable during the night, but we almost froze riding home the next day. Although we got no buffalo meat, we were glad that we went; we passed through a very fine country and it was well worth such a trip to see the huge monsters."[83]

Winter weather was a constant danger for the hunters. Manhattanite John Tennant wrote of another bison hunt in November 1858 that ended with a blizzard. After spending some time hunting and preparing bison meat, Tennant's party was on its way back to camp when a blizzard suddenly struck. He wrote that the hunters "unhitched, fastened our oxen to the wagons and camped where we were so as not to lose our bearings; and put in the night walking to keep from freezing." Trying to keep warm, Tennant soon found himself in trouble:

> I tried during the night to rest by rolling myself up in my green buffalo hide with the hair on the inside. It seemed a good idea. I was warm and comfortable for a time till I felt cramped and tried to turn over; when I found I could not move hand or foot. The hide was frozen stiff with me inside! I could never have got out alone. My friends had a hard time to get me out as it was.[84]

Despite difficulties, the hunting trips were exciting and proved popular. They also served a practical use: one settler explained that the trips were taken not only "for adventure or pleasure but for the prosaic purpose of getting a supply of buffalo meat."[85] When the hunters returned to Manhattan, they would "distribute the meat in the neighborhood which would then be fairly well supplied with meat for the winter."[86]

Closer to home, Manhattan's residents also continued to have frequent interactions with the native peoples of the area, despite the federal government's forced removal of most Native Americans from the territory. Although relations between Manhattan's settlers and the Native Americans were "generally peaceable," there was always the unsettling question of whether ongoing conflicts in nearby locales could lead to unrest.[87] For example, on September 3, 1855, a contingent of U.S. troops from Fort Riley and Fort Leavenworth attacked a nearly defenseless Sioux village in southern Nebraska Territory, killing eighty-five men, women, and children.[88] So, for Manhattan's white settlers, the proximity of Native Americans sometimes meant fear of attacks — even though such hysteria proved misplaced every time. One settler later recalled of the early years of settlement: "From time to time there had been 'scares' of Indian depredations and every one capable of bearing arms was trained for defense, and signals were planned to call the citizens together."[89] Settler Amos Powers added that in his opinion "an Indian was always dangerous if you made him mad and had no gun. Carrying a gun was a good way to keep them away."[90]

Most often, Manhattan's settlers regarded the presence of the Native Americans as simply "a nuisance," particularly when they stopped at settlers' cabins to "beg or buy" supplies.[91] A number of settlers' accounts (colored by racial and cultural biases) provide their point of view of these interactions.

For example, Amos Powers later wrote: "For years they passed this place every spring and fall, going and returning from their hunts or visits to other tribes. We could see them coming, a dark line on the hills, miles away. Some of them would stray off from the file and steal anything they could get their hands on, even the dog."[92] Similarly, Manhattanite Samuel Wendell Williston recalled his mother confronting several Native American men who came to drink from the Willistons' well in his youth, and "rapped on the door and demanded a cup to drink from." Williston wrote that his mother told them to drink from the bucket: "But they grew impudent and threatened by their actions to beat the door in. My mother hustled my aunt and us children into the loft and took the ladder away, and then seized my father's shot gun which hung over the fireplace, and thrust its muzzle through a crack between the logs, and threatened to shoot them. They went off laughing and saying 'heap squaw.'"[93]

The summer of 1857 was particularly stressful for the townspeople, with several rumors of nearby attacks by Native Americans.[94] Ellen Goodnow, who held a view of Native Americans that was enlightened for its time (she wrote that "they were more civilized, and even Christianized, than some of their [white] neighbors"), recounted the story of the most sensational event of the summer in August.[95] Ellen wrote that her neighbor Samuel D. Houston woke her "in the dead of the night" to tell her that a band of Cheyenne Indians had "murdered several whites" near Fort Riley and that families were fleeing the area.[96] Houston borrowed Ellen's horse so that he could go to "enlist a camp of Delaware Indians" to "go immediately to the Fort and prepare to fight the Cheyenne." Meanwhile, William Goodnow was summoned to retrieve Ellen and her niece Harriet from their cabin and to take them to safety in town. Ellen and Harriet immediately grabbed breakfast, packed a few items, and locked up the house, "thinking in all probability that our goods and home would be burned ere we returned as reports said they had sworn to exterminate the whites."[97] While they were still waiting for William, Ellen later recalled, "I looked into the garden and exclaimed to Hatty, 'The Indians are right upon us.' Shutting up the drawers, trunks and house I went out without anything on my head and met them. To my great joy they were the Delawares that were going up to [defend] the Fort the shortest way and wanted to go through our yard."[98]

It was soon determined that no white settlers whatsoever were murdered or otherwise involved in the incident, which concerned warring tribes of

Potawatomi and Sioux near Fort Riley.[99] But before discovering that it was a false alarm, U.S. troops were dispatched on a hasty march from Fort Leavenworth, which made the matter significant enough to draw national attention — a full account of the event was published in the *New York Times* on August 21, 1857 — and it brought the new Territorial Governor Robert Walker to Manhattan to thank the townspeople "for the promptness with which they turned out for the assistance of the Fort when it was supposed to be in danger."[100] After relief set in, Ellen wrote, "Such a Sabbath I never spent and I hope that in like weakness and fear I shall ever be preserved."[101]

Part of the townspeople's constant apprehension of Native Americans almost certainly stemmed from a deep reservoir of prejudice against the natives in both proslavery and antislavery whites.[102] For example, Manhattan had only one doctor who would treat Native Americans during the 1850s: Dr. William Stillman.[103] As stories of encounters with Native Americans show over and over again, the experiences were always fraught with tension due to settlers' distrust and a failure to appreciate the natives' culture. A final tale from Manhattan's early days demonstrates the point in stark terms. In September 1855 an area settler named James Bishop was arguing in a market in Pawnee over the price of watermelons that a group of Kansa men wanted to purchase.[104] The argument intensified to the point that Bishop smashed a melon over the head of one of the Native Americans. Wiping the melon from his face, the Kansa man drew a knife and chased Bishop around the store. At this point the account devolves abruptly from semicomical to tragic, as Bishop grabbed a rifle and shot the Kansa man dead. Bishop immediately jumped on a horse while the rest of the Kansa mounted their horses and chased him to Juniata — where Bishop was given a fresh horse — before Bishop finally escaped back to his native Missouri.[105]

In all events, the Native Americans had little hope for a bright future in the northeastern section of Kansas. Between 1855 and 1860 the number of white settlers tucked into the eastern part of Kansas Territory grew from 8,601 to 107,206. Meanwhile, the entire territory remained home to only 10,000 Native Americans.[106] And the native numbers were shrinking as a result of the obliteration of their traditional lifestyle and the spread of communicable diseases.[107] By 1859 the Kansa tribe was reduced to 1,035 members, a loss of 200 people from just one year before.[108]

1858

"WE DO NOT DESPAIR OF A FREE STATE YET"

The year 1858 dawned with Kansas Territory and the Free-State question at the forefront of national politics, and with yet another round of balloting on the state constitution. The proslavery provision in the Lecompton Constitution had been approved by voters the year before because Free-Staters boycotted the vote. Now, the second Territorial Legislature — with Free-Staters newly in the majority — decided to hold a special referendum on accepting or rejecting the Lecompton Constitution as a whole.

The referendum was held on January 4, 1858.[1] This time the proslavery faction boycotted, and the vote went in favor of rejecting the entire constitution.[2] Isaac Goodnow wrote in his diary: "'Lecompton' is about dead! Thank God! Right will triumph."[3] But Goodnow's joy was premature. U.S. President James Buchanan disregarded the January vote and on February 2 submitted the Lecompton Constitution, with slavery, for congressional approval. President Buchanan asserted matter-of-factly that Kansas was "as much a slave state as Georgia or South Carolina." An enraged Thomas Wells wrote from his Manhattan home in February 1858: "The Lecompton Constitution, if confirmed by Congress, will *never* be submitted to by the people of Kansas, *civil war first.* . . . We do not despair of a free state yet. The people of Kansas *will not* be the slaves of the administration or the South. There are wise heads here as well as in Washington and the plans of the slave power for our subjugation will be thwarted, *peaceably* if they can be, *forceably* if they must — at all events Kansas must be free."[4]

Because the two votes in Kansas on the Lecompton Constitution had both been boycotted by various factions, Congress ultimately refused to approve it until it was put to a third vote. Prompted by this impasse several

Free-Staters, including Manhattanites Isaac Goodnow and George W. Higinbotham, met in Leavenworth in March 1858 to draft another alternative constitution. The Leavenworth Constitution these men drafted would have disallowed slavery and granted the right to vote to African American men in Kansas.[5] In fact, the proposed constitution made no mention of race anywhere, thus making no distinction whatsoever between the rights of white men and African American men. (It did not, however, extend the right to vote to women — suffrage for women was more unthinkable than rights for African American men in this era.)[6] Goodnow worked hard at the convention in favor of including rights for African Americans, and he celebrated the triumph afterward in his diary: "Close debate on Free suffrage! . . . succeeded! At last!"[7] After the delegates approved the constitution, Goodnow also helped to coauthor an "Address to the American Public," which stated, "You have it within your power to reject and defeat the hateful Pro-slavery instrument by endorsing this new Free-state Constitution."[8] But the proposals in the charter were too radical, and the U.S. Congress rejected the Leavenworth Constitution; it was a rare example of overreaching by Goodnow and other usually cautious Free-Staters.

The next round in the constitution debate was a third vote on the proslavery Lecompton Constitution, held on August 2, 1858, in which both sides fully participated. The political atmosphere in the territory was now running heavily against slavery. Tellingly, one month before the vote, former Territorial Governor Frederick Stanton, who previously had been the scourge of Free-Staters — famous for saying that resistance to the proslavery legislature would meet "war to the knife, and the knife to the hilt" — gave a speech in Manhattan taking a position "very strong anti Lecompton."[9] Thus, it was not a surprise when the Lecompton Constitution was finally and conclusively killed by Kansas voters in the August election. The vote in Riley County for this round of balloting was decisively Free-State: 258 against the document and 22 in favor.

The ultimate solution to the constitutional standoff proved to be yet another constitutional convention, held in the summer of 1859, this time with Samuel D. Houston representing Manhattan.[10] This convention met in Wyandotte City, Kansas, to draft a fourth and final constitution. Houston played a significant role in the debates, giving a number of eloquent speeches and arguing that women should be allowed to address the full convention to advocate for their voting rights (an argument he lost) and that the borders of the state of Kansas should extend "to the summit of the Rocky Mountains," in part so that Kansas would be a large, self-reliant state in the event of civil war (another losing argument).[11] In the end, this constitution, under which Kansas was ultimately admitted to the Union in 1861, barred slavery and granted women the right to vote in local school district elections, but it did not extend any voting rights to African Americans.[12] After the framers had done their work, the citizens of Kansas Territory ratified this charter by a vote in July 1859.

Early in 1858, Goodnow predicted that all of this political wrangling would soon put an end to violence, writing, "Rest assured the days of Border Ruffian invasions are *numbered*."[13] But the use of politics and the ballot box in 1858 did not mean that violence was concluded. Far from it. On May 19, 1858, a posse of Missourians called the "Bloody Red" rode into Kansas and took a number of Kansas settlers captive. In Marais des Cygnes, Kansas Territory, the posse fired on their unarmed captives, killing five and wounding five more.[14] The incident became known as the Marais des Cygnes Massacre, and it reignited violence throughout the territory. Afterward, violence flared up periodically throughout the year, and when John Brown returned in the fall, "suddenly, it was 1856 again."[15] Though violence raged throughout the territory, the frontier village of Manhattan was nevertheless spared once again due to its proximity to Fort Riley. Notably, for a short time in 1858, John Brown himself reportedly took advantage of Manhattan's relative peacefulness to hide there from his multiple pursuers.[16]

By 1858 a distinct village had been imprinted in the tallgrass prairie at Manhattan. Settler Thomas Wells observed in February 1858: "The first two or three years are always pretty hard in a new country, but it is getting old very fast. It is nothing like it was two years ago."[17] In May 1858 pioneer Julia Lovejoy, who had moved away from Manhattan in 1856, returned to visit her daughter and was amazed by growth in the new county seat: "O how changed! Our little log cabin, the first cabin built in Manhattan, has been removed to the banks of the Blue, and sacrilegiously converted into a stable, and near its former site is the tastefully built residence of Hon. Mr. Thurston, of Maine, one of the original proprietors of the town."[18] Upon touring the town, she "noticed some beautiful private residences, large hotels, a number of costly stone buildings, for various purposes, and a large two-story stone building, for school purposes. The Methodists have a stone church they hope soon to have completed, and the Episcopalians and Congregationalists intend to build immediately, we were told."[19]

In February 1858 Thomas Wells predicted that the town's progress would continue during the coming year: "We expect one or two more churches will be built during the coming season at Manhattan and a good many other houses, stores, &c."[20] But Manhattan grew but little during 1858, due to the unsettling return of Bleeding Kansas chaos along the Missouri border.

The most notable physical additions to Manhattan during the year were two stone churches in different stages of construction. The first, completed in June, was the First Methodist Church, at the corner of Juliette Avenue and Pierre Street.[21] The Methodist church featured a memento from the recent founding of Manhattan: the bell from the steamship *Hartford.* The bell came into the possession of the church after the *Hartford* burned and sank in the Kansas River on October 10, 1855.[22] (The cause of the fire that sank the *Hartford* remains one of history's mysteries: several sources report that it was caused by a prairie fire or Native Americans, but many others suspected that the fire was started by William Osborn, the bitter proslavery man who was detained on the boat by Free-Staters in June 1855.)

The second stone church under construction in 1858 was the Congregational, at the corner of Poyntz Avenue and Juliette Avenue, which was started that summer and completed in 1859.[23] Donations for construction of the church were solicited in the East by the Congregational minister Charles Blood, and among those donating money were Stephen A. Douglas and Abraham Lincoln, each of whom provided a five-dollar donation in the midst of engaging in their famous debates during the 1858 Illinois Senate election.[24] When nearly finished, the church was unroofed and "broken up" by a tornado in May 1859, but it was quickly rebuilt and dedicated on July 24, 1859.[25]

The town's housing stock also continued to slowly improve during the year from the original untidy collection of tents, dugouts, and primitive cabins. To cite one example, Thomas Wells and his new wife, Ella, built a new two-story house west of Manhattan, and the possessions in the house reflect a quantum leap forward from 1855. In the sitting room, Ella Wells wrote they had a clock (although it "chooses not to go"), a large stuffed chair ("which is quite a luxury"), a bookcase, a mirror, and a table with five chairs. The old tent that Thomas Wells had camped in after arriving in 1855 was now used to line the ceiling in the sitting room ("by much hard rubbing I got the tent so

*Photo collage showing Manhattan's Congregational Church, built in
1858–1859, with Rev. Charles E. Blood (top left) and Mary Blood (top right).
The year 1858 was inscribed above the church's entryway to commemorate
the year construction began. The church has been significantly renovated and
expanded since that time, but it is now the oldest building in Manhattan other
than early limestone cabins. (Courtesy of Kansas State Historical Society.)*

it looks quite white").[26] Nevertheless, even newer cabins such as the Wellses'
were not yet plastered and proved so drafty that snow and dust blew in from
outside.[27] Reaching the housing standards of the East would take several
more years.

Of greater long-term significance for the town than any new buildings
in 1858 was the incorporation by the Territorial Legislature of Blue Mont
Central College just outside Manhattan — the institution that would ultimately transform into Kansas State University.[28] (The "Central" in the name
of the school is commonly omitted; it was included based on the belief that
the school was located very near the center of the United States.)[29] The enterprise had been in the works since April 1855, when the idea for a college in the town was first raised in an address given by George S. Park to
the old Boston Town Association. Soon thereafter, Goodnow became an

indefatigable advocate for the college.[30] In April 1857, at a meeting of the Methodist Church Conference in Nebraska, Goodnow inaugurated an official plan for the college.[31] Finally, on February 9, 1858, the college was incorporated by act of the new Free-State Territorial Legislature and Governor Denver, thereby becoming one of the first three institutions of higher learning established in Kansas Territory.[32] In July the New England Emigrant Aid Company's Thomas Webb wrote a note of congratulations to Isaac Goodnow, stating that education at all levels in Manhattan "will aid materially in promoting the mental, moral and physical well-being of those who may be trained under its auspices, and thus impart a healthy and vigorous tone to the community."[33] However, while funds were raised and a building erected, another two years passed before the first classes could be held.

Despite the forward momentum, just three years into the town's existence, Manhattanites in 1858 still spent much of their time taming the wilderness to provide for their needs. The work was oftentimes dangerous, and frontier life had a way of continually reasserting its raw nature. The following passages taken directly from the diary of Juniata resident Chestina Allen in August 1856 serve as an example of the casual brutality of everyday life on the Kansas frontier:

> 23rd Mr Green was killed in a well by a stone falling on him.
>
> A man in Leavenworth asked another where he was from? He replied Lawrence the former shot the latter dead. They proved to be both proslaveryites.
>
> John cut his foot with an ax. Abbie fell down the ladder.
>
> 31st Heard of the death of my cousin Mrs. Jesse Stone of Topeka. Mrs W. Dyer has just been presented with a fine daughter this week. The wolves are becoming troublesome, they bite calves so that they die, we have lost one, wild animals catch the poultry. Mrs Arnold, who lives at the mouth of the Blue has been bitten by a Copperhead snake, it was under her pillow and as she put up her hand it bit, it was exceedingly painful, but she recovered.[34]

Along the same lines, Manhattanite Amos Powers recorded the dreadful tale of his neighbors, the Shaffer family, all of whom separately succumbed to the frontier's dangers during 1858. First, while Mr. Shaffer was away on a buffalo hunt in March, their cabin burned down, killing their four children.[35] Months later, Mr. Shaffer died of "rheumatism," and when the newly widowed and childless Mrs. Shaffer subsequently decided to move deeper into Kansas Territory, she was killed by Native Americans.[36]

The Goodnows likewise recorded tales of woe. In April 1857 Isaac Goodnow's sister Lucinda died in Manhattan, leaving her husband William Parkerson alone with two daughters.[37] (Easing his burden, Ellen and Isaac Goodnow took in one of the girls, Harriet, and raised her as their own.)[38] The following summer, in August 1858, Ellen Goodnow's brother Joseph Denison lost his wife to typhoid fever, leaving him alone in Manhattan with five children.[39] After Ellen heard that yet another woman she knew had lost her husband while traveling to Kansas, Ellen mourned, "Oh how swiftly we are passing away."[40] Two weeks later she added, "How sad and strange that so much of my time is spent over careing for the things of the dead."[41] Strength in the face of tragedy was the order of the day on the frontier.

Even day-to-day activities like travel to church or the market carried risks for the settlers, since there were no good roads, and high grasses on the treeless rolling hills could hide the few trails. Isaac Goodnow, for example, recorded two occasions in his diary when he was returning to his own home but was forced to camp out a mile from his cabin when he lost the trail.[42] Another settler reported to friends back East in 1856: "We missed our way upon the prairie and were as much confused as you would be in a skiff on Long Island Sound, out of sight of land."[43] Inadequate trails also posed other dangers. On one occasion, a settler was returning home from a trip to a market in Manhattan with her child and two workmen in her wagon when the wagon was swept into the Big Blue River while passing along a flooded trail next to the river. The woman managed to throw her child ashore, but she was nearly swept away, and one of the workmen drowned trying to rescue her.[44]

Travel was particularly foreboding at night: once the pioneers stepped outside, their only source of illumination was the moon. Chestina Allen wrote after visiting a neighbor four miles away: "I was obliged to travel by moonlight. I never had been there and was uncertain whether I was in the right direction as I could not discern the house from a tree."[45] Likewise, the sixteen guests at Thomas Wells's 1856 wedding "all had to come from one to five miles over the prairies in the dark and several of them got lost and wandered about for half an hour or more before they could find the house."[46] Above all, bad weather could make traveling completely impossible, confronting travelers with impassable rivers and streams.[47] Fittingly, an 1859

Hand-Book to Kansas Territory famously advised immigrants to test their traveling trunk "by throwing it from the top of a three-storied house; if you pick it up uninjured, it will do to go to Kansas. Not otherwise."

The rough life of the frontier was inevitably reflected in the settlers' dress. At the time that Manhattan was settled, antebellum fashions on the East Coast had reached the pinnacle of extravagance. Steel hoop skirts became the norm for eastern women, together with gloves, fans, and aprons embellished with lace, fringe, and ribbon. Eastern men of the time wore tall silk top hats, high black boots, and black three-piece suits. Meanwhile, on the frontier formality was unknown, and Manhattan's settlers adopted more utilitarian clothing. Thomas Wells wrote in 1857 that the settlers were "freed in a great measure from the demands of fashion, and the customs of a too aristocratic and extravagant east . . . and you could live more *simply* and *cheaply,* yet no less *comfortably,* and not lose caste in the best of society around you."[48] But even on the frontier a head covering remained essential for decency for both sexes; women wore bonnets and male settlers wore broad-brimmed straw or felt hats.

The pioneers' diet was a similarly lackluster variation on what was eaten in the East: "Bread, pork, and potatoes in their variations constituted the fundamental basis of nutrition."[49] River water was a staple drink. Another New Englander wrote of dining in Kansas: "Our butter looks precisely like hog's lard, and does not taste like any thing in particular. Milk we only see occasionally, and potatoes are few and far between; dried peaches are very common, but the cooking of everything is bad. I would be glad to compromise my entire rations daily for one meal from home."[50] Only occasionally the basic diet could be "supplemented by milk, cream, butter and eggs, and by green vegetables in season."[51] The chief complaint by the settlers was a lack of beef and the monotony of the meals. Amos Powers recalled, "We were always glad to find anything new to eat," and A. F. Grow sourly observed, "Corn bread is good, but even that after 'fifty or sixty meals' got to be a trifle monotonous."[52] Early settlers also confronted a lack of fresh produce and because of their limited diet suffered from scurvy—a disease more common to sailors lost at sea than to settlers homesteading on land.[53]

Still, the rough frontier experience was often enlivened by social activities, chiefly frequent visits with each other. One settler later recalled, "Our cabins were full at all times."[54] The rigid conventions of the East were also leveled down in this area. Washington Marlatt wrote: "The town knew no 'upper or lower tandem;' all were on a happy equality. There was a freedom in social intercourse from the usual conventionalities of life."[55]

Music played a large role in lightening the mood during Manhattan's earliest days. A barbershop quartet and a children's choir were quickly established in the settlement.[56] Among the contemporary songs performed by such music groups in America during these years, Stephen Foster's songs such as "Camptown Races" and "Jeanie with the Light Brown Hair" were particularly well liked. (The Romantic composers then active in Europe — including Wagner, Liszt, and Verdi — were not widely appreciated in the United States.)[57] Musical instruments were rare on the frontier, but Isaac and Ellen Goodnow had a melodeon in their cabin, and Isaac wrote that he was fond of polkas and waltzes.[58] At the same time, however, a frequent lament in the social realm was that men could find few dancing partners on the frontier. One early settler later wrote: "Here in Manhattan bachelors were plenty, but there was a very great scarcity of girls. . . . I remember it was no uncommon thing for three or four boys to go to see the same girl; not, of course, at the same time, but they took turns at it, so that sometimes the girl's time was pretty well taken up."[59]

Manhattanites also organized societies aimed at the betterment of civilization, such as were common in New England. One example was the Manhattan Institute, an organization that sponsored educational lectures. A representative address was Isaac Goodnow speaking on "Chemistry & Philosophy of the Atmosphere" on February 25, 1857.[60] Meetings for the Institute were held at Manhattan's first public hall, a prefabricated *Hartford* building that merchant Ira Taylor fixed up next to his store on Poyntz Avenue.[61] The building was not grand — it was twelve by twenty feet, built of light cottonwood, and sealed with brown paper — but it worked well enough for the frontier, and the settlers used the hall extensively for social events and religious meetings.[62]

Even the occasional arrival of steamboats at Manhattan's landing held potential for entertainment of a sort. According to the historian Donald Parrish in *This Land Is Our Land,* Manhattanites welcomed such events as "a break in the hard life on the frontier. Residents hurried to the landing, perhaps greeted a few arriving passengers, heard news of the outside world, and watched freight being unloaded. Then with cheers and good byes, they saw the boat depart."[63] When the boats tied up overnight in Manhattan, they often hosted dances onboard.

Kansas is actually one of the sunniest states in the United States, but thanks in part to *The Wizard of Oz,* it is now far better known for its destructive tornadoes. Indeed, Kansas averages forty-eight tornadoes per year.[64] But when the Free-State settlers arrived in Kansas Territory, they did not necessarily know much about the weather that awaited them. Charles Boynton's guidebook, *A Journey through Kansas* — much relied upon by New England settlers — contains a chapter on weather but does not mention tornadoes or the violent thunderstorms that regularly batter the state.[65]

The settlers learned quickly. Tornadoes and thunderstorms appear often in the early chronicles of Manhattan.[66] Julia Lovejoy wrote poetically of a thunderstorm in Manhattan in May 1855: "On a sudden the heavens are overspread with black angry clouds, and seem for hours to be wrapped in a sheet of flame, heavy thunder, as if the whole artillery of heaven was at once discharged, when the rain not only falls in drops but in copious streams, deluging the earth."[67]

According to Amos Powers, the first tornado to hit Manhattan struck in 1857 or 1858. He recalled that "it blew several lightweight houses into the Blue river," and during the same storm, "a house belonging to Mr. Chambers, built of light cottonwood timber, was literally blown to pieces."[68] Another, far larger tornado struck on the evening of May 15, 1859, causing widespread destruction.[69] Rev. Charles Blood wrote of the 1859 storm: "A real *tornado* passed through our quiet town. It unroofed our Church, blew down the Cotton boarding house, utterly destroyed Williston's shop & [many homes]. . . . The Chimney to the Emigrant Aid Co's Mill blew into the river."[70] Samuel Wendell Williston wrote of the same storm: "There came up one evening one of those 'cyclones' for which Kansas was long notorious. It threatened to blow down the house, and did destroy the house from which we had just moved, distributing some of its timbers quite into our back yard. My father and cousin had not returned from the shop which also was blown to pieces, and my mother was greatly distressed and nearly wild in her anxiety."[71] Inevitably, tragedies happened. In July 1860 another reported tornado blew the roof off a Manhattan house, "and a young man named Logan, who was staying there at the time, ran out of the front door just as the south gable fell, and his back was broken, thus crippling him for life."[72]

But severe storms were not the only form of extreme weather to challenge settlers in Kansas Territory. Temperatures can be severe — both hot and cold — and there are always winds. Manhattan settler A. F. Grow later recalled that "Kansas never does anything 'by halves.' . . . her winds generally cannot be accused of letting up when only half through blowing."[73] Author William Least Heat-Moon described the "nearly constant" wind in Kansas as "a faceless force, usually for destruction, the power behind terrible prairie wildfires, the clout in blizzards and droughts, and, most of all, in tornadoes that will take up everything, even fenceposts."[74] One New England immigrant noted in 1856 that the persistent wind of Kansas was "spoken of by some of our men as constituting the most serious objection to the country."[75] Amos Powers also complained of the wind: "The continual wind, so often mentioned, kept the dust in the air and made my housekeeping . . . anything but a success, especially as to cooking. . . . Flapjacks were my chief article of diet. When the wind blew hard by the time the underside was done enough to turn, its top was a dark gray color."[76] Yet, the settlers learned to adjust. By April 1856 the *Lawrence Herald of Freedom* resorted to sarcasm, noting in a one-sentence report, "The 'Kansas breezes' are now in their glory."[77]

The Kansas winds also brought dramatic and unpredictable changes in the weather. In 1875 Kansas Senator John J. Ingalls joked that "the stranger [to Kansas], if he listened to the voice of experience, would not start upon his pilgrimage at any season of the year without an overcoat, a fan, a lightning rod, and an umbrella." Kenneth S. Davis, an author and historian raised in Manhattan, remarked on the extremes of the weather in the Midwest in a 1949 article in the *New York Times Magazine,* noting that the "temperature ranges annually through 130 degrees Fahrenheit — from twenty or more below zero to almost 110 above — often leaping, in the late spring, from frost to 100 above in a month or less."[78] Davis continued: "Add to this the average violence of winter blizzards and summer thunderstorms and you have a weather which wears the visage of a community enemy and might well cause people to band together in self-defense."[79]

Finally, not to be forgotten among Kansas's extensive repertoire of extreme weather, are flooding and drought. For example, a notorious drought hit the area in 1860, laying waste to much of the new farmland that the settlers had laboriously planted. There was virtually no rain that year until November.[80] But it is flooding that Manhattan — perched on the banks of two rivers — is particularly prone to. Regular floods have deluged the area, with the most momentous hitting Manhattan in 1903, 1951, and 1993, and before the town was founded, in 1844. When the town erected a sign across Poyntz

Avenue following the 1951 flood declaring "Manhattan Will Rise Again!" locals joked, "So will the Kaw!"

The 1951 flood, striking shortly before the town's centennial, was one of the most calamitous events in Manhattan's history. It inundated the entire downtown business district and more than 200 blocks of residential homes.[81] Two deaths were reported, and property damage was estimated at $20 million, including wrecked buildings, cracked water mains, sewer lines plugged with sand, and massive craters gouged in the streets.[82] A marker showing the height of the floodwaters downtown is now engraved in the front of the building at 311 Poyntz — it is five feet six inches above the sidewalk. Because the biggest floodwaters seem to come only once every fifty years or so, the timing of the town's founding perhaps provided the settlement several decades to develop before the dangers of building on a floodplain became fully apparent. Nonetheless, one observant visitor to Manhattan in January 1856 wrote to his brother in Massachusetts: "The whole town is situated on the Kanzas bottom, but a few feet above the water, and liable to be overflowed at any time."[83]

On top of the effects of the weather, Manhattan's founders also unwittingly selected a location that is one of the most seismically active in the region. In fact, the two strongest earthquakes in the state's recorded history had their epicenter near Manhattan.[84] The first struck at 2:32 P.M. on April 24, 1867. The Manhattan newspaper reported that "the sound was like that of heavy thunder which was immediately succeeded by a rocking of 'the old beldame Earth' which called the entire population out of doors in an instant."[85] The paper added, "The house seemed to sway to and fro, mirrors and crockery were toppled down; the Blue River Bridge rocked about on its piers like 'a thing of life.'" When the shock hit the water of the Kansas River, it "rolled in a wave at least two feet high."[86] The second major earthquake struck at 6:16 P.M. on January 7, 1906, causing greater property damage — toppling chimneys and shattering plate glass windows in businesses downtown — but no loss of life. Once again, townspeople "rushed out of the house thoroughly frightened and called to their neighbors."[87]

1859
"A FLOURISHING YANKEE SETTLEMENT"

Ever since the icy flood in February 1856 destroyed Juniata's bridge, the informal overland route through Kansas Territory to Denver and the Rockies passed through Manhattan.[1] The arrangement was formalized in 1859 when Manhattan became an official wagon stop on the new Leavenworth and Pike's Peak Express Company.

Travelers heading into the West in 1859 entered Manhattan by taking one of two ferries across the rivers — the upper ferry on the Big Blue or the lower ferry on the Kansas — or simply by fording through the rivers' waters.[2] By 1859 Manhattanites were also discussing plans to build a wooden plank bridge across the Big Blue and debating where on the river it should be located.[3]

The need for a bridge into Manhattan was underscored early that year when traffic through town exploded with prospectors following the Smoky Hill–Republican Trail to the Rocky Mountains to mine gold, discovered there late in 1858.[4] Around the same time, Bleeding Kansas violence was also ending as proslavery forces realized that the population of Kansas Territory had permanently tilted in favor of the Free-Staters and gave up the fight — or as Manhattan carpenter A. F. Grow later colorfully put it, "the incarnate fiends who deluged the land in blood slunk back to their dark caves, and freedom triumphed."[5] With these factors in place, Manhattan was poised to enjoy a miniboom.

As the weather turned warm, the prospectors started coming. Thomas Wells wrote in April 1859: "Hundreds and I don't know but I might say thousands of people are passing through here continually for Pikes peak. They come from all parts of the country, from various classes in society and they travel in all sorts of ways. Some come with horses, mules, or oxen, and others come drawing hand carts, rolling wheelbarrows, or lugging packs on their backs."[6] And they kept coming. The next month the traffic continued: "The travel to Pike's Peak continues passing through our town without any sign of diminution. Often two hundred teams will cross our ferries in one day. The mode of travel is exceedingly diversified, and sometimes truly laughable."[7] On May 11, another Manhattanite wrote in amazement, "There are more folks on the road to Pikes Peak than ever and there seem to be more coming every day."[8] Ultimately, the gold rush of 1859 would draw twice the numbers that more famously went to California in 1849.[9] Very few locals, however, joined the flocks heading west to the Rockies. Manhattanite Samuel Whitehorn had worried in November 1858 that "two-thirds of the settlers around Manhattan" would leave to mine gold in 1859, but Kansas newspapers questioned the accuracy of the gold claims over the winter, and only a small number actually departed Manhattan in 1859.[10] Indeed, Thomas Wells astutely observed in April 1859, "I am afraid, however, that very many of them [the prospectors] have much more *gold* in their possession now than they will have six months hence."[11] In all events, money was more easily made by selling supplies and services to the miners flooding through Manhattan than by prospecting in the mountains with a pick and shovel.

In addition to the prospectors arriving in Manhattan by private means, two four-horse stagecoaches from the Leavenworth and Pike's Peak Express Company began making semi-weekly stops in Manhattan in 1859.[12] Although stagecoach travel was vastly preferable to pulling a handcart across the prairie, it was still trying—the coaches were basically bone-jarring wooden boxes on wheels. One Manhattan passenger complained of the experience, "The vehicles themselves are uncomfortable and crowded, and the horses never make more than four or five miles an hour."[13] Primitive trails added to the difficulties. One passenger recounted the details of an evening stagecoach west out of Manhattan to Junction City on a cold winter night in 1862: "At Wild Cat we ran into a top of a tree which had been cut down the day before and fallen across the road. We were half an hour in working that coach through the brush and timber around that obstacle. . . . Twice in passing over Eureka bottom the team came to a dead standstill, and the passengers joined in pelting the horses." The party finally reached their Ogden stop, and when ready to depart again the driver "cracked his whip and larruped those horses for ten minutes before they started, and then they ran with all their speed for a mile or so. At Three Mile they balked again. The passengers alighted, gathered brush, and argued with that team." Finally, at 5 A.M. the coach reached the Junction City ferryboat, which promptly got stuck in the middle of the freezing Republican River. The passengers reached their final destination only after the slush ice solidified; "we took a few planks from the bottom of the boat, laid them across the ice walked over and into town."[14]

Despite the difficulties of stagecoach travel, it was significant that Manhattan was included on the express line, and the coaches provided more regular delivery of parcels and letters to the town. Meanwhile, riverboat traffic also continued to stop at Manhattan's landing (the levee) at the base of Poyntz Avenue.[15] One typical arrival was the *Colonel Gus Linn,* which tied up overnight in Manhattan on May 16, 1859, on its way up the river to Fort Riley. The log of the *Gus Linn* recorded that it "moored right in full view of the flourishing young city of Manhattan. Here we found Hon. A. J. Mead, Col. W. M. Snow, Rev. Mr. Blood and other influential citizens waiting to receive us." The log continued: "News of our arrival spread like wildfire through the town, and in less than fifteen minutes the boat was literally taken by storm. Though somewhat blue over the havoc caused by a furious tornado the day before, everybody expressed themselves delighted with the boat." After dinner was served on the boat, "the cabin was quickly cleared, and music and dancing filled the programme till long after midnight, when the company dispersed with three cheers for the '*Gus Linn* and all her hands.'"[16] Unfortunately for Manhattan, the riverboat era in Kansas Territory would soon come to an end, as the Kansas River proved too shallow to navigate.

All of this traffic through town created a brisk trade for merchants, and it was actively promoted by business owners and town fathers.[17] Andrew Mead, for example, wrote back East to encourage a freight company to utilize the river crossing at Manhattan.[18] The growth of commerce in turn resulted in a little building boom in town. In April, Thomas Wells wrote, "Manhattan continues to grow and improve, some buildings are going up all the time."[19] The following month another Manhattanite observed, "Warehouses, stores, &c., are constantly multiplying in our midst."[20] By May it was estimated that there were "upwards of a hundred dwellings" in Manhattan, and a visitor from Boston that month described the town as "a flourishing Yankee settlement of two or three hundred people."[21] Finally, as part of Manhattan's growth, a third limestone church was also being erected — St. Paul's Episcopal — on two Poyntz Avenue lots donated by the Cincinnati company,

St. Paul's Episcopal Church. Due to the scope of the plans for the
church and the intervening Civil War, it was not fully completed
until 1867. (Courtesy of the Riley County Historical Society.)

one block from the Congregational church. The neo-Gothic church was designed by noted architect Richard Upjohn's company and was described when completed as "one of the very best and most beautiful edifices erected anywhere west of St. Louis."[22]

Furthering the boom atmosphere, on the afternoon of May 10, 1859, the cornerstone was laid for a home for the college incorporated in Manhattan the year before, Blue Mont Central College. A jovial ceremony was held on the occasion, attended by 300 people, who converged on the college's sunny hilltop location from all directions by carriage and horse.[23] The ceremony was presided over by Joseph Denison and featured speeches by area dignitaries, including Samuel C. Pomeroy.[24] Washington Marlatt wrote afterward, "The ceremony of laying the corner stone was all we had wished and hoped for."[25]

The site selected for the college was about three miles northwest from the developing core of Manhattan, at the top of a gently rising hill, later known as College Hill. Rev. Charles Blood noted, "Blue Mont never looked more charming. I doubt whether our country affords another location from whence the landscape in every direction is more beautiful than from our college site in the beautiful month of May."[26]

The fund-raising effort for the college building was Herculean, and it continued long after the cornerstone was laid. Agents to collect donations were appointed in New York City, Boston, and other major U.S. cities. Additionally, Isaac Goodnow personally spent large parts of every year from 1857 to 1860 in the East soliciting funds.[27] The undertaking was so massive that even after the cornerstone ceremony, in June 1859, George S. Park, who had initially proposed a college for Manhattan, wrote to Goodnow suggesting that the entire project might be set aside: "I think you are too fast. That country hardly wants a college yet. We perhaps had better have waited until times are better. Yet under the circumstances if you can financier it through you will certainly be entitled to great Credit. It is a noble enterprise."[28] Park was not alone in expressing concern. Marlatt noted around the same time, "Even *now* many of the *friends* of the enterprise looked upon it as altogether impracticable, if not chimerical."[29] Marlatt also confessed his fears to Goodnow: "I am almost frightened when I think of the labor before us to be done in so short a time. But then it was neck or nothing, do or die. I sincerely hope and pray that you will succeed in raising the needful to prosecute the undertaking to a triumphant completion."[30] Goodnow himself remained positive but admitted in his diary that it was a struggle finding donations.[31]

While soliciting funds, Goodnow offered to name the building or a professorship after "some liberal donor," but evidently no donors gave liberally enough to merit the honor.[32] The largest single donation, $2,500 worth of lots, was given by John M. S. Williams, of Cambridge, Massachusetts, co-founder of the Emigrant Aid Company and future Massachusetts congressman.[33] Many local residents also gave generously, and considerable funding for the building was also provided by Manhattan's founding organizations.[34] The New England Emigrant Aid Company sold twenty of its town lots in Manhattan and donated half of the proceeds to Blue Mont College.[35] Similarly, the Manhattan Town Association granted the school one hundred lots and fifty shares of MTA stock.[36] The Cincinnati and Kansas Land Company initially promised to donate one hundred lots, with certain conditions, but the Cincinnati emigrants generally showed little enthusiasm for the college, and it appears this pledge was never fulfilled.[37] Indeed, the Cincinnati emigrants Mead, Pipher, George Miller, and William Snow formed the core of a faction in town that essentially opposed the college, apparently because they feared it might prevent their land on Poyntz Avenue from becoming the commercial center of town.[38] Washington Marlatt complained about this faction in a series of letters to Isaac Goodnow. He first wrote in June 1859: "Everybody almost is expecting *favors* from the College. I don't see how they would have lived at all if it were not for the College. Manhattan is horribly dull, between the boat and the College it just manages to sustain life, and yet Mead and Pipher remain as great Asses as ever. It is a pity that such men are tolerated in the world."[39] A year later, Marlatt complained to Goodnow: "Nothing has been done by the Cincinnati Company for the College. Mead . . . has opposed this College from its very inception. Never intended to give anything nor suffer it to be built even if he could help it. He must be remembered in future."[40] Finally, in August 1860, Marlatt exploded: "Pipher nor Miller have done nothing by way of donation of lots to the college. Jack asses both of them."[41]

Despite the obstacles, construction moved quickly on the college building following the cornerstone ceremony. Marlatt helped to supervise the construction, and in another letter to Goodnow in September 1859 he suggested that he undertook this role in his typically abrasive manner: "Matters in connection with the College Building have moved frightfully slowly from our not getting lumber and iron according to order and promise. I have almost come to the conclusion that it is the normal condition of man to lie. I have been deceived so often in promises of lumber, that I have hired a man to go down to the mill, and stand there pistol in hand till it is sawed out."[42] By whatever means, the building was sufficiently complete by the end of 1859 to allow the school to open in January 1860, although major construction work continued through at least November 1860.[43]

When completed, the building was the largest educational facility in the territory: a three-story white limestone edifice, with a bell tower and an arch above a window that contained the words Blue Mont College, each letter inlaid with gold leaf.[44] The first two floors of the building contained classrooms, offices, a library, and a laboratory, while the third floor was occupied by a grand chapel hall capable of seating 500 people.[45] One visitor in 1863 was positively stunned by the appearance of such a building far out on the prairie, writing: "I was prepared to see a pretty respectable building, but nothing like the reality." He continued with a detailed description: "It is of

Blue Mont Central College building. (Courtesy of Kansas State Historical Society.)

large size, three stories in height, substantially and tastefully constructed, and on a commanding site. The rooms are large, well arranged and finely finished. . . . It has quite an extensive and judiciously selected library, a good stock of philosophical, chemical and astronomical apparatus, and a fair assortment of minerals. In the tower hangs a large and clear-toned bell, the gift of a benevolent Massachusetts gentleman."[46]

On May 25, 1859, intermingled among the passengers on one of the semi-weekly stagecoaches arriving in Manhattan was future presidential candidate Horace Greeley, already notable at that time as editor of the *New-York Tribune*, though perhaps best remembered now for the exhortation "Go West, young man." Greeley was a genuine hero to Free-Staters for fervently advocating their cause in the *Tribune* and was visiting Manhattan as part of a triumphant tour of the West. Manhattanites had advance notice of Greeley's arrival, and as soon as his coach crossed the ferry into Manhattan, Greeley was met by eager townsfolk and enthusiastically welcomed by a delegation of three local officials, including new mayor Samuel G. Hoyt.[47] (Previous mayor E. M. Thurston's death in office in March 1859 left Samuel D. Houston as the only one of the original six pioneers from Polistra and Canton still residing in Manhattan.)[48]

Greeley spent the next two days in Manhattan, during which time he gave a speech at the First Methodist Church, described by one listener as "full of good sense and valuable ideas."[49] After his first day, Greeley posted a report to the *Tribune* describing the four-year-old settlement as "an embryo city of perhaps one hundred houses." He wrote that the town was well situated "on the flat, deep bottom in the forks of the rivers, with a high limestone bluff, affording capital material for building, just behind it." Greeley had arrived just ten days after the 1859 tornado struck Manhattan, and he also reported that several buildings "were unroofed and three or four utterly destroyed. . . . Several families deprived of home and shelter by the hurricane are temporarily lodged in the basement of the new hotel [the Manhattan House] . . . , a three-story building 55 by 33, with limestone walls and black-walnut finishing."[50]

The following day, Greeley posted another report to the *Tribune* from Manhattan that remarked upon the town's frontier location. In his closing, Greeley bade farewell to Manhattan and, as he traveled west beyond Manhattan, he wrote: "Adieu to friendly greetings and speakings! Adieu for a time to pen and paper! Adieu to bed-rooms and wash-bowls!"[51]

On May 27 Greeley left Manhattan on the Pike's Peak Express coach, together with Albert D. Richardson, a correspondent from the *Boston Journal* who had arrived in Manhattan separately. Richardson later reported in the *Journal*: "At Manhattan Horace Greeley after a tour through the interior to gratify the clamorous settlers with speeches, joined me for the rest of the journey. His overland trip attracted much attention. A farmer asked me if Horace Greeley had failed in business, and was going to Pike's Peak to dig gold! Another inquired if he was about to start a newspaper in Manhattan."[52]

Fittingly, at nearly the same time that the noted newspaperman Greeley visited Manhattan, the first newspaper for the town was issued by abolitionist Charles Francis de Vivaldi. Indeed, Greeley noted for his readers that "*the Manhattan Express* is about to be issued here by M. Vivalde, an Italian exile and a devotee of universal liberty, who will of course sustain the republican cause. I commend him and his journal to the confidence and patronage of all who would like a weekly bulletin from the Far West."[53] De Vivaldi was an Italian native who had edited a newspaper in Torino, Italy, in the 1840s and had taken part in the 1848 revolution in northern Italy—the region's failed effort to gain independence from the Austrian Empire.

On May 21, 1859, four days before Greeley arrived in Manhattan, De Vivaldi published the first issue of Manhattan's first newspaper, the *Kansas Express*.[54] By way of introducing the weekly paper, De Vivaldi wrote in the first issue: "The cause of Free Kansas, so noble and inspiring in itself, and so glorious in its gallant defenders, is emphatically the cause which we pledge ourselves to sustain with all our energies and powers. We hate slavery in all its forms, and shall always denounce it as the most criminal usurpation of the sacred and natural rights of man, no matter if his skin be black, red, or white." With the cornerstone for Blue Mont Central College having been laid earlier the same month, it proved to be an extraordinary time for the young town. It also represented the full realization of the "trophies" described by Eli Thayer in *Kansas Crusade* as the goals for Free-State towns: "churches and schools, printing presses, steam-engines, and mills."

The first issue of the *Express* was actually printed in Wyandotte City, Kansas, and shipped to Manhattan, and while a press was transported up-river to Manhattan a two-month delay ensued before the second issue was published.[55] The press finally arrived in Manhattan on the steamship *Colonel Gus Linn* on June 24, 1859, and four days later, Rev. Charles Blood wrote a letter to Isaac Goodnow—back East at the time raising funds—to report that the press and De Vivaldi had arrived in Manhattan, and to celebrate that the town's newspaper at long last "is a *fixed* and *permanent* fact."[56]

Manhattan welcomed the advent of the newspaper with particular enthusiasm. It had been delayed several times during the first four years of settlement, and citizens had grown "most tired of waiting for it."[57] The first delay occurred when proslavery vigilantes destroyed George Park's press in Parkville in April 1855, which Park had planned to use to print a newspaper in Manhattan. Another delay was caused indirectly by the destruction of the *Herald of Freedom* press in Lawrence by Sheriff Jones in 1856. After that event, Manhattanites reportedly sold a press in their possession to Lawrence so that the *Herald of Freedom* could be reestablished.[58] By January 1857, Samuel D. Houston was driven to plead: "We need one [a press] in Manhattan.

We need it to marshal the hosts of freedom; we need it to encourage our friends, and press to the wall our enemies; we need it to answer the least and last arguments of the slaveholder's blighting, deadly curse of the land."[59]

Yet, in the two years following Houston's plea Manhattanites witnessed only false starts toward establishing a newspaper.[60] By 1858 Goodnow had resorted to raising funds to finally entice a newspaperman to Manhattan with financial payments.[61] Thus, when De Vivaldi was recruited in 1859, he was lavished with stock in the Manhattan Town Association and the Cincinnati and Kansas Land Company, as well as being provided a printing office on Poyntz Avenue.[62] Still concerned, on May 5, 1859, Goodnow wrote to Reverend Blood that Manhattanites "must be liberal with Mr. Vivaldi" to ensure that he stayed in Manhattan: "He has full favorable opinion enough of our people. I hope his expectations will be met! An office for his press should be secured immediately, also a house for him to live in. . . . The Editors family wants must be cared for, or they will get homesick."[63]

As it turned out, De Vivaldi remained in charge of the newspaper for only a relatively short time — until September 1861, when he ceded control of the paper to the transplanted Englishman James Humphrey.[64] (Humphrey acquired full ownership of the paper in May 1863, when a jury trial determined that De Vivaldi owed unpaid wages and loans to Humphrey.) Over the next few years, the newspaper continued changing ownership and names numerous times: it became the *Independent* (1863); the *Manhattan Standard* (1868); and finally the *Nationalist* (1870), which decades later was fully merged into its rival, the *Manhattan Mercury*, in 1943.[65] Although there were sweeping changes in the newspaper landscape in Manhattan following the founding of the *Express* in 1859, the town was never again to be without one.

12

1860–1865
DROUGHT, VIOLENCE, AND VICTORIES

As the 1850s closed, Manhattan was visibly prospering, and "all looked forward to the future with hope."[1] The sound of the times was a cacophony of banging hammers and blacksmith shops, the din of carousing Pike's Peak prospectors, and the creak and rattle of horse and wagon. A man-made hum now overwhelmed the eternal, subtle murmur of the two rivers intersecting next to the settlement. In the final months of 1859, "three or four buildings [were] going up nearly all the time."[2] The adjective used most often by visitors to describe the town in 1859 was "flourishing." The small Poyntz Avenue commercial area was bustling with blacksmiths, stables, hotels, and saloons catering to traffic passing through town.[3]

The population of the town had doubled since 1857 to about 300, with a total population of over 600 in the immediate vicinity.[4] In addition to erecting buildings, the settlers began to change their environs by planting trees on the surrounding highlands, where only grasses had prospered before.[5] Municipal governance was also taking hold as the city council imposed control over local matters: assessing taxes, taking charge of elementary education, arranging for the grading of Poyntz Avenue and ferry landings, and establishing fines for nuisances such as bathing nude in the rivers within city limits.[6]

The town also had bright hopes for the future, which were tied to the railroad. The editor of the *Express,* Charles de Vivaldi, was a great booster for routing a railroad through Manhattan, and he wrote of a grand vision in May 1859: "Soon there will be a rail road up the Kansas River extending on to the Pacific, and without a doubt, before many years elapse, there will be a road cross this at right angles at Manhattan, coming from the Gulf of

Mexico and running up the Big Blue, opening up Northern Kansas and Nebraska." De Vivaldi was confident of his vision: "No one can doubt this who is at all acquainted with the geography of our Western country. Who can doubt, then, that Manhattan will make one of the most influential and populous cities in the West."[7] In fact, in large part because of a successful lobbying campaign by Manhattan's boosters, the Corp of Engineers for the Union Pacific Eastern Division (better known as the Kansas Pacific) surveyed a track line west through Manhattan in August 1859.[8] It seemed that almost anything was possible for the booming little town as the 1850s closed.

The promising new decade started with an appropriately grand occasion: a ball on January 2, 1860, featuring the Manhattan String Band.[9] More significantly, one week later, on January 9, 1860, Blue Mont College opened outside of Manhattan with an initial enrollment of twenty-nine.[10] Notably, the college was open to enrollment by girls and boys, making it one of the very few coed options in the United States, with the college's constitution stating that the "College and its Preparatory and other Departments shall be open alike to students of both sexes and to all denominations of Christians."[11] It is unclear whether the school was also open to enrollment by African American students, but none are known to have attended. (Isaac Goodnow thoroughly supported education for African Americans, but in July 1857 he cryptically wrote to his wife, "I don't think much of making Bluemont a colored school.")[12]

But as the new decade opened, problems were already looming that would bring the boom times in Manhattan to a grinding halt. First, gold prospectors were no longer consistently taking the Smoky Hill–Republican Trail through Manhattan to the mountains. The route received a bad name after several parties of prospectors who followed it in 1859 discovered that there was no trail beyond Junction City, became desperately lost, and died on the Kansas plains — with one party notoriously resorting to cannibalism.[13] When Manhattanite Richard Kimball was in Denver on business in 1860, he was warned by a Denver merchant, "If we were going that way [the Smoky Hill trail] we had better make our wills before we started."[14]

Even worse than the loss of this traffic was the onset of a punishing drought: from June 1859 until November 1860 almost no rain fell in eastern Kansas Territory.[15] One year into the "most unprecedented" drought, in June 1860, Nathan Starks, a tenant farmer in Kansas Territory, wrote: "The drought is very severe. I never saw anything to compare. . . . The hot wind

Blue Mont Central College faculty and boosters in 1863. Seated in the
front row (left to right) are Washington Marlatt, Joseph Denison,
and Isaac Goodnow. (Courtesy of Kansas State Historical Society.)

sweeps over the land blinding one with the dust or blistering the skin. The
sun rising and setting daily only at long intervals obscured by a flying cloud,
no rain no hope."[16] That same month, Manhattanite Thomas Wells tried to
put an optimistic spin on the situation, writing, "Times must improve, however, before long, they cannot grow much worse."[17] But things did get worse.
In July, Kansas was blasted with abnormally hot winds, and in August, when
there still was little rain, one Manhattanite wrote in dismay, "The springs are
all most all dried up; the creek has stopped running and the water stands

in holes."[18] In the fall, Dr. Charles Robinson observed from Lawrence, "We are left to eke out an existence where *starvation* is said to stare the whole populace in the face."[19] "Oh I see suffering enough every day to make me sick — sick at heart," lamented Manhattan physician John Winter Robinson.[20] Before the drought finally broke in November, an estimated 30,000 settlers abandoned their claims in Kansas Territory. And even after the drought ended, massive crop failures left many Kansas families (and their livestock) on the verge of starvation through the first half of 1861.

Other problems also bedeviled Manhattan during 1860. As the year progressed, cattle and horse rustling became a growing problem in and around Manhattan.[21] A final predicament in Manhattan, as in many frontier towns, was that it remained "wealth poor," as it had been since its founding — in part because most newly arriving settlers spent their savings on land and supplies before arrival — and now the drought made matters worse.[22] The Manhattan newspaper noted in late 1860, "Owing to the failure of the crops, and the most calamitous drouth, to which this section of the country has been subjected, money is very scarce with us."[23] Citizens complained in letters that year that "money is not here — no one has it," and that it was "next to impossible to get any money at all."[24] The city government was forced to use a scrip system to make payments, promising funds out of future tax receipts.[25] The citizens of Manhattan addressed this shortage by resorting to the barter system amongst themselves — paying for goods or services by providing other goods or services in return.[26] The cash shortage would remain an issue in Manhattan until after the Civil War ended in 1865.[27] (When cash was available in Manhattan, it took the form of bank notes issued by an assortment of northern banks, there having been no central U.S. bank to issue paper currency since antigovernment Democrats disestablished the central bank in 1836.)

Although Manhattan suffered through a very difficult year in 1860, at least one encouraging event did occur: in November pilings were driven into the ground and stones were laid for the base for Manhattan's first bridge.[28] Andrew Mead and the Cincinnati company organized the efforts to build the bridge, and they ensured that it led onto Poyntz Avenue to keep traffic passing by the businesses they owned on the south side of that street.[29] The bridge, which opened on May 20, 1861, was an eight-foot-wide floating wooden pontoon bridge over the Big Blue River, which could be removed if necessary for riverboats.[30]

Manhattan's pontoon bridge over the Big Blue River, 1867. The bridge provided a welcome supplement to ferry boats. (Courtesy of Kansas State Historical Society.)

The bridge was a welcome addition; under bad conditions the ferry had been unable to operate, sometimes forcing travelers to camp out or cross in a small skiff, leaving wagons and horses behind until conditions improved.[31] The bridge was also part of a larger effort — encouraged by the territorial government — to build a continuous road between Manhattan and Denver to connect the eastern and western settlements of Kansas Territory.[32] Communities all along the length of the route in Kansas Territory funded improvements for the primitive road. Manhattan participated by volunteering men and levying a tax to provide funds for the bridge and other roadwork.[33] In Manhattan the effort fulfilled a long-term vision of building a bridge and developing a westward route through town — following Poyntz Avenue, skirting Wildcat Creek, and continuing off into the western hills — and it raised hopes that the village could recapture the Pike's Peak prospectors' traffic.[34]

The election of Republican Abraham Lincoln to the presidency in November 1860 provided even more cause for cheer in Manhattan. Dr. John Winter Robinson, president of the Manhattan Town Association, wrote that "no portion of the Confederacy rejoice[d] with a more heartfelt earnestness than the people of Kansas" at Lincoln's election.[35] For Manhattan's Free-Staters, it was a triumphant end to an incredibly difficult year.

On January 29, 1861, Kansas was admitted into the United States as a free state under the Wyandotte constitution. Manhattanites celebrated the news, hoping that additional capital improvements — most important, a railroad — would appear now that Kansas was officially part of the Union.[36] But the American Civil War was coming fast, and the country's grand plans for a railroad into the West had to be set aside. Further, although Kansas was now part of the United States, it had hardly before been more isolated. The historian Craig Miner wrote eloquently of the era in *Kansas: The History of the Sunflower State, 1854–2000,* noting that "the Hannibal and St. Joseph Railroad, the state's only connection with the 'bread-giving East,' might be shut down if Missouri seceded. The river route was again closed. . . . There were two hundred miles of border with Missouri, full of unfriendly elements, and twice that number of miles of Indian frontier to the West, with the tribes well aware of the opportunity the white man's war provided."[37]

Although Kansas was the thirty-fourth state to be admitted into the United States, only twenty-eight states remained after Kansas was admitted, because six slave states had already seceded from the Union. Five more Southern states would secede quickly thereafter, as the Confederate States of America was formed and civil war — having already cut a swath through Kansas Territory — broke out into open combat in the rest of the country.

Remarkably, during the secession dispute, the new state of Kansas was so preoccupied with its own heated fight over the distribution of aid for the 1860 drought that limited attention was paid to the actions of the Southern states. Thus, the most newsworthy incident in Manhattan in March 1861 was a "ruffianly attack" on Charles de Vivaldi by Manhattan's state legislator William H. Smyth, which was incited by a newspaper story about the local allocation of aid.[38] The local grievances were most vividly expressed in writing by Washington Marlatt, who in his typically blunt manner opined: "There are a few really deserving ones that need assistance, or may need it. But they will be the last to receive it. The other lazy idle vicious loafers deserve to starve till they get humble."[39]

The focus in Kansas changed abruptly on April 12, 1861, when the first military engagement of the American Civil War took place at Fort Sumter, South Carolina. In fact, during the confusing first week of the war, while the U.S. Army was splitting into two, men from the brand-new state of Kansas stepped into a leading role. Kansas Senator James H. Lane immediately organized a "Frontier Guard" to serve as President Lincoln's personal bodyguard in the White House, composed mostly of Kansans.[40] Having taken brief leave from his position as editor of Manhattan's *Express*, Charles de Vivaldi was one of about 120 men conscripted to serve in the guard.[41] De Vivaldi wrote to his wife, "I intend to serve my dear adopted country as a patriot; if I should perish in the battle, be assured that I shall have died fighting for the honor of the Stars and Stripes, and the safety of the Country."[42] However, the Frontier Guard saw little action, and as soon as regular Union troops arrived, the unit was disbanded because it was no longer needed. As a reward for de Vivaldi's service, in December 1861, President Lincoln named him consul to Santos, Brazil. So, de Vivaldi ceded control of Manhattan's newspaper to James Humphrey, and the Italian newspaperman moved on to yet another continent.

In the year following the start of hostilities, several Manhattan men volunteered to serve in the Union Army. Most Manhattanites serving with the Union forces were in the 2nd, 6th, and 11th Kansas regiments.[43] The 11th Kansas Infantry Regiment, which had the largest contingent of Manhattanites, was formed in August 1862, drilled for two months at Fort Leavenworth, and then marched south, where the men saw action in several battles, including at Cane Hill and Prairie Grove in Arkansas.[44]

Among Manhattanites killed while fighting for the Union were William Sanders, killed in October 1862; John Thompson and John Miller, killed in December 1862; and Grenville Gove, killed in November 1864.[45] (The town's fallen Union soldiers were memorialized by two monuments in Manhattan's Sunset Cemetery, and Gove County, Kansas, was named in memoriam to Grenville Gove.) Additionally, La Roy Prentice, one of the thirteen New Englanders who raced to Goodnow's camp in time to cast a Free-State vote on March 30, 1855, died while fighting with a New England regiment at the

Battle of Fredericksburg in 1863.[46] Meanwhile, William H. Smyth, after serving one term as Manhattan's first member of the Kansas House of Representatives, joined the Union Army and was captured in 1863 and held as a prisoner of war in Richmond, Virginia.[47]

In October 1864 other Manhattanites joined a state militia that was quickly raised to confront Confederate troops under General Sterling Price that were threatening to invade Kansas. Amos Powers was among the volunteer militiamen who rallied to support the Union troops that successfully turned back the Confederates at the Battle of Westport. He later wrote of the experience: "We left Manhattan in corn-making time. Those that 'skulked' going got a good crop of corn, those who went raised a crop of 'corns.'" Powers reported that the militiamen "went lively for Kansas City," and when they reached Kansas City, "we could see Price's men very plainly." Nevertheless, the Manhattan militia saw no action: "Governor Harvey realized our incompetence and would not take us into the engagement, but kept us in Kansas City in case of need."[48]

Other Manhattanites during the war joined gangs of "Jayhawkers," groups of unsanctioned mercenaries that waged guerilla war against suspected Confederates in Missouri and Kansas. Unbound by military codes of conduct, the Jayhawkers were deeply hated and feared in Missouri. They were also widely disliked in Kansas, where they raided farms to support themselves. The *Manhattan Express* opined in 1861 that Jayhawkers were "mean dirty thieving miscreants" and later wrote: "The people in Western Kansas are almost unanimously down on horse stealing and Jayhawk villainy. It cannot and will not be tolerated. Men who engage in it with very few exceptions will steal from *anybody and anything.*"[49]

During the Civil War era, Manhattanites serving in uniform faced dreadful hard times, but those remaining in Kansas experienced comparative quiet. The Bleeding Kansas violence had mostly ended in 1859, the same year that John Brown died in Virginia, and only two Civil War battles were fought on Kansas soil: the Battle of Baxter Springs in 1863 and Mine Creek in 1864.[50] On August 17, 1863, the editor of the *Manhattan Independent* was moved to observe: "No state in the Union is at present more favored by Providence than the bleeding, famine stricken Kansas of former times. . . . War has receded from our borders."[51] Unfortunately, only four days after this opinion was printed, a gang of Missouri guerrillas led by William Quantrill—Missouri's answer to the Jayhawkers—raided Lawrence, burning the town and killing 150 citizens. The next edition of the *Independent* carried a marked change of tone: "Kansas has been invaded and many of her best citizens murdered by rebel outlaws from Missouri. Justice cries aloud for vengeance and expiation. The destruction of Lawrence must be avenged."[52]

Quantrill's bloody destruction of a fellow Free-State town naturally created in Manhattan "not a little fear that the 'bush-whackers' would come as far west as our town."[53] As in 1856, the U.S. Army responded to an attack on Lawrence by boosting the defenses of Manhattan, issuing eighty muskets to the town's citizens.[54] The mayor of Manhattan, Moses J. Gove, also arranged for the town's businesses to close and its citizens to drill in the days following Quantrill's raid, warning, "To prevent such an occurrence here, we must organize immediately."[55] In the end, however, the distance from the Missouri border and the nearness to Fort Riley once again conspired to spare Manhattan from proslavery violence.

For many in Manhattan, the closest they would actually come to experiencing the Civil War was reviewing the regiments of Union soldiers and batteries of guns that regularly passed though the small town. Throughout June 1861, regiments of Union soldiers from the east marched through Manhattan on their way to secure Santa Fe.[56] In 1862 Union troops marched back in the other direction.[57] This pattern continued throughout the war. On yet another occasion, in May 1862, Manhattanites were also allowed to watch 4,500 Union soldiers on military parade at Fort Riley.[58] But through it all Manhattan remained at a safe remove from the hostilities.

The relative quiet during the war years allowed Kansas to fully establish the apparatuses of statehood. In Manhattan, Samuel D. Houston took office in 1861 as the first state senator for Riley and Pottawatomie counties.[59] Manhattanite William H. Smyth represented the town in the first session of the Kansas House of Representatives.[60] In addition, Manhattanite John Winter Robinson, formerly president of the Manhattan Town Association, was elected Kansas's first secretary of state. (Later, in the wake of a bond scandal in 1862, Robinson was impeached, convicted, and removed from office — becoming the first state executive officer impeached and removed from office in U.S. history.)

Some of the earliest decisions confronting the new Kansas government concerned the location of the state capital and state university, both of which were mandated in the Kansas constitution. To the victors went the spoils: only towns home to the triumphant Free-State viewpoint (principally

This watercolor by Union soldier John Gaddis shows long lines of troops from Wisconsin marching west through the village of Manhattan toward Fort Riley on April 24, 1862. (Courtesy of Kansas State Historical Society.)

Manhattan, Lawrence, and Topeka) were serious contenders for these prizes. Manhattan's newspaper celebrated at the time, "All of these Border Ruffian towns are as dead as the cause they once sympathized with."[61] Isaac Goodnow — befitting his lifelong emphasis on education — proved to be a dogged advocate for Manhattan as the location of the state university.

Unfortunately for Manhattan, its first legislative delegation of Houston and Smyth (guided behind the scenes by Goodnow) immediately began to butt heads with the first governor of Kansas, Charles Robinson of Lawrence.[62] Robinson, who was intent on making Lawrence the state capital, reportedly sought Goodnow's promise that Manhattan's delegation would support his goal in 1861. However, Goodnow had already thrown his support behind a bill that would result in Topeka becoming the state capital. Robinson allegedly offered to guarantee the state university to Manhattan if Goodnow changed the Manhattan delegation's position, but Goodnow refused the deal. As a result, Governor Robinson sought revenge and decided to try to prevent Manhattan from getting the university.[63]

The Manhattan delegation of Houston and Smyth during the 1861 session had sponsored a bill to reorganize Blue Mont Central College in Manhattan into the state university. The bill sailed through both houses of the Kansas Legislature with large margins, despite vigorous opposition from the Lawrence delegation.[64] Moreover, a legislative commission sent to Manhattan in April 1861 to look at Blue Mont determined that the college was perfect for the purpose.[65] But in May 1861, when Governor Robinson received the bill putting the state university in Manhattan, he vetoed it.[66] An effort to override the veto failed by two votes. James Humphrey later complained in the *Express*, "The Governor assigns several feeble reasons for this act, which merely amount to the fact that he wants to put in a bid himself at a future time."[67] Whatever the reason for Robinson's veto, his action single-handedly killed Manhattan's hopes for a year.

The next year, in 1862, Manhattan's new delegation reintroduced the bill to reorganize Blue Mont as the state university. By now the effort was driven in part by the fact that Blue Mont was failing — enrollment had dropped and no college-level classes were even being offered.[68] (Such failures were common in frontier educational institutions during the nineteenth century.)[69] By the time the bill was reintroduced in 1862, the political winds had shifted, with Goodnow serving in the state House of Representatives and Governor Robinson having been impeached for the same bond scandal that cost John Winter Robinson his position as secretary of state, and with a trial pending in the Kansas Senate.[70] With Robinson weakened and preoccupied, the time seemed right for success on the university bill.[71] Yet after the Kansas House of Representatives easily passed the university bill in a 45–16 vote, it was unexpectedly killed by a 12–11 vote in the Senate.[72] Still, it was never in Goodnow's nature to accept defeat, and he would try again the next year. Following the Senate vote, he heatedly wrote to his wife: "Another year's battle is before us! Three times & *out!*"[73]

In 1863 the confluence of three events allowed Manhattan to finally find success in establishing a state institute of higher education. First, Governor Robinson, although he survived his impeachment trial, was voted out of office. Second, Goodnow was elected to the position of state superintendent of public instruction, lending him added influence in the arena. Finally, and most significantly, by 1863 the U.S. government had passed the Morrill Land Grant Act, which gave each state remaining in the Union tens of thousands of acres of land that it could sell for the purpose of endowing a state agricultural and mechanical university. With this recipe for success in place, on February 16, 1863, Kansas finally passed a bill reorganizing the assets of the private Blue Mont Central College into a state institution, under the land grant provisions. By separate legislation on April 3, the school was named Kansas State Agricultural College (KSAC), eventually to become Kansas State University.[74] Isaac Goodnow wrote from Topeka that "there were strong elements of opposition," making establishment in Manhattan of the state's first public institution of higher learning "a great & satisfactory victory."[75]

On July 2, 1863, Blue Mont Central College and one hundred acres of surrounding land were ceremoniously transferred to the state. The event was marked by a dinner and a celebration held in the chapel hall on the third floor of the college building.[76] Isaac Goodnow, who could be a bit of a scold, wrote to his wife that he wanted the celebration held in accordance with old Methodist principles, meaning for him, "no dancing!" He added that he hoped the organizers would charge a fifty-cent entry fee to "keep out the *rabble,* who go simply to circulate without contributing anything."[77]

Exactly two months after the celebratory transfer ceremony, on September 2, 1863, KSAC opened with fifty-two students for the first term — twenty-six men and twenty-six women.[78] After the college opened, college president Joseph Denison wrote that access to the school delivered "the hour for which so many worthy pioneer parents have waited; the hour when their sons and daughters can enjoy full educational privileges, at a very reasonable rate, in their own State."[79] In fact, KSAC brought a remarkable breadth of educational opportunities to Manhattan; it was only the second fully coeducational public college anywhere in the United States.[80] Celebrating the school's inclusiveness, the *Manhattan Independent* commented, "This institution demonstrates what we have long believed, that the female mind can cope with the male in those branches which require profound thought as well as in the lighter studies."[81] The college was also open to African Americans, making it doubly remarkable, although the first African American student would not graduate from the school until George Washington Owens earned a diploma in June 1899.[82] During the first year, base tuition per term ranged from four to ten dollars, with additional fees required for use of the college's piano or melodeon.[83]

After the college successfully completed its first semester in December 1863, Kansas governor Thomas Carney delivered a celebratory address that complimented the vision, persistence, and ultimate success of Manhattan's settlers:

I will candidly confess to you that however much I was surprised at the beauty of the scenery, and other natural advantages of the country in this region of Kansas, as an agricultural country, I was still more surprised to hear your early and intelligent settlers discussing the question, and, in fact engaged in the act of erecting a college in the neighborhood. When I recall that day, and remember too, that you were poor, I could not but think that you would have been considered, in the older countries, enthusiasts indulging in dreams that would never be realized.[84]

By the time of Governor Carney's speech in December 1863, Goodnow had succeeded in securing for Manhattan the finest educational facilities in the state of Kansas — a large primary school and the only public college operating in the state — fulfilling Goodnow's ideals, as well as the goals of Eli Thayer and the New England Emigrant Aid Company.

But, returning again to February 1863, the Kansas Legislature was not finished with educational matters when it established the land grant college in Manhattan. Prodded by former governor Charles Robinson, the legislature determined that the land grant college was distinct from the state "university" required in the state constitution, which was the prize that Goodnow had sought in 1861 and 1862.[85] So, on February 20, 1863, four days after creating KSAC in Manhattan, a law was enacted conditionally establishing a state university in Lawrence, if that town was able to raise $15,000 and acquire land for the school.[86] After Lawrence met these conditions, the university was opened there on September 12, 1866.[87] As a result, Manhattan was thwarted in obtaining the precise goal that it initially pursued, and an enduring rivalry was born between Kansas State University in Manhattan and the University of Kansas in Lawrence.

For a time in the 1860s, while the Civil War raged and the struggle to establish a university in Manhattan was being fought, the character of the town shifted distinctly. Change was ushered in by the gold-hungry prospectors that streamed through Manhattan in 1859, together with stores and saloons that opened to serve them, all of which put a greater emphasis on the more commercial and profane elements in the village. On the heels of this traffic more criminal elements appeared, and in the following years Manhattan began to suffer from the rowdiness and unlawful activity generally associated with the frontier. Manhattan physician Samuel Whitehorn later summed up

The earliest known photograph of Manhattan, taken in 1863 by photographer George Burgoyne. The view looks east down Poyntz Avenue toward the Big Blue River crossing. Burgoyne took a series of photos from this viewpoint over the next three years. (Courtesy of the Morse Department of Special Collections, Hale Library, Kansas State University.)

the era in the town: "Drunkenness grew to be a fearful blemish on the public. A spirit of plunder and rapine broke out among all who were not firmly established in sound principles of justice and [equity], and too often the record was marred by fierce vindictive, cowardly retaliations." Continuing with a litany of woes, Whitehorn wrote, "Cheap lawyers and stolid Justices set criminals free, to run riot and plunder. . . . For a long time, citizens made no attempt to defend each other but with all that contemptible indifference to mutual welfare, would allow armed ruffians to insult and threaten individuals, and thus half the [population] were abused, annoyed, bullied and maltreated."[88]

The 1860s were not, of course, the first time that Manhattan had seen outbreaks of violence. In 1855 townspeople resorted to mob violence to drive William Osborn and Isaac Hascall from plots of land. They then formed the Manhattan Invincibles in case further action was needed. Likewise, in February 1859, after "a miserable fellow" named Frith jumped a land claim in Manhattan, an unknown vigilante shot and killed Frith through the window of his cabin.[89] But beginning in 1860 and lasting through the Civil War years, crime and its attendant "frontier justice" reached a degree previously unknown in Manhattan.

*Looking north from Poyntz Avenue toward Bluemont Hill, 1864. Claims remained
scattered in the town during this Wild West era of Manhattan's history. (Courtesy of the
Morse Department of Special Collections, Hale Library, Kansas State University.)*

The illegal activity started with cattle and horse rustling, which became
a serious problem in and around Manhattan in early 1860. However, the
true signal shot for the Wild West era came in October 1860, when Newton
Sarber, a Manhattanite and "an inoffensive young man," was attacked by a
Pike's Peak prospector named Munroe. Sarber was having his hair cut in a
Manhattan saloon when, as the *Western Kansas Express* reported, "Munroe
being somewhat in the liquor commenced pouring whiskey down the back
of Sarber's neck, Sarber told him to stop it or he would knock the glass out
of his hand, but he persisted." According to the newspaper's account, Sarber
then knocked the whiskey glass out of the prospector's hand and against
his forehead, causing a deep gash. Munroe "became greatly enraged by this,
drawed a revolver and threatened to shoot Sarber who apologized to him by
saying that he did not intend to knock the glass against his forehead. A man
who was present interfered, and took the revolver away from Munroe; and
Sarber left and went to Taylors Saloon." After Sarber left, Munroe pledged
his word not to shoot Sarber, and his revolver was given back to him. But
Munroe "soon after followed Sarber to Taylors Saloon, and, on meeting him,
accosted him thus. 'You have drawn my blood and I'll Kill you,' at the same
time pointing the pistol at him; Sarber instantly grabbed hold of it and succeeded in pointing it down towards the floor. Munroe fired: the ball struck
Sarbers ankle and lodged in his foot."[90]

Sarber survived the shooting, but later incidents proved more fatal. In February 1861, in a shootout on the streets of Manhattan, a man named Branch from New York shot and killed a "desperate character" from California named Wheeler.[91] Then, at the end of that year, on December 7, 1861, Oliver Langworthy, a Manhattanite who had joined a gang of Jayhawkers, was gunned down in Manhattan while being arrested with five other Jayhawkers.[92] James Humphrey reported in the *Manhattan Express* that the gang had recently been "especially active and bold in their nefarious operations," adding, "This gang, knowing that the community were down on their thieving and plundering were running their Stock to places of safety outside of town, and when returned from their plundering expeditions on the border, would take especial pains to be vile, insolent and abusive to persons who might be suspected to disfavor Jayhawking." Humphrey concluded: "Very vile whiskey added to a total loss of self respect rendered a part of these men not only obnoxious but exceedingly dangerous to the community. They gloried in their crimes and defied the civil authorities, until becoming utterly intolerable."[93]

Although finding the Jayhawker gang "intolerable," Humphrey was still also upset about Langworthy's fate: "Oliver, long known in this community, has been a peaceful and hard working citizen . . . and but for his unfortunate connection with the Jayhawk band would now have been enjoying life."[94] Manhattan physician Samuel Whitehorn similarly noted that Langworthy was a Civil War veteran and lamented: "It had been better had he died on the field made glorious by himself and associates in arms."[95]

James Humphrey used his position as editor of the *Manhattan Express* to condemn the crime wave, and he also played an active role in pursuing outlaws as Manhattan's marshal and acting county sheriff in 1860. Because of his crusading activities, Humphrey himself "was threatened with dire calamity and waited on by outlaws."[96] At least once, Humphrey's activities made him the target of an attempted assassination attempt while sitting in his home.[97] Referring to the attempt on his life, he angrily wrote in 1861, "If you are so unfortunate as to think that you live in a free country, and exercise your freedom in denouncing villainy, attempted assassination in the darkness of the night is the result."[98]

During the 1860s, Manhattan also acquired many of the physical trappings of a Wild West town, with liquor shops and rollicking saloons featuring ten-pin tables, billiards, and full hitching posts outside. One noteworthy

Manhattan saloon was originally built as a general store, but in the early 1860s one-half of the building was converted to a saloon, while the other half was run by the undertaker.[99] A competing barkeep warned visitors: "Be sure to order your coffin before you take your drink, for you will sure need the coffin if you take the drink."[100] Another indication of the free-wheeling conditions in town at this time is that two of the most common issues in city council meetings during this era were requests for licenses to sell "intoxicating liquors" and complaints about swine running wild in the streets.[101] Indeed, after several liquor licenses were granted, on December 29, 1860, the council received a petition from disgruntled Manhattanites "praying the Council to grant no more licenses for the sale of liquors."[102] It was ignored. Surveying the rowdy scene, the *Manhattan Express* complained in 1862, "The sale of the killing rot gut which finds its way into our midst is in itself a violation of all decency."[103] The next year, the newspaper despaired, "Multitudes of our young men are gliding into the habit of tippling."[104] The young town was threatening to become unrecognizable to Isaac Goodnow and its other decorous founders.[105]

Then, in 1862, the criminal elements in the town ran headlong into a revived strain of vigilantism that had lain mostly dormant in Manhattan since the days of the claim-jumpers and the Manhattan Invincibles in the 1850s. In December 1861, Humphrey used the newspaper to pointedly suggest that Manhattan needed "a more summary and less expensive method of justice."[106] His request was answered soon afterward with several public lynchings.

From 1862 to 1864 Manhattan featured at least one hanging of an outlaw each year — the only location in Kansas so afflicted during that time.[107] First, on October 1, 1862, two horse thieves named Stephen Branch and Jack Dixon were lynched near Manhattan while being transported as prisoners to Fort Leavenworth by five soldiers from Fort Riley. The soldiers were camped north of town when a vigilante lynch mob from Manhattan ambushed the group and hanged Dixon and Branch. No regret was ever expressed for the unsanctioned killings. To the contrary, one Manhattanite later wrote, "Of all the unfortunates of our past anarchy lawlessness, Jack Dixon is the only one who should be accused of pure cussedness, perverseness, and essential devilishness."[108] The *Manhattan Express* reported three days later, "The only solution of the strange affair, (for no one seems to know anything at all about it,) is, that a great number of citizens were determined to make an example for the contemplation of those who feel inclined to indulge a propensity for horse stealing."[109] Two months later, in December, two more suspected horse thieves were shot by vigilantes east of Manhattan.[110]

The next summer, in July 1863, a horse thief named Monroe Scranton was caught in Manhattan and, after a speedy hearing in front of a "citizen's court," he confessed to rustling and was sentenced to hang — a sentence that flatly violated Kansas law, which did not allow for the death penalty in such cases. That night, Scranton was taken across the Big Blue River to the east bank, where he was publicly hanged from a leaning willow tree in front of 200 citizens.[111] Finally, in May 1864, another posse of vigilantes from Manhattan ambushed and lynched a man named E. H. Wetherell outside Manhattan for stealing cattle.[112] The *Junction City Union* reported, "the mob left him hanging, and he remained in that condition all that night and all day Tuesday."[113]

Although the lynch mobs were ostensibly on the side of law and order, by 1864 many had grown weary of Manhattan's frontier justice. The Junction City newspaper labeled the lynching of Wetherell a "most diabolical and cowardly murder."[114] Even more meaningfully, the same month that Wetherell was hanged, the brigadier general of the Kansas state militia, Samuel N. Wood, harshly reprimanded the citizens of Manhattan in the *Manhattan Independent*: "Whatever may have been the necessity in the past, there is certainly now no necessity or justification for Mob Law or Vigilante Committees." Wood insisted that Manhattanites must begin to observe the law: "At this place there is an institution of learning, designed as a State Institution. It will not do to ask the people of Kansas to send their sons and daughters for an education, when the civil law is powerless, or insufficient to punish crime, and protect life and property." Finally, Wood closed with a plea: "Whilst good men may have been drawn into acts that they must regret and deprecate in the past, let all resolve at least for the future, to support, stand by, and uphold the civil law."[115] The new editor of the *Manhattan Independent*, Josiah Pillsbury, added to the chorus and declared the following week: "this thing must cease now and forever — Henceforth all offenders will be dealt with according to law."[116]

Wetherell would in fact prove to be the last man lynched in Manhattan during this era. Years later, looking back on these events with some regret, Manhattan physician Samuel Whitehorn wrote, "The manner of [Wetherell's] death grates harshly on the memory, and one can feel that an uncalled

Poyntz Avenue, June 28, 1865, with U.S. cavalry troops crossing the Big Blue River. The cavalry was converting from a Civil War force into a frontier Indian fighting unit. (Courtesy of the Morse Department of Special Collections, Hale Library, Kansas State University.)

for and stupid crime was committed."[117] Dr. Whitehorn also opined: "The hanging of Scranton was another piece of cruel stupidity. A petty thief and half fool. . . . Several men who urged on his death, were fierce, vindictive and moreover not of immaculate character themselves."[118]

Fortunately, the era of disorder in Manhattan proved to be relatively brief, ending entirely by 1866. There were several reasons for the end of the era. The unrelenting westward march of civilization certainly played a role. By 1863 Manhattan itself was no longer the frontier; the *Junction City Union* reported that year that the discernible frontier line had moved ninety miles west of Manhattan.[119] Meanwhile, the arrival of the railroad and telegraph in Manhattan in 1866 reoriented the town toward the civilizing and lawful influences of the East. It is not without irony that notoriously hard-drinking railroad men helped bring this era to a close. Indeed, in one fairly typical evening in 1866 while they were building the railroad bridges into Manhattan, the newspaper reported that a railroad contractor spent an evening "quaffing the social glass" and "walked off the abutment to the old bridge into the Blue river and was drowned."[120] At around the same time, cow towns farther west in Kansas, such as Abilene and Wichita, descended into anarchy with the opening of the Chisholm Trail in 1867. Outlaws undoubtedly saw better opportunity for mischief elsewhere.

Reversing their earlier hands-off stance, city officials also did their part to end the disorder by passing ordinances establishing Sunday and nighttime closing hours for liquor shops and saloons — and at one point even making it illegal to be drunk in Manhattan.[121] In December 1866, the town also enacted an ordinance to dishonorably expel any city councilman who attended meetings drunk.[122] Finally, not least of all, a religious revival swept through the town in 1866, and moral pressure was brought to bear on the problem of rowdiness. By August 1866 one former resident returned and observed a clear change in Manhattan: "Unlike many new cities which I have visited even in Kansas, it has no Institutions, half hotel-half liquor shop, where a lazy crowd of loafers guzzle whiskey and squirt tobacco juice on the floors. This is much to the credit of the place and is an improvement on days of 'lang syne.'" The reason for Manhattan's superior condition seemed clear to the writer: "Religion and her daughter, education, have here temples erected to their honor. The College upon the hill looks down upon the commodious School House & the 4 Church edifices, all of elegant proportions and of solid masonry, and Providence is plainly saying to the people of Manhattan 'By these conquer.'"[123]

From 1866 onward, Manhattan remained at a remove from the widespread drunkenness and violence of Kansas's Wild West era. In March of 1866, the *Manhattan Independent,* which had despaired of the town's situation three years earlier, wrote: "We beam with pleasure, that a revival of religion is progressing in town. . . . May the good work go on until truth, sobriety, honesty and kindness shall prevail and evil practices all be banished from the community."[124]

Nevertheless, despite strict laws and a strong homegrown temperance movement, Manhattan would not be completely rid of all saloons until a statewide Prohibition amendment took effect in 1881.[125] Indeed, when a delegation of high federal officials on business for the railroad visited Manhattan in June 1867 — including acting Vice President Benjamin Wade and seven U.S. senators — some of the officials apparently used their visit to the Western town as an opportunity to get drunk and go carousing.[126] The *Independent* later derided the town's youth for following the example of the visitors: "Those foolish young men about town ... are exceedingly proud and boastful of their feats in drinking, since the senatorial excursion and the subsequent scandals of drunkenness attending it. We beg to inform these simple, silly creatures that even if the two highest functionaries of our government were addicted to drunkenness, it by no [means] follows that the same vice will elevate them to the same heights."[127]

POST-CIVIL WAR
TRIUMPH OF THE YANKEES

Manhattan celebrated the end of the Civil War in the spring of 1865 with a fireworks display "commemorating the surrender of the Rebel Army."[1] The celebration marked not only the cessation of a bloody war, but also the end of the slavery system in the United States. For Manhattan's early settlers, the event was an opportunity to revel in victory in the struggle against slavery they themselves had faced on the prairies of Kansas Territory.

The celebration also happened to mark the passage of a full decade since Manhattan was established. Although ten years had now passed, hardly a year had gone by that Manhattan had not been harassed or troubled with a significant calamity of some sort: the town was dragged through the gauntlet of Bleeding Kansas, the 1860 drought, the Civil War, and frontier violence. Yet Manhattan persevered. The newspaper in neighboring Junction City noted in May 1865: "Manhattan needs no apology or advertisement. There she stands, and will continue to stand, like the eternal hills with which she is environed, till its rich valleys and country around has built up a city, magnificent in literary as well as commercial proportions."[2]

Moreover, the Manhattan that emerged following the Civil War and purge of Wild West lawlessness was remarkably like the pious Yankee village that Isaac Goodnow had dreamed of years before. Of all the Free-State settlements, it was Manhattan—located deep in Kansas Territory on a shallow stretch of the Kansas River—that remained after the war as perhaps the purest example of the New England Aid Company's ideal. (Lawrence, the other Kansas town directly founded by the New England Emigrant Aid Company, had grown more diverse by this time.) Over half of Manhattan's 1865 population was originally from New England or other "Northeastern culture" states such as New York — the largest percentage of Yankees in any town established in Kansas.[3] One visitor in 1866 noted that Manhattanites seemed "mostly of New England birth or origin," and settler James Humphrey recalled of the town during the era that "its leading characteristics were of the New England type."[4] Several advertisements in Manhattan's newspaper catered explicitly to the Yankee population, and Culbertson's Bakery in Manhattan specialized in traditional baked beans and brown bread for "sons of New England."[5] Further, most of the non-Yankees in Manhattan were white Free-Staters from the Upper Midwest who shared a similar cultural outlook.

Manhattan displayed Yankee orderliness both in its citizens' actions, which heavily stressed religion and education, and in its physical layout, which had many of the trappings of a New England village, while making concessions to the rough Western frontier in which it was located. As one Civil War soldier from upstate New York would observe of the town during a march into the West in 1862: "All at once, as if by magic, a beautiful village rose around us, with large commodious churches, hotels, stores and schoolhouse. We were surprised and delighted to see, where we supposed at most a few settlers cabins, a village combining the neatness, thrift, and comfort of New England, with the freshness and fine natural scenery of the West." The soldier exclaimed: "Such is Manhattan, standing at the advance guard of civilization, bright prophecy of culture, refinement and progress soon to cover the fields of the far West."[6]

Conspicuous among the non-Yankees residing in Manhattan in 1865 were a handful of African Americans. None of the members of the original parties of Manhattan settlers were African American, and the historical record does not reveal precisely when the first African American settlers arrived. (Although there were enslaved African Americans living in neighboring Juniata and Fort Riley before Manhattan was settled, Thomas Wells noted in December 1856 that there were no African Americans living in Manhattan, a situation that apparently prevailed for several years thereafter.)[7] The first African Americans to settle in Manhattan were probably Southerners — likely ex-slaves — who arrived during the Civil War. By the end of the war in 1865, 9 of the 347 residents of Manhattan were African American.[8] One of the town's first African American residents was Edam Thomas, a laborer and hotel porter, who named a son Abraham Lincoln Thomas in 1863, to honor the Great Emancipator. Another early settler was William T. Breakbill, who

*A George Burgoyne photo from 1865, with military wagons on
Poyntz Avenue. (Courtesy of Kansas State Historical Society.)*

moved to Manhattan from Kentucky with his wife, Sally, a former slave who
had been sold away from her prior husband.[9] Despite the small numbers,
by 1866 Manhattan's African American population was beginning to establish roots in the town, and that year the wood-frame Second Methodist
church was erected to serve the town's African American citizens.[10] Just over
a year later, on January 1, 1868, the African American community rented
out the town's first theater (Gove's Hall) for a New Year's celebration. The
Manhattan Independent wrote a report of the attendees at the event that was
kindhearted and optimistic, albeit somewhat condescending: "From the
degradation poverty and the listlessness of slavery, many of them have in
two or three years residing among us acquired the bearing of free men and
women, a competency of this world's goods, and a degree of sharpness and
vivacity. . . . We rejoice that they are possessing themselves of real estate,
and teams for labor. By doing so they are laying the foundation of future
comfort and independence."[11]

On top of the eradication of slavery, Manhattanites also found cause
for joy following the Civil War in the return of the U.S. government's interest in building railroads into the West. The Manhattan newspaper had
reported in 1863 that the town was positively "aching" for a railroad connection, and by 1865 it seemed finally to be coming.[12] Remarkably, there even

appeared to be a possibility for a time that the main transcontinental line connecting the East and West coasts might pass up the Kansas River valley through Manhattan, just as Charles de Vivaldi had proposed in the *Kansas Express* in 1859.[13] Although a more northerly route for the transcontinental line — through Nebraska — ultimately prevailed, the Kansas Pacific railroad did start work in 1864 on a road along the line it surveyed through Manhattan, which would serve as a key conduit to the Rockies and the Southwest.[14] Alert to the importance of the railroad for the future health of the town, when the Manhattan City Council heard in July 1865 that it was definitely coming, the council expressed "hearty appreciation of the efforts of the Superintendent and managers of said road to furnish this great and important enterprise forward, deeming it of vital interest to the future growth and prosperity of our town."[15]

By the summer of 1866, the western end of the Kansas Pacific railroad was nearing Manhattan, and exuberant newspaper reports began appearing. On June 23, 1866, the *Manhattan Independent* wrote: "Sound the Hew-gog and Ring the Tong-jong! The long hoped for — the long prayed for — and long time coming Railroad is within twelve miles of us."[16] The next month, the tracks had reached the eastern shore of the Big Blue River opposite Manhattan, and another local paper rejoiced, "The gap will soon be closed up and good bye trouble!"[17]

The actual arrival of the railroad in Manhattan was delayed for another month while Kansas Pacific workers built bridges for two tracks over the Big Blue River.[18] (It was possible at that time to erect permanent bridges over the river because the state legislature declared that the Kansas and Big Blue rivers were unnavigable for riverboats in 1864.)[19] Manhattan offered the Kansas Pacific right-of-way along any course it wanted through town, and the railroad decided to route its line through the southern part of town — apparently at the urging of Andrew Mead, who was still looking to guard the value of his investments in that neighborhood.[20] Accordingly, the railroad's bridges were built leading into Battery Park, near the base of Houston Street. The parkland was donated to the Kansas Pacific and would serve from that time forward as the town's railroad hub.[21] While the bridges were being built, the railroad was also busy that summer building a freight depot and engine house in Battery Park.[22]

Just days before the railroad bridges were completed, on August 11, 1866, a correspondent from the *New York Times* passed through Manhattan on

Poyntz Avenue, August 4, 1866, two weeks before the railroad started running into Manhattan. The steel trusses for the nearly completed railroad bridge are visible at the far end of Poyntz Avenue. (Courtesy of the Morse Department of Special Collections, Hale Library, Kansas State University.)

an overland trip to the Pacific. The correspondent noted that, at the time, rail service from the East Coast terminated in Wamego, sixteen miles east of Manhattan, "but [the track] has been completed as far as Manhattanville, and only waits a bridge to cross the Blue Water there, and come on to Fort Riley."[23] For lack of a railroad, the *Times* correspondent had to travel west out of Wamego—all the way to California—by stagecoach, a prospect that he deemed "uninviting." The first stop on the stagecoach line was Manhattan, and his report provided a look at the conditions of stagecoach travel on a sticky summer day in Manhattan, just as the era was about to end: "At Manhattanville, 16 miles from Wamego, we exchanged horses, dropped a few of our passengers, and packed all the rest into one coach for Junction City. It was a long low vehicle, on leather springs, with three seats, a canvas cover, and four indifferent horses; yet this was made to take nine passengers inside, (three to a-seat,) three outside, and nearly a half ton beside of baggage and freight." Despite the crowded, uncomfortable condition, "the agent at Manhattanville had the assurance to ask if there wasn't 'room inside for some express packages,' withstanding the nine pairs of legs there, and the thermometer well up to 100°. My friend L. says [the Manhattan agent] was answered with profane ejaculations, and I am not prepared to dispute it."[24]

Nine days later, on August 20, 1866, the railroad bridges were completed and the first passenger train entered Manhattan.[25] The line allowed travelers from Boston to reach Manhattan in five days — compared to seventeen days for the New England emigrants' 1855 trip — while those coming from St. Louis could make the trip in just eighteen hours.[26]

Together with the railroad also came the telegraph, along which news could travel even faster, so that Manhattan for the first time was fully intertwined with the wider world.[27] Manhattanites would no longer have to make do with days-old news, "savoring of old age," as the *Manhattan Independent* put it.[28] The arrival of the telegraph was perhaps as significant as the railroad, and as the telegraph lines continued their steady march toward Manhattan that summer, one area newspaper had observed: "When the wires are stretched, whoop-ty-deedle-doo, we have close connection with 'Ameriky,' Austria, Italy. . . . The movements of the Old World in less than an hour will be known in Manhattan. Toot!"[29]

With the arrival of the new technologies, Manhattan would see an immediate and striking change in lifestyle — an explosion of growth and quickening of society. Tellingly, the headline of the newspaper article announcing the arrival of the telegraph in Manhattan declared: "Time and Space Annihilated."[30]

The transformative effect of the railroad was striking. During the post–Civil War era, Manhattan would become an oasis on the frontier, bustling with growth. The town had experienced very little population growth from 1860 to 1865, stalling just below 350 citizens. Longtime resident A. F. Grow recalled these as the "years of stagnation" in Manhattan.[31] But in anticipation of the arrival of the rail line in August 1866, an unprecedented number of people began settling in Manhattan. From 1865 to 1870, the population multiplied from 347 to 1,173, with growth truly exploding upon the arrival of the railroad in the summer of 1866. The town also saw a major building boom. The *Manhattan Independent* observed in late 1866, "From July to Christmas, our town will probably have doubled in size. It is thought by most that it has nearly doubled in population since the same date."[32] The newspaper reported that fourteen new buildings were under construction in May 1866, and nineteen were under construction in mid-July, filling up vacant lots along Poyntz Avenue.[33] Another report in July stated, "Brick blocks are going up, stone, mortar and other building material line the streets on every side, and the unceasing sound of the saw and hammer are heard above

*The view upon arriving at Manhattan's Poyntz Avenue in 1867 at the
Big Blue River crossing. The Manhattan House hotel is on the left.
(Courtesy of Kansas State Historical Society.)*

the din of business and the hum of our thrifty town."[34] Propelled by the new
arrivals, new single-family houses were also developing around Poyntz Avenue—by the end of the decade residential areas would arise with "new
houses and bright, painted fences, and fine gardens."[35] In October 1869, a
visitor noted, "not only have the people added greatly to the comforts of
their houses, but residences of great elegance have been erected."[36] Manhattan was still dotted with original settlers' cabins and the prefabricated buildings that arrived on the *Hartford,* but these primitive reminders of a more
rugged past were all slowly falling away. The *Standard* reported on May 8,
1869: "The old log house on the John Pipher farm, adjoining the city—the

original house in which he pre-empted about twelve years ago — was blown down last Sunday. *Sic transit.*"[37]

The railroad also quickly changed the face of business in Manhattan. The rail provided an influx of capital and a means to transport large goods, so several Manhattan businesses that opened in 1866 were industrial in nature for the first time. That year the *Manhattan Independent* reported, "There are several manufactories in our town, among which may be numbered those of Tin, of Furniture, of Carriages, Harnesses, Boots, Shoes, Clothing, and other articles too numerous to mention."[38] By 1867, after a year of growth, the town had between thirty and forty houses of business on Poyntz Avenue, plus a tannery, a large paper mill, and a sawmill under construction along the Big Blue River.[39] The din of machinery, the clanking of trains, and the factory steam whistle had arrived in Manhattan. At the same time, the railroad's connection to the East also brought a civilizing influence, reflected in two additional businesses that opened in Manhattan in 1866. The first of these was a second newspaper for the town, called the *Kansas Radical.* The second business was the town's first bookstore, opened on Poyntz Avenue in August 1866 by two new arrivals from Leavenworth, Simeon Fox and Howard Kimball.[40]

Simeon Fox later recalled that, upon his arrival, Andrew Mead of the old Cincinnati company was still the leading influence in the town's commercial development. And whereas Washington Marlatt would have Mead's name shrouded in historic shame for not supporting Blue Mont College, Fox believed that Mead should be remembered positively for building the town's commerce: "General A. J. Mead was the skilled gentleman to whom the town owes its greatest debt — that is in a business way."[41]

Meanwhile, in yet another sign of development, the town's rutted and muddy streets were paved with gravel in 1866 for the first time. Poyntz Avenue was the first to be graveled, extending up to the very end of the business district, at Fifth Street.[42] Ten-foot-wide sidewalks of flagstone were also installed in 1866 in front of businesses on Poyntz — though locals complained that merchants often blocked these paths with piles of grain or straw.[43] Soon, several cross streets throughout town were also paved with gravel and lined with sidewalks. In November, the city council provided fire protection for the first time, purchasing three ladders and fifty tin buckets.[44]

Although the town experienced remarkable growth during this era, it could have been even greater. The population exploded statewide in Kansas

Fox's bookstore on Poyntz Avenue. (Courtesy of Kansas State Historical Society.)

following the war, and many of the Civil War veterans and Catholic European immigrants flooding into the state were leery of the Manhattan Yankees' cold, aloof, and moralistic attitude.[45] This leeriness was reciprocated. The *Manhattan Independent* suggested in February 1867 that "the time has already arrived when if we will maintain our former preeminence and continue to attract the more discrete class of Emigrants, we must put forth effort." The paper opined, "The Rabble may and will resort to that town where most Billiard Tables and Beer Saloons are found and where Loafers are best kept in countenance by numbers; but discerning men will not make for themselves homes nor place their families in a town where vice predominates over virtue."[46] Pressing a similar point, the *Manhattan Nationalist* subsequently observed about potential emigrants to Manhattan: "Those of the other [better] class want new *homes* where they can make money without sacrificing all the advantages of civilized life. They must have church privileges and educational facilities, and will not leave their eastern homes unless they are sure of these."[47] Plainly, the Manhattanites' original impulse to maintain a discrete populace still remained. This was a healthy enough inclination during the Bleeding Kansas era, but at this point a preference to keep "the Rabble" at bay may have also kept the town's growth artificially low.[48]

Yet the Yankees could not hold out forever — their influence in Manhattan inevitably waned as their proportion of the town's population was relentlessly diluted by native Kansans and new arrivals from closer regions of the country. One of the last hurrahs for the Manhattan Yankees was the fight for full suffrage in Kansas leading up to a vote on the issue in November 1867.

In the summer of 1866 Kansas Republicans proposed two amendments to the Kansas constitution to allow women and African Americans to vote in Kansas elections. These would be put to a vote in 1867 — the first time the question of female suffrage was put to a direct ballot anywhere. Such rights were unheard of elsewhere in the United States, but the progressive Manhattan Yankees came out strongly in favor, along with a statewide Impartial Suffrage Association that formed in Topeka, including the lieutenant governor, Nehemiah Green, of Manhattan.[49] Even before the amendments were offered, the editor of the *Manhattan Independent*, Josiah Pillsbury (an old Free-State activist), argued in favor of women's rights in January 1866: "We say to women take courage, a brighter day is dawning. The old civilization, in which force ruled by its own power is giving way to a higher one. . . . The power of women is irresistible if she will but use it. She has but to demand her rights and she will take them at once."[50]

When the suffrage amendments were proposed, a group of leading Manhattan citizens promptly published an address to "all Kansans" in support of the amendments on August 18, 1866.[51] Over the next fifteen months, countless editorials and letters in the *Independent* called for free suffrage, and every suffrage activist of note came to speak before large crowds in Manhattan: Lucy Stone and Henry Blackwell on April 22, 1867; Susan B. Anthony and Elizabeth Cady Stanton on September 7, 1867.[52] Anthony was particularly blunt, stating in her speech that any man who would vote against free suffrage was a "blockhead."[53] Finally, the month before the vote, in October 1867, a group of sixty-one Manhattan women published a profemale suffrage declaration in the *Independent* that stated in part, "We believe that we have a right to a voice in the government that we are compelled to obey, and taxed to support; that our rights are derived from the same source and are of the same nature and extent as those of our fathers, husbands, and brothers; that to yield to us our withheld right to the elective franchise will prove a blessing to us, and an advantage to the State."[54]

Unfortunately for the suffragettes, in the summer of 1867 the Republican Party made a cynical decision to turn against its own proposal for female suffrage in Kansas and to more strenuously pursue rights for African American men. (The Republicans felt their party could better rely on votes in the future from African Americans than from women.) Bickering over this decision probably doomed both proposed amendments. The proposals were at last put to a vote (of white men) on November 5, 1867. Manhattan's Riley County voted in favor of suffrage for blacks — one of only four counties in Kansas to vote favorably — but against women's suffrage.[55] Statewide, both amendments were overwhelmingly defeated. The *Independent* was unbowed by the loss, writing: "Take courage Radicals. One more effort and we will place the Kansas State Constitution on the bed rock of Republican principles, that governments must derive their power from the consent of the governed, without distinction of race, color, sex or class."[56] But the *Independent* was wrong to be so optimistic. While African American men would earn the right to vote in all elections under the Fifteenth Amendment to the U.S. Constitution in 1870, women would have to wait forty-five more years, until 1912, to gain the right to vote in Kansas state elections. Writing in the 1870s, Manhattan physician Samuel Whitehorn observed, "We shall live to wonder at this campaign. . . . Brains and intelligence should vote, and not sex."[57]

Manhattan's development into a Yankee village during this era was all the more remarkable given its proximity to the very heart of the West. Just fifteen miles to the west of Manhattan, at Fort Riley, the U.S. cavalry was training to convert from a Civil War force into a frontier Indian fighting unit under the command of Lieutenant Colonel George Armstrong Custer. At the same time, "Wild Bill" Hickock served as a deputy U.S. marshal at the fort. The cavalry stationed at Fort Riley would soon take a leading role in the Indian Wars that began on the central and western plains of Kansas in 1867 and 1868.[58]

There were thirty-one engagements between the U.S. Army and Native Americans in Kansas in 1867 and fifty-eight more in 1868, many along the Kansas Pacific railroad line that was working its way toward Denver. These battles were brought even closer to home in Manhattan by the reporting of Manhattanite Alfred Lee Runyan, who enlisted under Custer and reported his experiences in the *Manhattan Standard*.[59] In one dispatch, on April 17, 1869, Runyan complained, "We had to 'hoof it' to Fort Dodge 25 to 35 miles per day, which was the utmost cruelty on the men, almost all with blistered feet. Custar *may* gain a name for making long marches in short periods, but he wears out men and animals in doing so. He has few friends among the privates."[60]

These battles with Native Americans generally resulted in decisive victories for the U.S. Army and were nearly the last stand for the natives of Kansas. Certainly, few tribes remained resident anywhere in eastern Kansas after the Civil War. Although the Kansa tribe remained on a reservation south of Manhattan, near Council Grove, in 1866 the U.S. House of Representatives ordered the Kansa Nation to either become full U.S. citizens or be removed from the state that had taken their name.[61] Subsequently, on May 27, 1872, the U.S. government simply ordered the Kansa tribe to be permanently removed from Kansas to Indian Territory (the future state of Oklahoma). The chief of the Kansa Nation, Al-le-ga-wa-ho, who was born and raised in the bucolic Kansa riverside village where Manhattan now stands, sadly observed: "The white people treat the Kon-zey like a flock of turkeys — they chase us from one stream and then chase us to another stream, so that soon they will chase us over the mountains and into the ocean." That same year, the song "Home on the Range" was written in Kansas, to which this lesser-known fourth verse was fittingly soon added:

The red man was pressed from this part of the West,
He's likely no more to return,
To the banks of Red River where seldom if ever,
Their flickering campfires burn.

Yankee Manhattan was notably also located only forty miles east of the notorious cow town of Abilene. Abilene was the endpoint of the first cattle drive up the Chisholm Trail in 1867, and home to the cowboys, saloons, brothels, and gambling parlors of Old West lore.[62] Anarchy reigned in the town during these years, and after marshal Tom Smith was gunned down and beheaded in Abilene in 1870, "Wild Bill" Hickock was brought in as the new marshal to try to rein in the violence.

Part of the reason Manhattan succeeded in staying isolated from this frontier lawlessness was a quarantine line adopted by the Kansas Legislature before the first Texas cattle drive in 1867.[63] The law was enacted to guard against tick fever that Texas longhorns carried north, which decimated herds of northern shorthorn cattle.[64] The law required that Texas cattle stay west of Abilene, which also helped to keep the cowboys at bay. Nonetheless, despite the law, immense herds of Texas cattle from the first drive up the

Chisholm Trail in 1867 ended up wintering just west of Manhattan in the Eureka Valley.[65]

Although discerning Manhattanites tried to keep "the Rabble" from settling in their town after the Civil War, they also worked hard to bring into the settlement as much commercial traffic as possible — to become the market town for the surrounding area, the place where farm families could procure the goods or services of a doctor, baker, shoemaker, blacksmith, carpenter or wheelwright. To this end, the consuming civic preoccupation of the era was increasing the means of transportation into the town.

First, new dirt roads were built heading north and south of town, leading into the surrounding farm communities. Next, Manhattanites worked to get new bridges built into town over the Big Blue and Kansas rivers. Although a fixed railroad bridge into Manhattan was built in 1866, those traveling by horse or wagon were still forced to enter town by ferry across the Kansas River or on the floating wooden pontoon bridge across the Big Blue, first installed in 1861. In 1867 the *Manhattan Independent* pleaded, "We *must* have a bridge over the Kansas. . . . We are fully convinced that no other enterprise now [under consideration] is calculated to enhance so greatly the business of our town."[66] But no bridge was built in 1867 — nor in 1868 or 1869. The newspaper returned to the topic repeatedly in 1869, opining in August of that year: "The time was when the slow and old-time ferry boat would satisfy the demands of those wishing to cross the Kaw and Big Blue at this point. But that time is now fully passed."[67] On another occasion in 1869 the newspaper wrote: "The people living on the opposite sides of these rivers, from Manhattan, are already turning their attention away from us. . . . Shall we permit the trade that naturally belongs to us, to be turned away to other locations, for want of a bridge?"[68] Despite several town meetings on the topic, the decade would close with no improvements in river crossings.

Many Manhattanites also sought in the second half of the 1860s to develop additional railroad service into town. The most prominent idea was to build a line running northeast of town to Chicago. Meetings were held in Manhattan to encourage support for this Chicago & Manhattan Rail Road, which was envisioned to have a terminus in the town. But the idea required financing, and the Riley County commissioners refused to even allow a vote on a proposed $150,000 bond for the county's segment of the rail line, effectively killing the idea.[69] Soon after the Riley commissioners refused the vote, heavy rainstorms in Kansas stranded trains on the Kansas Pacific line in

Manhattan in July 1869, flooding the town with captive passengers, and the Manhattan newspaper took the opportunity to complain, "The advantages of making Manhattan a railroad terminus have been demonstrated during two weeks last, but yet some of our fogies don't see it."[70] In September a bitter letter-writer again wrote on the topic in the *Manhattan Standard*: "We have as a city been cursed with that class of men who are always opposed to anything in the line of progress."[71]

Although it did not help to deliver visitors, to close the decade, Manhattan did witness the arrival of one entirely new mode of transportation — the bicycle, or velocipede, as it was known in its earliest days. In 1869 a firm called Basley & March opened in Manhattan making velocipedes. The editor of the *Manhattan Standard* wrote that year: "We go it on two wheels. The steed is not yet thoroughly broken, but on trial last week did very well, and this week has been much better."[72]

As the town worked on developing its tools for commerce, a number of its merchants were rising to prominence. One of the most successful businessmen in Manhattan in the post–Civil War era was Major Nathaniel A. (N. A.) Adams, who had originally moved to the town in early 1859. Major Adams served in the Union army during the Civil War and was the commanding officer at Fort Riley from 1863 to 1864.[73] Upon his return to Manhattan after the war, Adams built a large warehouse by the railroad track and depot as part of the 1866 building boom.[74] He quickly parlayed this prime commercial location into success as a dealer in lumber and livestock. In 1870 Adams also constructed the three-story Adams House Hotel on Poyntz Avenue and Second Street, which was widely recognized as one of the grandest hotels in the area — "a hotel that is equal to any west of St. Louis."[75]

With his comfortable earnings from these businesses, Adams built one of the most elegant residences in town, a small mansion on the corner of Juliette and Houston Street.[76] Adams also pursued political interests: he was elected Manhattan's mayor in 1869 and 1880 and mounted an unsuccessful run for governor of Kansas in 1876.[77] Sadly, little physical evidence remains of Adams's legacy; his grand hotel burned down in May 1884, and his mansion was torn down in 1981.[78]

Another — even more successful — businessman of the era was Edward Benton (E. B.) Purcell, a Pennsylvania merchant who arrived with the railroad in Manhattan in 1866 at the age of twenty-nine, looking for business

*Detail from a photo by Robert Benecke showing Manhattan in 1873, taken from the
top of Mount Prospect. The* Topeka Commonwealth *wrote of Manhattan that year,
"It has the substantial appearance of a New England village." The Kansas and
Big Blue rivers, which intersected next to the town, are both visible in the photo.
(Courtesy of DeGolyer Library, Southern Methodist University, Dallas, Texas.)*

opportunities.[79] E. B. Purcell started with a small shop, but he had an eye for
opportunity. He quickly bought out older merchants in Manhattan — the
Higinbotham brothers in 1866 and John Pipher in 1868 — and then consoli-
dated his ventures into several new buildings on the south side of Poyntz
Avenue, at Third Street.[80] In order to expand, Purcell demolished several
older buildings, including John Pipher's old wooden store from 1856, raising complaints in the mid-1870s that he was "ruthlessly" tearing down old
town landmarks.[81] (Many of Purcell's buildings were in turn destroyed by a
fire in 1927.)[82] By 1873 Purcell was doing over $1 million a year in business,
and by 1888 he had developed control over the largest stock of merchandise
in Kansas.[83] His emporium sold dry goods, hardware, groceries, clothing,
boots, patent medicines, coal, farm machinery, lumber, livestock, and feed,
among other items and services.[84] He took the name "Dealer in Everything"
for his slogan, and an 1881 catalog of Manhattan merchants stated that this
slogan was "literally true."[85]

E. B. Purcell's block of buildings on Poyntz Avenue after completion in 1876. Purcell begin construction on his block of stores in 1869. His motto is on the side of the building: "Dealer in Everything." (Courtesy of the Riley County Historical Society.)

As Purcell's finances grew, so did the scope of his business ventures. His first nonretail project was erecting an oak dam and gristmill on the Big Blue River at the old Rocky Ford crossing in 1867–1868.[86] In 1870 he also established the second bank in town, the Manhattan Bank.[87] Purcell then established the American Land and Cattle Company, which purchased cattle in western Kansas, brought them to the Flint Hills for fattening, and then shipped them to Kansas City for sale.[88] As part of his burgeoning empire, Purcell also purchased the Topeka Daily Capital Publishing Company, which printed the newspaper in the state's capital.[89] Finally, Purcell served a long term as a director of the Atchison, Topeka & Santa Fe (AT&SF) railroad company.[90] In recognition of his service, the first engine to run on an AT&SF spur rail line heading south from Manhattan in 1880 was named in his honor.[91] Purcell was also provided with his own private furnished railcar for his travel needs.[92] As part of his work with the AT&SF, Purcell was responsible for arranging the intersection of rail lines running east-west and north-south in Indian Territory (Oklahoma), and the town of Purcell, Oklahoma, which arose at the intersection, is named in his honor.[93]

However, Purcell was nearly wiped out by a drought and run on his bank in 1890. The bank crisis was capped when the British Land and Mortgage Company of America, which had its U.S. offices in Manhattan, demanded immediate repayment of a large loan from Purcell's Manhattan Bank — perhaps a ripple effect from a crippling bank panic in England that year.[94] Reporting on the event, the *Chicago Daily Tribune* called Purcell's bank failure "by far the worst disaster that ever befell the county."[95] Although Purcell was able to avoid complete financial ruin, his finances never fully rebounded. He did, however, retain a three-story brick mansion he built in 1869 at 206 South Juliette Avenue — the finest residence in the town at the time — and until his death in 1924 he traveled around Manhattan in an elegant carriage pulled by a team of horses.[96] Purcell's house was torn down in 1943 to erect a Catholic school.[97]

Around the same time, Manhattanite Nehemiah Green made his mark in the political arena, becoming the fourth governor of Kansas. Green was initially elected to the office of lieutenant governor in 1866 — Manhattanites celebrated his election with an oyster supper at the Manhattan House — before ascending to the governorship in an interim capacity from 1868 to 1869.[98] Before his election in 1866, Green served as a Methodist minister in Manhattan, a position to which he promptly returned after his term expired.[99] Green also worked as an instructor of military drill tactics at KSAC after finishing his term as governor in 1869. After several years outside politics, Green again returned to the field in 1880 when he was elected to the Kansas House of Representatives, where he served as Speaker pro tem until 1882. He died in 1890 of lingering complications from an illness incurred during the Civil War and is buried in Manhattan's Sunset Cemetery. The little town of Green, Kansas, is named in his honor.

14

1870S
"A LIVELY TOWN, FULL OF BUSINESS"

The 1870s were years of continued growth and significant change in Manhattan. To start the decade, there were 1,173 citizens in Manhattan, and the town was already prospering. Albert D. Richardson, a Boston writer who had repeatedly visited Manhattan, described it at the time as "a busy town of one thousand people, at the junction of the Kansas and Big Blue rivers." Noting that Manhattan "is within a few miles of the geographical center of the United States," Richardson also generously asserted: "On this remote frontier, beyond forty-nine fiftieths of our present population, is the hub of the continent, if not of the universe."[1] Richardson surely exaggerated, but Manhattan's development since the arrival of the railroad in 1866 was quite remarkable indeed. And the growth continued in the new decade, so that observers in the 1870s described Manhattan as "healthy" and "full of life" and wrote that it was "a lively town, full of business."[2] By 1878 the town's population reached 1,600 — finally matching that of the Kansa village that preceded it.[3]

One effect of this growth was that the percentage of Manhattan's citizenship born in New England was diluted down throughout the decade. As the 1870s opened, a letter-writer in the *Manhattan Standard* observed that "the [New England] element is still predominant, and gives tone to society."[4] Similarly, in 1872 William Goodnow wrote to a friend that Manhattanites enjoyed "New England privileges" — meaning Manhattanites could immerse themselves in values and institutions held dear in New England culture, such as churches and schools.[5] But by the middle of the decade, the percentage of Manhattan's families originally from New England and other

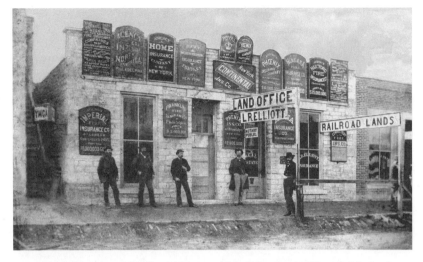

Land office on Poyntz Avenue. (Courtesy of the Riley County Historical Society.)

"Northeastern culture" states such as New York had fallen to 26 percent, and by the end of the decade the percentage had fallen further still.[6]

To complement the town's population growth during the decade, Manhattan at last addressed its simmering transportation issues. In 1870 the town issued bonds to build permanent iron bridges for wagon and foot traffic over the Big Blue and Kansas rivers.[7] The last plank on the deck of the iron bridge over the Big Blue was laid on the evening of March 23, 1871, and the bridge was opened to the public the next morning at ten o'clock.[8] The iron bridge over the Kansas River was completed the next month.[9] Previously, only those arriving in Manhattan by train were guaranteed to arrive "dry shod," but now all were able to cross the rivers dry — and for free.[10]

The following year, in 1872, the town authorized an even larger bond offering to help fund a railroad running north from town, up the valley of the Big Blue River.[11] Work on this Manhattan & Northwestern Railroad began that year, but the nation was hit by a financial crisis in 1873 and construction progressed slowly thereafter. By 1876 only a few miles of the line had been built, and in July of that year Dr. Samuel Whitehorn wrote with frustration that Manhattanites wished "we could cut the cord that binds it about our necks."[12] However, the railroad line kept slowly extending north, and the renamed Manhattan & Blue Valley Railroad eventually reached Marysville,

*Two sisters pose on the iron bridge built over the Big Blue River
in 1871. (Courtesy of Kansas State Historical Society.)*

Kansas, where it connected with a branch of the Union Pacific to Omaha
and ultimately proved its worth.[13] Meanwhile, the Manhattan, Alma & Bur-
lingame Railroad, a branch of the AT&SF, was also opened heading south-
east from Manhattan in July 1880.[14]

By the 1870s Manhattan was sufficiently well established for its citizens
to indulge in more leisure activities. As an example, Manhattan's annual fair
in the City Park, which began in 1869 as mainly a livestock and crop exhibition, evolved in the decade to include entertainment for fairgoers such as
baseball games, minstrel performances, sack races, and slow mule races.

Manhattan's men in the decade often pursued their leisure outdoors. The
town's "young fellows" entertained themselves by "fishing, shooting, swimming, or horse-running."[15] They also filled their free time with countless
games of baseball. After Manhattan's first baseball club was formed in August 1866 — the Blue Mont Base Ball Club — games were held regularly from
that point forward, teaming off the men of the town in nearly every possible
combination: northsiders against southsiders, fat men against skinny men,
etc.[16] As for the town's women, a Manhattan newspaper reported that they
"are as cultural as any in the land. Music and painting interest them; they

Poster for the tenth annual fair in Manhattan in 1879.
(Courtesy of Kansas State Historical Society.)

have their literary and science clubs, too."[17] Victorian standards precluded women from participating in vigorous outdoor games, but croquet provided a genteel way for women and men to mix in good-natured competition.[18] Indeed, the town's youths were always on the watch for social opportunities that fit into constricted Victorian mores. One young resident complained of the time, "the nearest approach to frivolity was an occasional 'sociable,' where boys and girls promenaded, chanting the 'Dusty Miller' [a Scottish reel]."[19] Other mixed-sex activities that were less sedate but still acceptable included horseback rides up Bluemont Hill for picnics in the warm months and ice skating on the Big Blue River when cold.[20]

More intellectual pastimes also existed, and Manhattan offered a large number of societies open to both sexes: "temperance, literary, musical, agricultural and social."[21] In February 1874, fifteen years after Charles Darwin's *Origin of Species* was published, one of the societies invited Manhattan native Samuel Williston to give a presentation on Darwinism and evolution.[22] The topic was of enduring interest in Manhattan. Thirteen years later, on May 9, 1887, another speech on the topic was given by Alfred Russel Wallace, the English naturalist who had copresented the theory of natural selection with Charles Darwin in the 1850s.[23]

Less innocent fun was to be found in the few saloons operating in Manhattan until 1881, when the Kansas constitution was amended to prohibit liquor. The *Manhattan Nationalist* observed in 1875, "Manhattan has her six churches at one end of the town and her six saloons at the other!"[24] Manhattan's German population also organized a beer garden during the 1870s, "in the woods near town, where all sorts of amusements were carried on, just the same as on the continent, — music, dancing, beer-drinking, card-playing, etc."[25] Undoubtedly, some of the beer garden's supply was provided by Manhattan's own small brewery, opened by German immigrant Charles Alten in the mid-1870s.[26]

Finally, the town's Fourth of July celebration continued to be a major event on the social calendar in Manhattan, as it had been since the settlement's first summer. In the woods near Manhattan an annual picnic was held with "speeches, music, dancing, and all kinds of games, followed in the evening by a grand display of fireworks."[27]

The 1870s also brought significant growth and change to the educational institutions founded in Manhattan in the 1850s. First, in 1873, the Manhattan school board recognized the overcrowding at the original two-story Avenue

*Poyntz Avenue around the end of the 1870s. Left, Allingham's large
Wines/Liquors shop. (Courtesy of the Riley County Historical Society.)*

School built in 1857 — essentially two little one-room schoolhouses stacked
on top of each other — and reorganized the town's public schooling. Since
the Avenue School was built, Manhattan had multiplied from 150 citizens to
nearly 1,500, and one commenter noted that the school "would pass toler-
ably well for the use of a school in the average country districts; but for a
thriving city like Manhattan, it is a poor apology."[28]

To address overcrowding, four new separate classrooms were opened in
rooms rented in buildings throughout Manhattan.[29] Three of the new classrooms were devoted to the youngest students, while in the fourth classroom,
housed in an African American church, the town segregated all African
American students for the first time.[30] The older white students were left in
the Avenue School classrooms, with the Manhattan High School occupying
the upper floor.[31] That same year, the high school also published a monthly
newspaper, the *Manhattan High School Monitor,* which was reported to be
the first high school newspaper issued by students in the young state of
Kansas.[32]

In 1878 the town opened the Central School, a handsome two-story limestone school building at Sixth Street and Leavenworth.[33] The town's school-
children, who had been scattered about in various buildings for the past
few years, were all brought back together at the Central School — including

The Central School, the second public school built in Manhattan, opened in 1878. Intermingled in the assembled crowd of kids are a handful of African American students. (Courtesy of the Riley County Historical Society.)

reintegration of African American students. In comparison to the large and modern Central School, the twenty-one-year-old Avenue School suffered. The Avenue School was small and had aged badly; over time the native timbers used for its rafters had warped, so that the back of the roof was "somewhat bent."[34] Thus it was with few regrets that the old school was closed in 1878, torn down two years later, and a new two-story schoolhouse opened on the site in 1882 to serve as the high school.[35]

In the midst of these changes to the town's public schools, the Kansas State Agricultural College moved in 1875 from the site of old Blue Mont Central College to its current location closer to central Manhattan.[36] Although the college had been some distance from Manhattan proper before the move, Manhattanites already recognized that the college was a great resource for the town. In a column in 1870, "Manhattan's Best Card," the *Manhattan Nationalist* opined: "This community owes much to Messrs. Houston, Goodnow, Denison, Marlatt, and others who established the College, and now it is our turn to do our share toward sustaining and improving it. Let every shoulder go to the wheel and push forward the enterprise."[37] With the move in 1875 the college established an even tighter link with the town. The move also strengthened the college, which benefited from more places to room its students.[38] In fact, the college saw a jump in enrollment from 143 students to 238 in its first year after moving.[39] The school was further aided in 1879 by the arrival of a dynamic new president, George Fairchild.[40] President Fairchild would increase enrollment at the college to 734 by his last year in 1896.[41] By 1887, the editor of the *Nationalist* wrote: "I presume that no citizen who thinks seriously about the matter will deny that Manhattan is a larger and better city with the college than it could possibly have been without it."[42]

The new Kansas State campus in 1875 initially consisted of two instructional buildings: a new "industrial workshop" and a large stone barn that was renovated and turned into classrooms.[43] After the move, the old Blue Mont College building continued to house the library and to be used as a student boardinghouse for a few years before it was abandoned and torn down in 1883.[44] Only a few reminders from the old college building were saved. The stone arch from below the eaves that says "Blue Mont College" was salvaged by Washington Marlatt and is now located over the central fireplace at the Alumni Center for Kansas State University. Also, the original 140-year-old bell that rang out from the cupola of the old Blue Mont building was preserved and now hangs next to Bluemont Hall on the Kansas State campus.

By the 1870s the Kansa and all other Native American tribes had been long since removed from the Manhattan area. But in a distant echo of earlier times, in 1877 — one year after Custer's last stand at the Little Bighorn — a sad band of Poncas passed near Manhattan on a forced march to Indian Territory from their homeland on the Missouri River, under the guard of U.S. troops. The Poncas were a peaceful, sedentary farming tribe who had helped Lewis and Clark when the explorers passed through the area, and the tribe remained friendly to the United States.[45] In response to this friendly attitude, the U.S. government entered into a treaty with the Ponca tribe in 1858, promising them protection from their enemies — the more contentious Sioux — and a permanent home in Missouri.[46] Despite these promises, the United States mistakenly gave the Poncas' land to the Sioux in an 1868 treaty and then ordered the Poncas off the land in 1876.[47] The order of removal was enforced by U.S. troops taking the Poncas on a forced march in May 1877.[48]

Holtz Hall, built in 1876. The first new building erected after Kansas State moved to its new campus, it was originally used as a chemistry laboratory. It is now used by career planning and placement services. (Courtesy of the Morse Department of Special Collections, Hale Library, Kansas State University.)

In mid-June, one month into the march, the Poncas camped south of Manhattan.[49] On Sunday, June 24, some Manhattan locals smuggled whiskey into the camp to sell, so the U.S. Indian agent leading the tribe quickly restarted the tribe's march that afternoon.[50] Subsequently, the *Manhattan Nationalist* printed a rather unfortunate report of the Poncas' activities, reflecting the full scope of the biases of the times:

> We saw "Hiawatha" making a Breton jacket. . . . We saw papooses of all sizes strapped upon dirty boards sleeping sweetly in blissful ignorance of soap and water. We saw Mrs. Lo with a short crowbar attached to her arm dexterously removing every particle of meat from a hide which was tightly stretched upon the ground, and with commendable economy carefully saving the tiny bits in a dirty looking kettle from which, no doubt, she produces a stew at dinner fit for — for — the Indians; and while she was performing this arduous task the noble red man of the forest sat by vigorously smoking his pipe.[51]

The next year, 1878, saw a last armed clash between Native Americans and the U.S. military in the far west of the state.[52] But this was essentially the end. As an 1881 book, *Historical Plat Book of Riley County, Kansas,* noted: "Years ago, the red man was driven — he and his squaw, his buffalo and his antelope — into the country still farther west. He has been continually pushed from his place, driven out by the spade and the plow, and kept at bay by the smoke of chimney fires. The exception hardly breaks the rule. A band of picturesque peddlers only may be occasionally seen."[53]

In 1879 Kansas was the destination for an exodus of African Americans out of southern states. These "Exodusters" were abandoning the South because U.S. Army troops had recently withdrawn from the South, ending the post–Civil War Reconstruction era and freeing white Southerners to unleash their violent racism.

None of the Exodusters initially reached Manhattan. Devious brokers in the South who promised to send the Exodusters to Kansas took all of their money for tickets and then delivered them by boat or train just across the Kansas border to Wyandotte City. There the Exodusters were left as a growing group, stranded and broke. The *Manhattan Nationalist* ruminated in April 1879: "What to do with them is a grave question. We fear they are not fitted to succeed in Kansas, but we cannot send them back if we would, and ought not to if we could. Under all the circumstances we think the best course to pursue is to scatter them over the State, wherever they can get employment."[54]

As the number of Exodusters multiplied in Wyandotte in April 1879, that town arranged to send the immigrants farther into Kansas by train.[55] On April 24 the immigrants were ordered out of town, and according to the *Kansas City Mail,* "Darkeys sprung from under every roof. They were packed in cars, and with evident happiness at going — they didn't care particularly where — they started. They were ticketed for various points in the happy land of Kansas, and were judiciously distributed."[56] Two railroad cars, containing approximately one hundred of the destitute Exodusters, were sent to settle in Manhattan.[57]

The Exodusters were well received upon arrival in Manhattan. The *Manhattan Enterprise* reported: "They were visited by a large number of citizens of both sexes, all ages and colors. Being entirely destitute, active measures were at once taken for their relief. The whole number were removed to the old paper mill, where they are at present. The accommodations are not great, but there is good shelter from the weather."[58] The day after their arrival, on

April 25, 1879, a meeting of Manhattan citizens was held to discuss care for the Exodusters. Free medical treatment was volunteered by one of the village's leading doctors, Dr. Eliphalet Leroy (E. L.) Patee.[59] A resolution was also issued after the meeting, stating in part:

> WHEREAS, A portion of the white citizens of the South have, for years systematically treated the colored people in their midst in an infamous manner, and the remaining portion has utterly failed and refused to punish the wrong doers and protect those who cannot protect themselves;
>
> AND WHEREAS, In consequence of this state of things, the victims of oppression and cruelty are now seeking homes where equal and exact justice is meted out to all; therefore,
>
> Resolved, That we would be untrue to our former history and the dictates of humanity, if we did not extend to them a cordial welcome to the free soil of Kansas, and pledge ourselves as far as we are able, to relieve their distress and aid them in finding employment and homes.

Exodusters continued to arrive throughout 1879 and 1880, quickly swelling the percentage of African American residents in Manhattan. By the time of the 1880 census, the population of African Americans in Manhattan had increased to 315 (out of 2,105 total citizens), as compared to approximately 100 five years earlier (out of 1,381 citizens).[60]

Upon arrival, the Exodusters continued a trend of African Americans settling in the south of Manhattan, particularly on Yuma Street.[61] (The south side of Manhattan had cheaper land and housing, because it was home to the town's sooty railroad and small industrial sector, but it also provided a closer proximity to railroad jobs.) The *Manhattan Nationalist* observed on January 30, 1880: "at the rate the colored people are building in the southwest part of town, they will soon have to have a separate city government. New houses are going up all the time."[62] Although the new arrivals were moving into segregated areas, this was not mandated by law; rather, it was driven primarily by income. To be sure, some African Americans lived in the wealthier parts of town, and some poor whites lived on the far south side of Manhattan.[63] Also, African American children and white children alike attended classes together at Manhattan's new Central School.[64]

Manhattan was certainly founded on progressive ideals, and the editor of the *Manhattan Nationalist* nicely stated admirable principles for the townspeople in 1875, writing, "*Justice* demands each individual, without regard to race, color or other facts that he cannot control, be given a free field."[65] Yet by the end of the decade there was a decisive racist element in Manhattan pushing for formalized segregation — recall that even many of the Free-Staters were segregationists. It was a situation familiar to most Exodusters in Kansas: "Not only did [Exodusters] in Leavenworth, Lawrence, Topeka, and Kansas City have to live in designated areas, but they had to endure discrimination in public services as well."[66] Indeed, even the enlightened *Nationalist* editor asserted that the majority of African Americans needed more time after emancipation to grow out of an "ignorant and vicious" state created by the slavery system.[67] In Manhattan, discrimination would soon grow even worse.

15

1880–1894
INTO THE MODERN ERA

By the 1880s Manhattan was an established middle-American municipality. Its steady population growth continued through the decade—growing from 2,105 in 1880 to 3,004 by 1890. Manhattan also succeeded during the decade in becoming the market town for the region, a position that it has retained into the twenty-first century. The *Topeka Capital* described Manhattan in the 1880s as "the entrepot of all the farming region about it," and a neighboring newspaper observed that "Riley [County] still serves as the tail to Manhattan's kite."[1] By the middle of the decade, Manhattan had railroads heading out in every direction, and in 1887 the last line servicing Manhattan, the Chicago, Rock Island & Pacific, was built through the town.[2] (Despite the various railroads, the town never became a national rail hub, as newspaper editor Charles de Vivaldi had optimistically predicted in 1859.)

Manhattan had also begun to decisively reshape its natural surroundings by this time. Trees that the settlers had planted years before in the town and on the surrounding hills had now reached maturity, and toward the end of the decade the Topeka newspaper described Manhattan as "shut in by the shade of great trees that have been planted."[3] Not all changes were positive, however. Bison on the plains west of Manhattan were hunted nearly to extinction, and wildlife as diverse as mountain lions and parakeets were almost entirely eliminated from the Manhattan area.[4]

Visitors to 1880s Manhattan routinely commented that the town presented a distinctive eastern appearance. A reporter from the *Chicago Inter-Ocean* was quoted in a Manhattan newspaper in 1881 as stating the town was "exceptional" because it was not western, rather being "largely of the

An overhead view looking west up Poyntz Avenue, early 1880s.
(Courtesy of the Riley County Historical Society.)

character of older eastern cities."[5] Another visitor remarked along the same lines that "the town has a substantial look, one that belies history, that it is comparatively a new town in a comparatively new state."[6] The "substantial look" of Manhattan arose primarily from its core, centered on Poyntz Avenue.

When Poyntz Avenue developed as Manhattan's central business district in the 1850s, it included a mixture of small wooden houses and small stores.[7] But the buildings erected on Poyntz Avenue in the late 1870s and 1880s were much more substantial: limestone and brick buildings, two or three stories tall. Some of these buildings have continued to house businesses on Poyntz Avenue into the modern era, including, for example, the First National Bank building, built in 1884 on the northeast corner of Poyntz and Third Street.[8] (The stones for the bank's vault were recycled from the Adams House hotel, which burned down earlier that year.)[9] Additionally, although many of these new business houses had residential flats upstairs, the ground floors of the new buildings were overwhelmingly commercial in nature, and Poyntz Avenue became far less of a mixed residential and commercial district. Instead, neighborhoods of single-family detached homes surrounding Poyntz swelled with the town's new residences. Houston Street, which was close

A crowd gathers on a chilly day to be photographed outside a Poyntz Avenue store, circa late 1880s. (Courtesy of the Riley County Historical Society.)

enough to Poyntz that residents could walk to shops and workplaces, was soon established as "the fashionable street in the town."[10]

Summing up the town in 1882, William Cutler wrote of Manhattan in his *History of the State of Kansas*: "Scattered over the town are modest cottages and palatial residences, tasty church edifices, store buildings of large and small proportions, banks, hotels, mills and elevators, while in the suburbs are many most beautiful and desirable homes."[11] The same year, a letter-writer in the *Manhattan Nationalist* bragged: "In Manhattan we do not find, as in most Kansas towns, the streets lined with farm implements, store boxes, tin cans, olds shoes and piles of ashes and an unmentionable variety of other nuisances, but the streets are kept clean and lined with beautiful shade trees. They do not plant a tree one day and make a hitching post of it the next. The lawns are not made a conservatory of farm implements."[12]

Yet, if the town presented something like the physical appearance of a tidy eastern village during the decade, its attitudes were no longer uniformly aligned with the progressive thought of New England. During the 1870s, the town's percentage of New England natives had dropped precipitously, and now in the 1880s Manhattan had apparently developed a more conservative outlook. At the start of the decade, the town's residents were still routinely described as "progressive."[13] But by 1887 one visitor was moved to comment, "Manhattan is an awful good town, solid and a beautiful place, but a little too conservative."[14]

Still, the progressive spirit in Kansas was not entirely extinguished. In 1887 the Kansas State Legislature extended to women the right to vote in local elections. The change brought Susan B. Anthony back to Manhattan. Speaking in October to female students at Kansas State Agricultural College, Anthony began by "contrast[ing] the educational advantages of our girls and the girls of her school days."[15] She then predicted that someday "a Kansas girl" would be a U.S. senator, which provoked a positive reaction from the crowd, and the newspaper reported that "all the 'strong-minded' lasses are candidates."[16]

One Yankee attitude that unquestionably remained in abundance in Manhattan was the founders' old impulse toward exclusion. As European immigrants were flooding into the United States — the Statue of Liberty and Ellis Island were built in New York City in this era — the *Manhattan Republican* rejoiced at the little town's exclusivity in 1887: "Our population is made up chiefly of the better classes of the surplus population of the Eastern and Northern States. We have some Swedes, Germans and other foreigners, but the percentage is small."[17]

The sweep of this exclusionary attitude was also reflected in relations with African Americans in Manhattan. African Americans are not frequently mentioned in the nineteenth-century records of the town.[18] But when they are referenced, it is often clear that they faced some difficult economic conditions. For example, Cutler's *History of Kansas* notes that one of the prefabricated *Hartford* buildings that remained in Manhattan in 1882 had fallen into disrepair and "now stands at the north foot of Poyntz Avenue, near the railroad track, and with its nine rooms is occupied by several colored families."[19] These apartments were later recalled as the "worst dive between Fort Riley and the Missouri."[20] Also, isolated incidents of harassment or violence against the African American community were an issue. The *Manhattan Nationalist* reported in September 1880: "The colored Baptist church people have crowded houses every night. But we are surprised to see young people who *call* themselves gentlemen and ladies go down there and make 'fun' and otherwise disturb the worshipers."[21]

Nevertheless, measured by the forlorn standards of the time, African Americans could find a relatively decent life in Manhattan at the start of the

1880s. There were three African American churches operating in Manhattan in 1882: the Second Methodist, Bethel A.M.E., and the Second Baptist (later known as Pilgrim Baptist). Moreover, African American children were still educated at Manhattan's integrated Central School. And the path to higher education at Kansas State remained open — as it always would — to African American students.

But as the 1880s wore on and the Exoduster presence continued to grow, white residents became less tolerant and the racial atmosphere began to grow stifling. By 1882 creeping segregation led to African American children being taught in separate classes at the Central School.[22] The trend toward segregation intensified in the next century, so that by 1904 a fully segregated elementary school was opened to provide education for the town's African American elementary school kids — although the secondary school remained integrated.[23] Indeed, in the coming years nearly all public places in Manhattan except the hospital became segregated.[24] African Americans could sit only in the balcony of the Wareham Theater, and they were permitted to use the city park and the city pool only on Emancipation Day (a holiday celebrating President Lincoln's emancipation of the slaves, celebrated in Kansas on August 2).[25]

The town's atmosphere was perhaps best reflected in a remarkable drop in Manhattan's African American population, beginning in 1885.[26] In the fifty-five years after 1885, the African American population in Manhattan declined consistently from 357 people in 1885 (representing 13 percent of the town's population) to 270 in 1940 (only 2 percent of the town's population).[27] The African American population did not rebound to its 1885 number until sometime in the 1940s — sixty years later — and in the 2010 census, African Americans still made up only 5.5 percent of Manhattan's population.[28]

The decade of the 1890s began with another significant step into the modern era for Manhattan — the arrival of electricity. On January 1, 1890, the Manhattan Electric Light Company powered up for the first time.[29] By the end of the week, eight arc lights were operating in downtown intersections, brightening streets previously lit by gas lamps. A total of 317 incandescent lights were soon also installed in businesses throughout downtown Manhattan.[30]

Manhattan continued to present a well-cultivated appearance as it entered the new era. A correspondent from the Topeka newspaper described Manhattan as it entered the 1890s as "a place where wealth directed by the good taste of refinement, had built up a city whose homes are not surpassed and whose business houses and public institutions have no superior in the state."[31] At the same time, an aristocrat newly arrived from England observed in her journal in October 1890, "Manhattan looked quite pretty—all the streets, except the main street, were avenues of green with houses peeping out of the trees and bushes on either side."[32]

By now Manhattan had also comfortably settled into an annual rhythm, linked to the passing of the seasons and the educational and agricultural calendars. Students arrived at the college each fall (enrollment was 593 in the fall of 1890), took rooms in town, and then departed the following spring.[33] Meanwhile, the small farmers surrounding Manhattan also provided a seasonal tide, coming to town each summer to have their wheat ground into flour at the mill, and then again each fall to market their livestock and crops. However, although agriculture remains important in the area in the twenty-first century, the impact of nearby family farms on Manhattan began a slow decline in the decade—many historians pinpoint the 1890s as the turning point when the United States became less agrarian and more mechanized, a shift symbolized by the establishment of Labor Day in 1894 as a national holiday in deference to the urban labor movement.[34] On the other hand, the annual ebb and flow of students at Kansas State University—now in the tens of thousands—still marks the seasons in modern Manhattan, as it has for more than a century.

Beyond broad national trends in the labor force, there was also a more immediate reason that Labor Day was established in 1894. As the calendar flipped to that year, the United States was reeling from the most punishing economic collapse it had ever experienced, from which Manhattan was not spared. The year 1894 brought the darkest days of the depression, with mass unemployment and a wave of violent strikes nationally.[35] Early that January, Manhattan's papers cheered unusually warm weather as a boon to newly poor people in town who simply had no means to keep warm.[36] Soon enough, however, record snows were falling, and the *Manhattan Mercury* reported "the jingle of the sleigh bell is heard in the land."[37]

Those with the means and leisure to visit Manhattan in early 1894 by wagon or horse-drawn sleigh—perhaps to attend a vaudeville show or a masked ball at the newly electrified opera house—arrived in a town that did not yet look like it does in the twenty-first century. Manhattan's growth had stalled at 3,000, and it would soon shrink back below that number, perhaps

The view looking west up Manhattan's Poyntz Avenue in the 1890s, showing a new electric light in the intersection. (Courtesy of the Riley County Historical Society.)

due to the hard economic times. What is more, Manhattan remained compact and walkable in 1894, reflecting the fact that automobiles had not yet gained purchase on its streets. The town had not yet even filled out the area of the map drawn up by the settlement's founders in 1856.

Nevertheless, Manhattan had certainly come far since its founding. It was now well forested — a major change from the original grassland. The rivers were bridged, and, as a Kansas State student observed in the *Nationalist,* "out from the midst of the city the railroads run in five diverging lines, like the spokes of a wheel."[38] The downtown area featured substantial multistory buildings, and a separate center for student life was also developing in the open land between downtown Manhattan and the Kansas State campus. (Over the coming decades, this student neighborhood would develop into an important alternative commercial and lodging district for students and professors who wanted to avoid the thirty-minute buggy ride to downtown Manhattan. The area was eventually called Aggieville, a name derived from the "Aggies" nickname used by the university's early athletic teams.)[39] In addition to electricity, Manhattan's citizens had also recently obtained

Kansas State Agricultural College in 1885, seen from the current location of Aggieville.
Soon after moving to its present location in 1875, the college built a wooden walkway to
the southeastern corner of campus to make the long trip to downtown Manhattan easier
for students and faculty. (Courtesy of Kansas State Historical Society.)

water service from an artificial reservoir built on top of Bluemont Hill in
1887.[40] As the *Mercury* proudly noted in January 1894, "Manhattan now has
a great many of the public conveniences that go to make a city desirable as
a residence."[41]

So, although Manhattan was not fully developed to the standards of eastern cities, it was certainly well established by 1894. The year also occasioned
the passage of forty years since the site of Manhattan was originally settled by European Americans in the Polistra and Canton camps. The fights
against slavery had passed, the Wild West era had passed, the Indian Wars
had passed, and the town thrived.

The year 1894 also represented something of another transition for the
town: it was the year that Isaac Goodnow died and a young entrepreneur
named Harry Wareham began building a commercial empire in Manhattan, the year that Manhattan passed into a more modern era. Goodnow, a
thoroughly nineteenth-century man, cleared the stage for Wareham, who
ushered in the twentieth century.

Isaac Goodnow died in his home west of Manhattan on March 20, 1894. In
his obituary in the *Manhattan Nationalist* he was described as "one of the

leading historical characters of the state of Kansas."[42] The *New York Times* agreed in its obituary that he was "one of the most prominent pioneers of Kansas."[43]

After choosing the town location in 1855 and spending two years getting his hands dirty with the hard work of building a settlement on the open prairie, Goodnow then shifted his focus to traveling and raising funds. Each summer from 1857 to 1860 he traveled through the Upper Midwest and New England fund-raising for Manhattan's Methodist Church and Blue Mont Central College. During his travels, Goodnow also found time for several diversions: visiting the original burned-out Mormon temple in Nauvoo, Illinois; visiting P. T. Barnum's museum and the renowned Five Points mission in New York City; soliciting the Reverend Henry Ward Beecher for funds (unsuccessfully) in Brooklyn; helping to raise funds for a slave to "buy himself" in Cincinnati; attending a clambake with Stephen A. Douglas in Providence and a rally with Senator Charles Sumner in Faneuil Hall, Boston; and, finally, calling on president-elect Abraham Lincoln in Springfield, Illinois, in January 1861.[44]

After helping to turn back slavery in Kansas Territory and to build Manhattan's institutions, Goodnow next turned to politics and to building Kansas in other ways. He served one year in the Kansas State House of Representatives (1862) and two terms as Kansas superintendent of public education (1863–1866). Goodnow also helped to found the Kansas State Teachers Association in 1863, served on the board of the National Education Association, and is justly known as the "Father of Public Education in Kansas."[45]

Two key attributes allowed Goodnow to repeatedly succeed at his work. First, he was an unyielding worker. At one point in the process of building Manhattan and Kansas State University, Goodnow took stock of his work and observed, "Hard work I believe agrees with me."[46] Agreeing with this assessment, the *Manhattan Express* observed that "obstacles to him are only an incentive to increased exertion, and success is to him almost a matter of course."[47]

Goodnow acquired this work ethic as a youth: after losing his father at the age of fourteen, he wrote that his childhood "was a laborious one attended by many discouragements, but, perseverance conquers all things."[48] And he maintained this attitude throughout his life. In 1890, when Goodnow was seventy-six years old, an encyclopedia of notable Kansans observed, "Though of slender build, he has by temperate habits, and a right

A parade on Manhattan's main street, Poyntz Avenue, in the 1890s.
The town stood on the cusp of the modern era, while just forty years earlier
the spot was open prairie. (Courtesy of Kansas State Historical Society.)

use of his mental and physical powers, preserved unimpaired his strength of body and mind, and is full of energy, and still capable of enduring much physical and intellectual labor."[49] According to the historian Julius T. Willard, it was this perseverance rather than any other natural gifts that allowed him to accomplish so much. Willard wrote that Goodnow "was not a man of deep learning, nor was he a good public speaker, but he became, by his sturdy, practical character and natural business abilities, at the very start, the indispensable manager and financier of the newly founded Blue Mont college, and afterwards of the Agricultural college."[50]

Secondly, Goodnow was also a natural consensus-builder. He demonstrated this ability from his first moments in Kansas Territory when he calmed the mounted and armed company of Border Ruffians that invaded his campsite in March 1855. In this role, Goodnow was also at times the glue that held together the early settlers of Manhattan, who could fall out over petty jealousies. The quarrelsome Washington Marlatt, for example, had problems with many of his fellow settlers, while John Pipher and Samuel Houston were said to have hated each other.[51] Goodnow's uniting spirit was eloquently demonstrated in the preface he wrote for Charles Robinson's history of the founding of Kansas, entitled *The Kansas Conflict.* Although Robinson and Goodnow regularly butted heads, Goodnow wrote a glowing description of Robinson and noted: "With a personal regard that has few equals, it has happened, fortunately or unfortunately, that ever since the war we have in most cases voted on opposite sides, yet without disturbing our personal relations. The world will never be quite right till we allow other people the same freedom of thought and action that we claim for ourselves."[52]

Meanwhile, at the time of Goodnow's death in March 1894, a young redheaded entrepreneur in Manhattan named Harry Pratt Wareham was hustling to sign up customers for an independent telephone system — the town's first — which he was proposing to build. Swimming against the tide of the economic depression, Wareham signed up enough customers by June 1894 to cover the costs of the enterprise, and he soon opened his telephone exchange, starting him on his way to assembling a commercial empire in Manhattan.[53]

Wareham would eventually become one of the most powerful businessmen in the town's history. Appearing every bit the Gilded Age baron, with a large moustache and dapper suits, he dominated the town throughout the early decades of the twentieth century. Although he passed away in 1939, his name presides even yet over downtown Manhattan, where the elegant Wareham Hotel and the marquee on the adjoining Wareham Theater remain the signature commercial features of Poyntz Avenue.[54] But Harry Wareham was also something more than a successful businessman; he was something almost entirely original in Manhattan's history — a wealthy socialite and bon vivant.

Wareham was born in Iowa on March 25, 1866, but his family moved to Manhattan four years later, and Harry spent the rest of his childhood in the rugged young town.[55] After his father died in 1875, his mother Sarah took over the family's dry goods store on the northwest corner of Poyntz and Second Street, across from the Adams House, and continued to run it successfully.[56] Harry Wareham demonstrated early on that he inherited his family's business acumen: as a teenager in 1884 he opened an icehouse alongside the

Big Blue River and a roller-skating rink in Manhattan (a popular pastime in Victorian America).[57] Later, using the profits from his family's various businesses, Wareham and his mother purchased H. S. Moore's opera house on Poyntz Avenue on August 17, 1893, renaming it Wareham's Opera House.[58] In a nod to the founding of the town, Wareham reportedly publicized coming attractions at the theater with a wagon ringing a small bell salvaged from the *Hartford*.[59]

Still only twenty-eight years old in 1894, Wareham parlayed these early successes into the development of the town's first telephone system (along with his business partner Charles G. Wood).[60] Five years later, on October 25, 1899, Wareham was awarded the franchise to build the town's first sewer system, which he promptly sold to the town once it was operational in 1908. After that, Wareham turned his attention to the Manhattan Ice, Light & Power Company, which he purchased in 1908 and then spent thousands of dollars improving.[61] (Wareham acquired much of the town's electricity from a new Rocky Ford power station built on the Big Blue River in 1909.)

At this point, Wareham also began acquiring and improving additional real estate on Poyntz Avenue between Fourth and Fifth streets — the block where he was already operating his opera house. He started in 1910 by remodeling his opera house so that it could show silent movies along with vaudeville stage shows, making the Wareham Theater the first movie theater in Manhattan.[62] The following year, Wareham built a four-story building (at that time the tallest in town) immediately west of the theater to house his telephone works and business operations. Because of the large crowds drawn to his theater, in 1912 Wareham also opened an outdoor theater alongside his two buildings, called the Wareham Airdome.[63] Several years later, in 1928, Wareham added his most impressive building, the six-story Wareham Hotel, built on the site of the former Airdome. A massive renovation of the facades of his theater and office building in 1938 completed the present appearance of Wareham's block of buildings.

As Wareham's commercial interests thrived, the lifelong bachelor also developed a reputation for entertaining well. He was singularly untroubled by the Kansas constitution's ban on alcohol — the alcoholic excess of his parties was one of the more open secrets in Manhattan. As a joke at one of his grand balls, a friend projected onto a wall a drawing of Kansas temperance activist Carrie Nation chasing Wareham with an ax. The colorful Wareham also kept a monkey and a crocodile as pets, and he had a fleet of flashy early

Seated on right, *Harry Wareham. (Courtesy of the Riley County Historical Society.)*

automobiles, including a Thomas Flyer, a Maxwell Runabout, and an eight-cylinder Cadillac.[64]

In addition to Wareham's activities, 1894 also offered yet another glimpse into the modern era with the beginnings of intercollegiate athletic competition at Kansas State Agricultural College, together with the start of a culture of spectatorship for athletics in Manhattan.[65] In modern Manhattan, Kansas State University sporting events have become important cultural occasions, and thousands of townspeople enthusiastically attend them. In fact, the school's football stadium is large enough to hold Manhattan's entire population.

Starting in November 1893, football was the first of today's major spectator sports to field an intercollegiate team at Kansas State.[66] It was immediately popular. The *Manhattan Mercury* reported on its front page after the first game: "About 30 spectators and lovers of the game accompanied our college foot ball team [by train] to St. Marys on Thanksgiving day and witnessed the defeat of St. Marys' college team by a score of 18 to 10. . . . The boys were nicely treated and feel good over their first game and victory."[67]

Six months later, in May 1894 Kansas State also began intercollegiate competition in baseball.[68] Although football was certainly popular, baseball

*Manhattan in 1890, as viewed from Mount Prospect. The railroad and
wagon bridges over the Kansas River are visible in the foreground. Many trees
have grown to maturity since a similar photo taken in 1873. (Courtesy of the Morse
Department of Special Collections, Hale Library, Kansas State University.)*

easily led all other intercollegiate team sports in interest at Kansas State
for many decades.[69] Baseball, of course, had the advantage of being the
most established sport, having already been played in Manhattan for decades—teams of college students had been playing baseball games against
local Manhattanites since at least 1873.[70] The sport of basketball, the last of
the three major modern spectator sports to arrive, would not appear on the
Kansas State campus until 1901.[71]

In 1894 Americans were marveling at entering a modern age. The Columbian Exposition the prior year had showcased a host of new wonders, and
the American frontier had been conclusively declared closed with the final
land rush of Sooners in Oklahoma in 1893.[72] Manhattan likewise witnessed
its own dividing line between one era and another. The stark contrast between the lives lived by Isaac Goodnow and Harry Wareham had much to
do with their differing personalities, but it also plainly illustrated that the
era of New England Free-Staters and crusaders in Manhattan had passed by
the turn of the century.

Nonetheless, Goodnow and the early settlers laid an enduring foundation that would influence the town into the present day. The *Manhattan Nationalist* observed in 1893: "[Manhattan] was settled at the beginning by some of the choicest spirits that came from eastern states to make Kansas free. . . . Starting with those high ideals the reputation of the town was assured from the very first."[73] Manhattan settler and longtime resident A. F. Grow added around the same time that the early settlers also complemented their ideals with strength and faith: "Some other cities may have had more wealth in an early day, but certainly there was none whose inhabitants showed more genuine grit and perseverance, mingled with unflinching faith in the future."[74] Indeed, Manhattan probably owes its present existence to the fact that all of these attributes were found in a combination of the town's founders. Looking back at the product of the settlers' work from the 150th anniversary of the town's founding in 2005, the *Manhattan Mercury* wrote with evident pride: "The pioneers have left a legacy of an education oriented city, a city with libraries, parks, tree lined avenues and streets, a city with well developed government services and infrastructure, a business community ready to instantly fill any want, and churches to supply any religious need."[75]

EPILOGUE

Twenty-first-century Manhattan is far removed from the lonely canvas tent erected on the spot by Isaac Goodnow in 1855. It has also changed much from the small village of 1894. Nevertheless, there are certain continuities running throughout Manhattan's history.

In a description that probably would have resonated with the citizens of 1894, Manhattan was described as a tree-filled town by the *WPA Guide to 1930s Kansas:* "Encircled by low hills, Manhattan is an oasis of green during the late summer months when the bluestem grasses that cover the hills are turned to an autumnal brown by the sun. With streets well-shaded by spreading elms, the city, seen from the adjoining countryside gives the appearance of a great park. Here and there the outline of one of the taller buildings is visible above the mass of green."[1] At the time that description was written, Manhattan had a population of 10,136. A similar description was again given in a *New York Times* profile in 1946 after the town had nearly doubled in size: "[Manhattan] is so embowered in shade trees, mostly elms, that it would be hard to see from the air, though a few handsome near-skyscrapers and some of the eighteen church spires might show through the rooftops."[2] In the past half century, Manhattan's population has multiplied again to 52,000, and the town has sprawled into the hills beyond the street grid mapped by the founders in 1856, but the above descriptions still ring true for the city center.

Similarly, while the physical center of the city retains an aspect familiar to earlier decades, the essential spirit of Manhattan still reflects the ideals and visions that New Englanders carried to the plains. Specifically, the influence of the Yankee founders can be seen in a continuing emphasis on religion and education.

Religious spirit is evident to outside observers. In describing the town's conservative nature in 2002, the *Christian Science Monitor* used religion as

An overhead view of Manhattan, circa 1950. The photo reveals a community that looks strikingly like the map produced by the founders a century earlier. (Courtesy of the Riley County Historical Society.)

metaphor, describing conservatism in Manhattan to be "as enduring as the native limestone blocks used to build many homes, public buildings, and churches. At the 121-year-old Pilgrim Baptist Church, the men's choir — six powerful, joyous voices — still sings 'Jesus Met the Woman at the Well' as if it had been written just this morning."[3] Manhattanites can sometimes also still display a conservative discomfort with outsiders or confrontation. After new Kansas State University professor Stephen Ambrose heckled U.S. President Richard Nixon over the Vietnam War during a speech in 1970, he was eventually driven from the school.[4]

And yet progressive sentiment is also readily apparent. As the *Monitor* also noted, "Over a cappuccino at the Espresso Royale Caffe just off campus, one still can read handouts from the Kansas State Socialists."[5] And although Ambrose faced repercussions from the Nixon incident, he and his wife were still gratified and surprised to find in Manhattan organized groups "trying to change America."[6] As humorist Calvin Trillin put it in the *New Yorker* in 1971, "At Kansas State, it is not always easy to tell if a pair of faded bluejeans is a symbol of the counter-culture or a leftover from the farm."[7]

A view of downtown Manhattan and Poyntz Avenue, 1953. It appears much the same today. (Courtesy of the Riley County Historical Society.)

Meanwhile, Manhattan's strong and enduring commitment to education was most recently reaffirmed by an overwhelming vote in November 2008 — in the teeth of another major economic downturn — approving a $97.5 million bond issue to improve public schools in the town, supported by 69 percent of Manhattanites.[8]

As it has since its founding, Manhattan has also continued to meet and surmount challenges in the past century. Not the least of these challenges was seeing U.S. Route 40 (later designated an interstate highway) rerouted eight miles south of the town in the 1950s, which removed the town from a major east-west transportation route for the first time since 1856.[9] For the previous century steamboats, horses, wagons, trains, and major highways had kept the outside world coursing through Manhattan. (The highway was rerouted primarily to address concerns that arose during World War II about having a major highway pass through nearby Fort Riley.) Although the town has continued to grow after the highway's move, Manhattan's core has perhaps retained a more timeless appearance — nineteenth-century limestone buildings with 1950s marquees — as a result of this decision.

Of course, Manhattan had never been entirely isolated. The *Christian Science Monitor* noted in 2002 that Manhattan has always had "some important windows on the world: Kansas State University, with hundreds of foreign students and professors, and nearby Ft. Riley, many of whose US Army personnel have served abroad or at the Pentagon."[10] And in a recent example of cosmopolitanism, the *Monitor* reported that, "instead of responding with fear and suspicion after 9/11, the community . . . rallied with flowers, notes and calls of support [for the town's mosque], and offers to accompany Muslim women shopping or to the playground with their kids."[11] Moreover, in the twenty-first century, the town has been decidedly reintegrated into the transportation grid, with daily commercial flights from its airport to Dallas and Chicago. (Isaac Goodnow's seventeen-day trip from Boston to Manhattan can now be accomplished in six hours.)

Through it all, Manhattan has in some ways remained at heart a small village — something like Isaac Goodnow and Eli Thayer pictured. The town certainly made nods toward recent trends that swept across the United States. A mall was constructed in the 1980s, which involved the demolition of ninety-three downtown buildings.[12] In the 1990s, coffeehouses appeared and a larger county jail was built. Big-box retailers invaded the town in the 2000s. Nevertheless, the town's livestock auction house and farm-implement dealers still ply their trades, a full order of biscuits and gravy at Bob's Diner downtown still costs just $3.99, and the solidity of Manhattan's citizens remains unfailing.

APPENDIX:
POPULATION IN MANHATTAN (1855–1900)

	Manhattan	Manhattan and Vicinity	Notes/Sources
April 1855		~60[a]	Before arrival of *Hartford*
July 1855		~150[a]	After arrival of *Hartford*
January 1856	~100[a]	~200[a]	
November 1856	~150		Governor Geary's secretary
March 1857		358	Local census of voters
1860	~300[a]	~620 (served by Manhattan post office)	U.S. census; imprecise
1865	347	873 (incl. Manhattan Township)	State of Kansas census
1870	1,173		U.S. census
1875	1,381	2,076 (incl. Manhattan Township)	State of Kansas census
1877	1,392		Township assessor[b]
1878	1,597		Township assessor[b]
1880	2,105	3,057 (incl. Manhattan Township)	U.S. census
1885	2,735		State of Kansas census
1890	3,004		U.S. census
1895	2,980		State of Kansas census
1900	3,438		U.S. census

[a]Author's estimates, based on compiled sources.

[b]*Manhattan Nationalist*, June 7, 1878.

NOTES

ABBREVIATIONS

KHQ   *Kansas Historical Quarterly* (the quarterly journal of the Kansas State Historical Society).

KSHS   Kansas State Historical Society.

KSU   Kansas State University, Hale Library, Morse Department of Special Collections.

KU   University of Kansas, Kenneth Spencer Research Library.

RCHM   Riley County Historical Museum.

RCHS   Riley County Historical Society.

CHAPTER 1. THE PEOPLE, THE PLACE, THE TIMES

1. Elizabeth Shor, *Fossils and Flies: The Life of a Compleat Scientist Samuel Wendell Williston* (Norman: University of Oklahoma Press, 1971), 17.

2. Henry Adams, *The Education of Henry Adams: An Autobiography* (Boston: Houghton & Mifflin Co., 1918), 53.

3. "Letters of a Kansas Pioneer: Thomas C. Wells Part III," *KHQ* (November 1936): 415 (hereafter cited as "Wells Letters III"). Kansas City was officially "the City of Kansas" until it was renamed in 1889, but it is called "Kansas City" throughout this history for ease of understanding.

4. "Letters of a Kansas Pioneer: Thomas C. Wells Part I," *KHQ* (May 1936): 154 (hereafter cited as "Wells Letters I"); see also "Letters of a Kansas Pioneer: Thomas C. Wells Part II," *KHQ* (August 1936): 308 (hereafter cited as "Wells Letters II").

5. David Reynolds, *John Brown, Abolitionist: The Man Who Killed Slavery, Sparked the Civil War, and Seeded Civil Rights* (New York: Alfred A. Knopf, 2005), 142: "'Free State' meant free of *any* blacks, whether slaves or not."

6. *Atchison Squatter Sovereign*, March 27, 1855: writing specifically of territorial governor Andrew H. Reeder.

7. The *Herald* reported that a planned Manhattan newspaper would be "neutral," but the proslavery *Herald* editor opined, "He that is not for us is against us." *Leavenworth Herald*, May 5, 1855.

8. Eli Thayer, *A History of the Kansas Crusade: Its Friends and Its Foes* (New York: Harper & Bros., 1889), 88–89; see also Daniel Walker Howe, *What Hath God Wrought: The Transformation of America, 1815–1848* (New York: Oxford University Press, 2007), 425–430; Reynolds, *John Brown,* 96; R. R. Palmer and Joel Colton, *A History of the Modern World,* 6th ed. (New York: Alfred A. Knopf, 1984), 538.

9. Thayer, *Kansas Crusade,* 32.

10. *Lawrence Herald of Freedom*, October 13, 1855; see also *Cincinnati Enquirer*, July 10, 1855, Riley County Clippings, vol. 1, KSHS: Intent of company was "not indeed to plant a colony of Abolitionists, but to increase their fortunes."

11. *Lawrence Herald of Freedom*, October 13, 1855.

12. "Letters of Julia Louisa Lovejoy, 1856–1864: Part 3," *KHQ* (November 1947): 383 (hereafter cited as "Lovejoy Letters III").

13. A letter-writer to the *Atchison Squatter Sovereign* argued that one particular town founder, George Park, was an abolitionist, writing: "You have frequently denied your abolition proclivities, yet keep company — are 'cheek by jowl' with the vilest and meanest of the gang." *Atchison Squatter Sovereign*, June 12, 1855.

14. W. Marlatt to Isaac Goodnow, June 14, 1859, KSU.

15. Howe, *What Hath God Wrought*, 570–588, 762–767, 835.

16. Leonard Pillsbury, "Why I Left New York City," Pillsbury Family Papers, KU.

17. *Manhattan Independent*, April 18, 1868: "The assertion of John Wesley [the founder of Methodism], that Slavery was the 'sum of all villainies,' would be more properly applied to Conservatism as Slavery was only one of its evil manifestations."

18. Ibid., April 21, 1866.

19. *Manhattan Standard*, September 4, 1869.

20. *Manhattan Mercury*, November 9, 1988.

21. "Brownback Victory Would Shift Kansas to Right," *New York Times*, October 21, 2010; "Moderates in Kansas Decide They're Not in GOP Anymore," *Washington Post*, October 19, 2006.

22. Thomas Schlereth, *Victorian America: Transformations in Everyday Life, 1876–1915* (New York: HarperPerennial, 1991), xii, 35.

23. James Shortridge, *Cities on the Plains: The Evolution of Urban Kansas* (Lawrence: University Press of Kansas, 2004), 9.

24. Thayer, *Kansas Crusade*, 31.

25. James Humphrey, "The Country West of Topeka Prior to 1865," *Transactions of the KSHS* 4 (1888): 292; *Manhattan Kansas Radical*, July 21, 1866; *Manhattan Independent*, January 26, 1867.

26. "Manhattan's Changing Complexion," *Manhattan Mercury*, March 13, 2011.

27. Sara Robinson, *Kansas: Its Interior and Exterior Life* (Boston: Crosby, Nichols & Co., 1856), 189.

28. C. B. Boynton and T. B. Mason, *A Journey through Kansas; with Sketches of Nebraska* (Cincinnati: Moore, Wilsach, Keys & Co., 1855), 65; see also *Leavenworth Daily Times*, July 29, 1863; Amos Powers, "Old Settlers Stories," Riley County Clippings, vol. 2, KSHS, 44.

29. H. M. Atherton, *The Great Flood of 1903* (Salina, KS: privately printed); *Manhattan Nationalist*, June 3, 4, 11, 1903; September 17, 1903; June 11, 18, 1908; Federal Writers' Project, *The WPA Guide to 1930s Kansas* (Lawrence: University Press of Kansas, 1984), 249.

30. John Frémont, *Report of the Exploring Expedition to the Rocky Mountains in the Year 1842* (Washington: Gales & Seaton, 1845), 13.

31. Robinson, *Kansas,* 189; see also Ellen Goodnow to T. H. Webb, July 10, 1855, KSHS; *Big Blue Union,* August 8, 1863, quoted in "Bypaths of Kansas History," *KHQ* (August 1939): 315; Louise Barry, ed., "Scenes in (and en Route to) Kansas Territory, Autumn, 1854: Five Letters by William H. Hutter," *KHQ* (Autumn 1969): 330–331.

32. *Leavenworth Daily Times,* July 29, 1863.

33. Joseph Collins, ed., *Natural Kansas* (Lawrence: University Press of Kansas, 1985), 91; Craig Miner, *Kansas: The History of the Sunflower State, 1854–2000* (Lawrence: University Press of Kansas, 2002), 31; "Letters from Kanzas," *KHQ* (February 1942): 39 (hereafter cited as "Lovejoy Letters from Kanzas").

34. J. H. Pillsbury to Mary Pillsbury, July 6, 1855, KU.

35. Isaac Goodnow, "Personal Reminiscences and Kansas Emigration, 1855," *Transactions of the KSHS* 4 (1888): 251; see also William Least Heat-Moon, *PrairyErth* (Boston: Houghton Mifflin Co., 1991), 12.

36. Richard White, "The Cultural Landscape of the Pawnees," in *Kansas and the West,* ed. Rita Napier (Lawrence: University Press of Kansas, 2003), 71–72; Charles Mann, *1491: New Revelations of the Americas before Columbus* (New York: Alfred A. Knopf, 2005), 250–252.

37. Boynton and Mason, *Journey through Kansas,* 77–78; James Griffing to Augusta Goodrich, November 24, 1854, KSHS.

38. Heat-Moon, *PrairyErth,* 13–14.

39. James Griffing to Augusta Goodrich, November 24, 1854, KSHS.

40. William Cutler and Alfred Theodore Andreas, *History of the State of Kansas* (Chicago: Western Historical Co., 1883), 1306.

41. Collins, *Natural Kansas,* 195–209; *WPA Guide to 1930s Kansas,* 13; Wells Letters III, 407; RCHS, *Log Cabin Days* (Manhattan, KS: RCHS, 1929), 24–25; White, "Cultural Landscape of the Pawnees," 69.

42. Boynton and Mason, *Journey through Kansas,* 65; John Gihon, *Geary and Kansas* (Philadelphia: J.H.C. Whiting, 1857), 203; George Willard to *Boston Journal,* January 7, 1855, quoted in Louise Barry, "The Emigrant Aid Company Parties of 1854," *KHQ* (May 1943): 148.

43. Frémont noted that the Kansa selected their villages based in part on a "fondness of beauty of scenery." Frémont, *Report of the Exploring Expedition,* 13.

44. "Account of an Expedition from Pittsburgh to the Rocky Mountains, Performed in the Years 1819, 1820," in *Early Western Travels, 1748–1846* (Cleveland: Arthur H. Clark Co., 1905), 14:188, 200 (hereafter cited as "Expedition from Pittsburgh"); Cutler, *History of Kansas,* 59; *Manhattan Nationalist,* July 16, 1903; Powers, "Old Settlers Stories," 40.

45. Elliot West, *The Contested Plains: Indians, Goldseekers and the Rush to Colorado* (Lawrence: University Press of Kansas, 1998), 19–31.

46. George Morehouse, "History of the Kansa or Kaw Indians," *Transactions of the KSHS* 10 (1908): 345.

47. Benjamin Dixon, "Furthering Their Own Demise: How Kansa Indian Death Customs Accelerated Their Depopulation," *Ethnohistory* (Summer 2007): 476.

48. Mann, *1491*, 109–111.

49. William Unrau, *The Kansa Indians: A History of the Wind People, 1673–1873* (Norman: University of Oklahoma Press, 1971), 92.

50. John Luttig, *Journal of a Fur-Trading Expedition* (New York: Argosy-Antiquarian, 1964), 36.

51. "Expedition from Pittsburgh," 190.

52. Luttig, *Journal of Fur-Trading Expedition,* 36–37; see also Dixon, "Furthering Their Own Demise," 476–477; "Expedition from Pittsburgh," 188–189.

53. Lela Barnes, ed., "Journal of Isaac McCoy for the Exploring Expedition of 1828," *KHQ* (August 1936): 255.

54. Ibid.; Unrau, *Kansa Indians,* 27–40; "Expedition from Pittsburgh," 190–191.

55. "Expedition from Pittsburgh," 190–191.

56. Unrau, *Kansa Indians,* 47–48; Dixon, "Furthering Their Own Demise," 492.

57. Unrau, *Kansa Indians,* 89; see also Morehouse, "History of the Kansa or Kaw Indians," 332.

58. Shortridge, *Cities on the Plains,* 14.

59. Ibid., 42–43, 51–53; Craig Miner and William Unrau, *The End of Indian Kansas: A Study of Cultural Revolution, 1854–1871* (Lawrence: Regents Press of Kansas, 1978), 5.

60. Shortridge, *Cities on the Plains,* 15.

61. Boynton and Mason, *Journey through Kansas,* 88.

62. Chestina Allen, "Journey from Mass. to Kansas," Pottawatomie County History Collection, KSHS, 17; Powers, "Old Settlers Stories," 40–41.

63. Powers, "Old Settlers Stories," 41.

64. RCHS, *Log Cabin Days,* 9.

65. The site was scoured of any archeological artifacts when the Big Blue River shifted location in 1908.

66. Stewart L. Udall, *To the Inland Empire* (Garden City, NY: Doubleday, 1987), 172–174.

CHAPTER 2. 1854: "A MOST APPROPRIATE TOWN SITE"

1. Daniel Walker Howe, *What Hath God Wrought: The Transformation of America, 1815–1848* (New York: Oxford University Press, 2007), 813–814, 816; J. S. Holliday, *The World Rushed In: The California Gold Rush Experience* (New York: Touchstone, 1981), 25–26, 53, 397.

2. William McKale and William D. Young, *Fort Riley: Citadel of the Frontier West* (Topeka: KSHS, 2000), 4.

3. James Shortridge, *Cities on the Plains: The Evolution of Urban Kansas* (Lawrence: University Press of Kansas, 2004), 59–60.

4. William Cutler and Alfred Theodore Andreas, *History of the State of Kansas* (Chicago: Western Historical Co., 1883), 1301; Elaine Olney and Mary Roberts, eds., *Pioneers of the Bluestem Prairie* (Manhattan, KS: Riley County Genealogical Society, 1976), 314; James Carey, "Juniata: Gateway to Mid-Kansas," *KHQ* (Summer 1954): 87–88.

5. Craig Miner, *Kansas: The History of the Sunflower State, 1854–2000* (Lawrence: University Press of Kansas, 2002), 33–34; Donald Parrish, *This Land Is Our Land: The Public Domain in the Vicinity of Riley County and Manhattan, Kansas* (Manhattan, KS: RCHS, 2003), 5.

6. An election for territorial representative to Congress was held in November 1854, but because that election "had no direct agency in state-making," it was not considered vital to the cause. Charles Robinson, *The Kansas Conflict* (New York: Harper & Bros., 1892), 92.

7. David Reynolds, *John Brown, Abolitionist: The Man Who Killed Slavery, Sparked the Civil War, and Seeded Civil Rights* (New York: Alfred A. Knopf, 2005), 140.

8. Carey, "Juniata," 89.

9. RCHS, *Log Cabin Days* (Manhattan, KS: RCHS, 1929), 37; Wells Letters I, 156.

10. Chestina Allen, "Journey from Mass. to Kansas," Pottawatomie County History Collection, KSHS, 11; *Parkville (MO) Industrial Luminary*, November 21, 1854.

11. C. B. Boynton and T. B. Mason, *A Journey through Kansas; with Sketches of Nebraska* (Cincinnati: Moore, Wilsach, Keys & Co., 1855), 78.

12. Louise Barry, ed., "Scenes in (and en Route to) Kansas Territory, Autumn, 1854: Five Letters by William Hutter," *KHQ* (Autumn 1969): 330.

13. Boynton and Mason, *Journey through Kansas,* 78–80.

14. Ibid.

15. *Parkville (MO) Industrial Luminary*, November 28, 1854; December 5, 1854; Cutler, *History of Kansas,* 1301.

16. *Parkville (MO) Industrial Luminary*, November 28, 1854; Barry, "Letters by William Hutter," 330; Boynton and Mason, *Journey through Kansas,* 81. The bridge was approximately 360 feet long by 18 feet, had one arch in the frame, and stood 25 feet above the water. *Lawrence Herald of Freedom*, March 31, 1855; George Willard to *Boston Journal,* January 7, 1855, quoted in Louise Barry, "The Emigrant Aid Company Parties of 1854," *KHQ* (May 1943): 148.

17. *Parkville (MO) Industrial Luminary*, November 14, 1854.

18. *Historical Plat Book of Riley County, Kansas* (Chicago: Bird & Mickle Map Co., 1881), 18.

19. Allen, "From Mass. to Kansas," 13.

20. "Slavery in Kansas," *Transactions of the KSHS* 7 (1902): 241.

21. Wells Letters I, 165.

22. Samuel Whitehorn, "Historical Sketch of Riley County," *Manhattan Nationalist*, July 7, 1876 (hereafter cited as Whitehorn, "Historical Sketch"); see also Central Committee's 1856 List of Voters in 7th Senatorial District, Blackman Collection, KSHS; Barry, "Letters by William Hutter," 330; *Manhattan Nationalist*, February 22, 1878.

23. Allen, "From Mass. to Kansas," 12, 13, 31; "Manhattan Twenty Years Ago," Marlatt Papers, KSU; Isaac Goodnow, "Personal Reminiscences and Kansas Emigration, 1855," *Transactions of the KSHS* 4 (1888): 247: Describing Juniata as "a little Pro-Slavery town" and noting "the rivalry of Manhattan."

24. Wells Letters I, 165.

25. *Kansas (Manhattan) Express,* May 21, 1859; Boston Town Association and Manhattan Town Association Records, KSHS, microfilm reel MS 123.01, January 7, 1856 (hereafter cited as MTA Records).

26. MTA Records, January 7, 1856; *Parkville (MO) Industrial Luminary*, December 12, 1854. The name is sometimes wrongly given as "Poleska" or "Poliska."

27. *Lawrence Herald of Freedom*, July 21, 1855; W. M. Paxson, *Annals of Platte Co., Missouri* (Kansas City: Hudson-Kimberly Publishing Co., 1897), 919.

28. Lovejoy Letters from Kanzas, 40; see also *Daily Cincinnati Gazette,* May 29, 1856.

29. *Lawrence Kansas Free State,* May 21, 1855.

30. George Martin, "Territorial and Military Combine at Fort Riley," *Transactions of the KSHS* 7 (1902): 380.

31. *Parkville (MO) Industrial Luminary,* July 4, 1854.

32. Ibid.

33. Ibid.

34. MTA Records, January 7, 1856; *Parkville (MO) Industrial Luminary*, December 5, #12 1854.

35. *Kansas (Manhattan) Express,* May 21, 1859; MTA Records, January 7, 1856. As to the location of the cabin, see Allen, "From Mass. to Kansas," 15; *Parkville (MO) Industrial Luminary*, November 21, 1854; December 12, 1854; and Goodnow, "Reminiscences," 247.

36. *Lawrence Herald of Freedom*, May 5, 1855: "The charge of abolitionism is false."

37. *Atchison Squatter Sovereign*, April 24, 1855; see also *Lawrence Kansas Free State,* August 27, 1855.

38. *Parkville (MO) Industrial Luminary*, January 1, 1855.

39. Ibid., November 28, 1854.

40. Olney and Roberts, *Bluestem Prairie,* 361; RCHS, *Log Cabin Days,* 85–86; see also Barry, "Aid Company Parties of 1854," 140, 149.

41. MTA Records, January 7, 1856.

42. David Ballard, "The First State Legislature, 1861," *Transactions of the KSHS* 10 (1908): 240.

43. *Kansas (Manhattan) Express,* August 3, 1859.

44. Ibid.

45. *Lawrence Herald of Freedom*, January 10, 1857.

46. Parrish, *This Land,* 22; S. Houston to F. G. Adams, January 2, 1888, KSHS; *Manhattan Nationalist*, March 24, 1871; Ballard, "First State Legislature," 240; Olney and Roberts, *Bluestem Prairie,* 360.

47. Parrish, *This Land,* 24.

48. William Connelley, *A Standard History of Kansas and Kansans* (Chicago: Lewis Publishing Co., 1918), 699. Johnston subsequently moved to Shawnee Mission, where the Territorial Supreme Court convened in 1855. In 1859 he was the losing Democratic candidate in the election for territorial delegate to U.S. Congress. He is buried in Arlington National Cemetery.

49. Sara Robinson, *Kansas: Its Interior and Exterior Life* (Boston: Crosby, Nichols & Co., 1856), 189; Barry, "Aid Company Parties of 1854," 140, 149; "List of Voters in the Tenth District of the Territory of Kansas, according to the census taken by M. F. Conway in the month of January and February, 1855," KSHS; Whitehorn, "Historical Sketch"; H. A. Wilcox to Isaac Goodnow, June 6, 1861, KSHS. Wilcox was a Baptist clergyman from Connecticut. *Hartford Daily Courant,* October 23, 1855. Thurston was a graduate of Colby College and a lawyer. Lovejoy Letters from Kanzas, 39; James Humphrey letter, *Manhattan Nationalist,* March 1, 1878.

50. Goodnow, "Reminiscences," 248; *Daily Cincinnati Gazette,* June 30, 1855; MTA Records, April 19, 1855.

51. Parrish, *This Land,* 23.

52. *Parkville (MO) Industrial Luminary,* December 5, 1854.

53. MTA Records, January 7, 1856.

CHAPTER 3. WINTER 1854–1855: A NEW ENGLAND CRUSADE

1. Isaac Goodnow, "Personal Reminiscences and Kansas Emigration, 1855," *Transactions of the KSHS* 4 (1888): 245; Diary of Isaac Goodnow, as transcribed by RCHM staff, January 9, 1856 (hereafter cited as Goodnow Diary).

2. *East Greenwich Weekly Pendulum,* December 30, 1854; D. H. Greene, *History of the Town of East Greenwich and Adjacent Territory, from 1677 to 1877* (Providence, RI: J. A. & R. A. Reid, 1877), 222.

3. Goodnow began researching a move to Kansas Territory in November 1854, first looking into the American Settlement Company, based in New York City. George Walter to Isaac Goodnow, November 22, 1854, KSHS. Thayer spoke unfavorably of the American Settlement Company, telling Goodnow: "One of their agents gambled away their money in going up the Missouri River" (Notes on Thayer lecture, Goodnow Collection, KSHS). The American Settlement Company did establish a settlement in Kansas Territory in 1854 called Council City, but the colony failed in 1856.

4. *Providence (RI) Daily Journal,* December 9, 1854; *Providence (RI) Freeman,* December 22, 1854.

5. *Providence (RI) Freeman,* December 6, 1854.

6. Isaac Goodnow to Stephen French, December 16, 1854, KSHS; Goodnow, "Reminiscences," 245.

7. J. Howe to Isaac and Ellen Goodnow, January 24, 1855, KSHS.

8. [Unidentified] to Isaac and Ellen Goodnow, January 25, 1855, KSHS.

9. Isaac Goodnow to Ellen Goodnow, March 30, 1855, KSHS; Goodnow Diary, April 5, 1855; Isaac Goodnow to Ellen Goodnow, April 8, 1855, KSHS: "I am now of the opinion that the sooner you can come on the better."

10. Goodnow, "Reminiscences," 245.

11. Isaac Goodnow to Stephen French, December 16, 1854, KSHS; Goodnow, "Reminiscences," 245; cf. Isaac Goodnow to Eli Thayer, May 24, 1858, KSHS: "You well know that we come to battle for Freedom & a pure Christianity, & now when the

victory in the Main is won we wish to make the results certain by seeing well to our Schools & Churches."

12. Samuel Wynn to Isaac Goodnow, February 28, 1855, KSHS.

13. Isaac Goodnow to Stephen French, December 16, 1854, KSHS; see also Charles Barnes to Isaac Goodnow, February 15, 1855, KSHS.

14. *Providence (RI) Freeman*, January 19, 1855.

15. *Providence (RI) Daily Tribune*, January 17, 1855.

16. Samuel K. Towle to Isaac Goodnow, January 30, 1855, KSHS; William Arnold to Isaac Goodnow, February 18, 1855, KSHS; J. Denison to Isaac Goodnow, January 18, 1855, KSHS.

17. E. Burdick to Isaac Goodnow, February 5, 1855, KSHS.

18. J. Howe to Isaac Goodnow, January 24, 1855, KSHS.

19. Ziba Loveland to Isaac Goodnow, January 26, 1855, KSHS.

20. Wm. Goodnow to Isaac Goodnow, January 21, 1855, RCHM.

21. Daniel Walker Howe, *What Hath God Wrought: The Transformation of America, 1815–1848* (New York: Oxford University Press, 2007), 617–626; David Reynolds, *John Brown, Abolitionist: The Man Who Killed Slavery, Sparked the Civil War, and Seeded Civil Rights* (New York: Alfred A. Knopf, 2005), 64, 121, 188.

22. Reynolds, *John Brown*, 222–224.

23. Howe, *What Hath God Wrought*, 166–185.

24. Ibid., 615. The founding of the New England Emigrant Aid Company was typical of the establishment of "societies" in New England during the era aimed at the betterment of civilization (168).

25. Some parties that departed during warmer months broke up the rail trip with a ferry across Lake Erie.

26. Isaac Goodnow was already scheduled for a March 6 departure by February 24. Goodnow Diary, February 24, 1855; see also Goodnow, "Reminiscences," 245.

27. *East Greenwich Weekly Pendulum*, April 28, 1855; Louise Barry, "The New England Emigrant Aid Company Parties of 1855," *KHQ* (August 1943): 234n4; Goodnow Diary, March 6, 1855.

28. Isaac Goodnow to Ellen Goodnow, March 5, 1855, KSHS.

29. Goodnow Diary, March 6, 1855; *East Greenwich Weekly Pendulum*, April 28, 1855; Elizabeth Shor, *Fossils and Flies: The Life of a Compleat Scientist Samuel Wendell Williston* (Norman: University of Oklahoma Press, 1971), 10; Letter of W. C. High, April 6, 1855, quoted in Barry, "Aid Company Parties of 1855," 235.

30. Barry, "Aid Company Parties of 1855," 234n4; Charles Robinson to S. Pomeroy, March 6, 1855, KSHS; Goodnow, "Reminiscences," 245; cf. Isaac Goodnow to Ellen Goodnow, March 5, 1855, KSHS: "We shall be accompanied by Mr. Lincoln, one of the first Pioneers, who wishes to settle down in *our company*, because he thinks it will be one of the *best* out!"

31. Thomas Webb to S. Pomeroy, March 6, 1855, KSHS.

32. Isaac Goodnow to Ellen Goodnow, March 5, 1855, KSHS.

33. Barry, "Aid Company Parties of 1855," 227; *Boston Daily Advertiser,* March 7, 1855; *Boston Evening Journal,* March 14, 1855.

34. Goodnow, "Reminiscences," 244.

35. Charles Robinson, *The Kansas Conflict* (New York: Harper & Bros., 1892), xiii, 87–88; Sara Robinson, *Kansas: Its Interior and Exterior Life* (Boston: Crosby, Nichols & Co., 1856), 24.

36. *Boston Evening Journal,* March 14, 1855.

37. Wells Letters I, 144; Eli Thayer, *A History of the Kansas Crusade: Its Friends and Its Foes* (New York: Harper & Bros., 1889), 56; *Boston Evening Journal,* March 14, 1855.

38. Carolyn Jones, *The First One Hundred Years: A History of the City of Manhattan, Kansas 1855–1955* (Manhattan, KS: privately printed, 1955), 19; see also Nicole Etcheson, "'Labouring for the Freedom of This Territory': Free-State Kansas Women in the 1850s," *Kansas History* (Summer 1998): 68–71. William Goodnow did return to New England several times for visits with his wife, first leaving Manhattan in August 1855.

39. *East Greenwich Weekly Pendulum,* April 28, 1855.

40. C. Lovejoy to Isaac Goodnow, January 13, 1855, KSHS. Julia Lovejoy gave birth to a son, Irving, after reaching the new settlement. He was the first child born in Manhattan.

41. Francis A. Abbott, "Some Reminiscences on Early Days in Deep Creek, Riley County," *Transactions of the KSHS* 12 (1912): 392; RCHS, *Log Cabin Days* (Manhattan, KS: RCHS, 1929), 51.

42. Wells Letters I, 143. It is never clear from the letters who "James" is.

43. Ibid., 144.

44. Barry, "Aid Company Parties of 1855."

45. Ibid., 234–235; Thayer, *Kansas Crusade,* 184.

46. *Boston Daily Advertiser,* March 20, 1855.

47. *Lawrence Herald of Freedom,* March 31, 1855; see also Ellen Goodnow to T. H. Webb, July 10, 1855, KSHS.

48. Hannah Anderson Ropes, *Six Months in Kansas* (Boston: John P. Jewett & Co., 1856), 12.

49. Lovejoy Letters from Kanzas, 31.

50. Barry, "Aid Company Parties of 1855," 268.

51. *Daily Cincinnati Gazette,* July 9, 1855.

52. *East Greenwich Weekly Pendulum,* April 28, 1855; see also Lovejoy Letters from Kanzas, 31; Ellen Goodnow to T. H. Webb, July 10, 1855, KSHS.

53. Wells Letters I, 145.

54. Reynolds, *John Brown,* 62–63.

55. *Lawrence Herald of Freedom,* March 31, 1855.

56. Ibid.; *East Greenwich Weekly Pendulum,* April 28, 1855; Goodnow Diary, March 10, 1855; Lovejoy Letters from Kanzas, 31, 33.

57. Wells Letters I, 146; J. Denison to "Bro. ___," April 19, 1855, KSHS; *Daily Missouri Democrat,* March 19, 1855.

58. Lovejoy Letters from Kanzas, 32.

59. Letter of W. C. High, April 6, 1855, quoted in Barry, "Aid Company Parties of 1855," 235.

60. Wells Letters I, 147.

61. Ibid., 146.

62. Alberta Prantle, "The Connecticut Kansas Colony: Letters of Charles B. Lines," *KHQ* (Spring 1956): 7.

63. Arthur Mecham to Charles Robinson, March 24, 1855, KU; Wells Letters I, 146.

64. Lovejoy Letters from Kanzas, 32.

65. "Journal," November 7, 1855, Isaiah Morris Harris Collection, KU.

66. Ibid.

67. Wells Letters I, 146.

68. RCHS, *Log Cabin Days,* 63.

69. *Atchison Squatter Sovereign,* March 6, 1855.

70. Ibid.

71. *Leavenworth Herald,* June 29, 1855.

CHAPTER 4. MARCH 1855: "DAMNED YANKEES" COME TO KANSAS

1. *East Greenwich Weekly Pendulum,* June 30, 1855; Isaac Goodnow to Ellen Goodnow, April 21, 1855, KSHS; J. Denison to "Bro. _____," April 19, 1855, KSHS.

2. *East Greenwich Weekly Pendulum,* June 30, 1855.

3. Ibid.

4. "Diary of Julia Lovejoy," Charles and Julia Lovejoy Collection, KSHS, 2; see also Hannah Anderson Ropes, *Six Months in Kansas* (Boston: John P. Jewett & Co., 1856), 34; Miriam Davis Colt, *Went to Kansas* (Ann Arbor, MI: University Microfilms, 1966), 35.

5. Colt, *Went to Kansas,* 34–35.

6. Lovejoy Letters from Kanzas, 34.

7. Sara Robinson, *Kansas: Its Interior and Exterior Life* (Boston: Crosby, Nichols & Co., 1856), 24; Edgar Langsdorf, "S. C. Pomeroy and the New England Emigrant Aid Company, 1854–1858," *KHQ* (August 1938): 232.

8. Robinson, *Kansas,* 24–25. The date of the election was set on March 6, but it was not well known until more than a week later. See announcements of election date in *Lawrence Kansas Tribune* on March 14, 1855; *Atchison Squatter Sovereign* on March 20, 1855; *St. Louis Daily Missouri Democrat* on March 21, 1855; and the *Boston Evening Transcript* on March 24, 1855. However, the approximate date for the vote was known further in advance. *Boston Evening Transcript,* March 9, 1855; *Atchison Squatter Sovereign,* March 6, 1855.

9. *East Greenwich Weekly Pendulum,* June 30, 1855; Isaac Goodnow, "Personal Reminiscences and Kansas Emigration, 1855," *Transactions of the KSHS* 4 (1888): 246.

10. Isaac Goodnow to Stephen French, December 16, 1854, KSHS.

11. Langsdorf, "Pomeroy and the Emigrant Aid Company," 232–233; Goodnow, "Reminiscences," 246.

12. Donald Parrish, *This Land Is Our Land: The Public Domain in the Vicinity of Riley County and Manhattan, Kansas* (Manhattan, KS: RCHS, 2003), 25.

13. Goodnow, "Reminiscences," 248; Goodnow Diary, March 27, 1855; Chestina Allen, "Journey from Mass. to Kansas," Pottawatomie County History Collection, KSHS, 15.

14. "Diary of Julia Lovejoy," 2; C. Lovejoy to Isaac Goodnow, January 13, 1855, KSHS; Goodnow Diary, March 20, 1855; Goodnow, "Reminiscences," 246.

15. Goodnow Diary, March 20, 1855; Lovejoy Letters from Kanzas, 35; *East Greenwich Weekly Pendulum,* June 30, 1855.

16. *East Greenwich Weekly Pendulum,* June 30, 1855.

17. Goodnow, "Reminiscences," 246.

18. *East Greenwich Weekly Pendulum,* June 30, 1855; *Lawrence Kansas Free State,* March 24, 1855.

19. Goodnow, "Reminiscences," 246.

20. "A Few Brief Sketches from My Diary" (1895), Charles H. Lovejoy Collection, KU.

21. Goodnow Diary, March 24, 1855; Isaac Goodnow to Ellen Goodnow, March 25, 1855, KSHS; "Diary of Julia Lovejoy," 3.

22. C. B. Boynton and T. B. Mason, *A Journey through Kansas; with Sketches of Nebraska* (Cincinnati: Moore, Wilsach, Keys & Co., 1855), 77–78.

23. Ibid. (emphasis omitted).

24. U.S. Congress, *Report of the Special Committee Appointed to Investigate the Troubles in Kansas; with the Views of the Minority of Said Committee* (Washington, DC: Government Printing Office, 1856) (hereafter cited as *Howard Report*), 1035; Goodnow, "Reminiscences," 247; Parrish, *This Land,* 59; "A Few Brief Sketches from My Diary" (1895), Charles H. Lovejoy Collection, KU.

25. Goodnow, "Reminiscences," 247; Goodnow Diary, March 24, 1855. The burial mound at the top of Bluemont Hill was exhumed in December 1879. *Lawrence Western Home Journal,* December 11, 1879.

26. *East Greenwich Weekly Pendulum,* June 30, 1855.

27. Isaac Goodnow to Ellen Goodnow, March 25, 1855, KSHS. For an example of Goodnow's later writings, see Goodnow, "Reminiscences," 247: "I felt like exclaiming *Eureka! Eureka!! I have found it!* I HAVE FOUND IT!"

28. Goodnow Diary, March 25, 1855.

29. Isaac Goodnow to Ellen Goodnow, March 7, 1855, KSHS.

30. Ibid., March 25, 1855, KSHS; see also Lovejoy Letters from Kanzas, 37: "The only thing we have noticed as being lacking to make this country all that could be desired, is a scarcity of good building material, such as spruce and pine."

31. Allen, "From Mass. to Kansas," 15.

32. Isaac Goodnow to Ellen Goodnow, March 25, 1855, KSHS.

33. *East Greenwich Weekly Pendulum,* June 30, 1855.

34. Goodnow Diary, March 26, 1855.

35. Goodnow, "Reminiscences," 248. Pomeroy probably informed Goodnow back in Kansas City that the Polistra and Canton claims were already located at the rivers' junction (Elaine Olney and Mary Roberts, eds., *Pioneers of the Bluestem Prairie* [Manhattan, KS: Riley County Genealogical Society, 1976], 263). Blood, who was showing Goodnow around the area, helped to build Park's cabin, so he certainly was aware of it. Goodnow reveals in his diary with no apparent surprise that he knew of Park and the Polistra claim on March 26, 1855, writing, "Walked down to Poliska a city site chosen by Mr Park."

36. Goodnow, "Reminiscences," 247; *East Greenwich Weekly Pendulum,* June 30, 1855.

37. Isaac Goodnow to Ellen Goodnow, March 25, 1855, KSHS.

38. J. Denison to "Bro. ___," April 19, 1855, KSHS.

39. Wells Letters I, 147.

40. Lovejoy Letters from Kanzas, 35.

41. *Lawrence Kansas Free State,* March 24, 1855.

42. Allen, "From Mass. to Kansas," 38.

43. Lovejoy Letters from Kanzas, 34–35.

44. Ibid., 35.

45. Handwritten Reminiscences of Mrs. George W. Lee, March 14, 1878, Riley County History Collection, KSHS (hereafter cited as Reminiscences of Mrs. George Lee); Allen, "From Mass. to Kansas," 9.

46. Alberta Prantle, "The Connecticut Kansas Colony: Letters of Charles B. Lines," *KHQ* (Spring 1956): 11.

47. RCHS, *Log Cabin Days* (Manhattan, KS: RCHS, 1929), 64.

48. Wells Letters I, 148–149; Allen, "From Mass. to Kansas," 15.

49. Wells Letters I, 148–149.

50. Sam Tappan to Ellen Goodnow, June 29, 1855, KSHS.

51. Wells Letters I, 148–149.

52. Ibid.

53. Edward E. Leslie, *The Devil Knows How to Ride: The True Story of William Clarke Quantrill and His Confederate Raiders* (New York: Random House, 1996), 11.

54. William H. Mackey, "Looking Backwards," *Transactions of the KSHS* 10 (1908): 646.

55. Allen, "From Mass. to Kansas," 15; Parrish, *This Land,* 26.

56. The *Squatter Sovereign* wrote on February 13, 1855, that Park was afraid to "show [his] face" on his claim "in daylight, for fear (as we are credibly informed) of a coat of Tar and Feathers."

57. Goodnow, "Reminiscences," 248.

58. Goodnow Diary, March 29, 1855.

59. *Howard Report,* 474–475; Isaac Goodnow to Ellen Goodnow, March 30, 1855, KSHS. The thirteen voters from the 1855 New England emigration that I was able to identify are Goodnow, Wright, Lincoln, Lovejoy, Wintermute (listed as Winterworth on the transcription of the voting rolls), Asaph Browning, Newell Trafton, John Flagg, A. La Roy Prentice, John Hoar, George W. Lockwood, J. Edgar Bissell, and Henry B. Gage.

60. *Lawrence Kansas Free State,* March 24, 1855; *Atchison Squatter Sovereign,* March 20, 1855.

61. Instead of Houston, the Free-Staters had hoped to nominate E. M. Thurston as their candidate for House because he had previously held office in Maine. But Thurston was absent from the nominating meeting on March 18. William Cutler and Alfred Theodore Andreas, *History of the State of Kansas* (Chicago: Western Historical Co., 1883), 1303.

62. Conway was one of the three principal agents working in Kansas Territory for the New England Emigrant Aid Company, along with Samuel C. Pomeroy and Charles Robinson. He was later elected as the first U.S. congressman for the state of Kansas.

63. Whitehorn, "Historical Sketch"; *East Greenwich Weekly Pendulum,* June 30, 1855.

64. *Lawrence Herald of Freedom,* April 14, 1855.

65. Federal Writers' Project, *The WPA Guide to 1930s Kansas* (Lawrence: University Press of Kansas, 1984), 47; cf. *Lawrence Herald of Freedom,* April 1, 1855.

66. The voters included Cyrus Garrett, Isaac Walker, and William Walker, a Wyandot who had ostensibly been elected provisional governor of the territory in 1852 (*Howard Report,* 475–476). William Walker was a Democrat and slaveholder (William Connelley, *The Provisional Government of Nebraska Territory and Journals of William Walker* [Lincoln, NE: State Journal Co., 1899], 13).

67. Amos Powers, "Old Settlers Stories," Riley County Clippings, vol. 2, KSHS, 38.

68. Ibid.; Daniel Walker Howe, *What Hath God Wrought: The Transformation of America, 1815–1848* (New York: Oxford University Press, 2007), 491.

69. The decisive overall Free-State edge in the voting in the combined ninth and tenth districts was provided by a large number of voters from Pennsylvania who were recruited to Pawnee by territorial governor Andrew Reeder. *Leavenworth Herald,* April 6, 1855; *Howard Report,* 267–269, 271; Samuel A. Johnson, *The Battle Cry of Freedom: The New England Emigrant Aid Company in the Kansas Crusade* (Westport, CT: Greenwood Press, 1977), 102; cf. Goodnow, "Reminiscences," 246.

70. *Atchison Squatter Sovereign,* April 19, 1855.

71. Whitehorn, "Historical Sketch"; *East Greenwich Weekly Pendulum,* June 30, 1855; Allen, "From Mass. to Kansas," 15–16.

72. Allen, "From Mass. to Kansas," 15–16; Goodnow, "Reminiscences," 248–249.

73. Allen, "From Mass. to Kansas," 15–16; Goodnow, "Reminiscences," 248–249; Goodnow Diary, March 30, 1855. A month after the camp invasion, the *Squatter Sovereign* (confusing the identity of the people involved) crowed that George Park had "receiv[ed] a sound drubbing from one of our squatter sovereigns, somewhere on the Blue river. It seems that Park attempted to jump some man's claim, but utterly failed, and if we are correctly informed, got badly 'jumped' himself. Park, we pity you" (*Atchison Squatter Sovereign,* May 1, 1855).

74. David Reynolds, *John Brown, Abolitionist: The Man Who Killed Slavery, Sparked the Civil War, and Seeded Civil Rights* (New York: Alfred A. Knopf, 2005), 96, 159–160.

75. *Chicago Daily Tribune,* August 26, 1857.

76. Goodnow Diary, March 31, 1855; Allen, "From Mass. to Kansas," 16.

77. Isaac Goodnow to Ellen Goodnow, March 30, 1855, KSHS.

78. Goodnow Diary, April 2, 1855.

79. MTA Records, April 6, 1855; Goodnow Diary, April 4, 1855: "Meeting to organize a city association, named it Boston. 24 present."

80. MTA Records, April 6, 1855. The official name for the BTA was the "Boston Association of Kansas Territory" (ibid.). Luke Lincoln was not a signatory; on April 3 Lincoln returned to New England to retrieve additional emigrants. Goodnow Diary, April 3, 1855; Allen, "From Mass. to Kansas," 16; *Lawrence Herald of Freedom*, April 7, 1855.

81. *Columbian History of Education in Kansas* (Topeka: Hamilton Printing Co., 1893), 190; Parrish, *This Land*, 60. Later that same year, Mary Blood became the first teacher in the town's history.

82. Parrish, *This Land*, 28.

83. *Lawrence Herald of Freedom*, April 14, 1855.

84. MTA Records, April 19, 1855; Lovejoy Letters from Kanzas, 40; "Reminiscences: Recollections of Ten Years on the Frontier," Marlatt Papers, KSU.

85. Louise Barry, "The New England Emigrant Aid Company Parties of 1855," *KHQ* (August 1943): 227–268; Samuel A. Johnson, "The Emigrant Aid Company in Kansas," *KHQ* (November 1932): 433.

86. Goodnow Diary, March 30, April 9, 1855; Isaac Goodnow to Ellen Goodnow, April 8, 1855, KSHS.

87. Goodnow Diary, April 6, 1855, see also April 9, 1855; Isaac Goodnow to Ellen Goodnow, March 30, 1855, KSHS: "This is trying times to our young men — It starts the tears even among the older ones at thoughts of those *left* behind!"

88. Wm. Goodnow to Harriet Goodnow, June 10, 1855, KSHS.

89. *Howard Report*, 1035; *Lawrence Herald of Freedom*, April 14, 1855: "The Boston Association is a joint stock company of fifty proprietors."

90. *Lawrence Herald of Freedom*, June 23, 1855.

91. MTA Records, April 18, 1855; Julius Terrass Willard, *History of the Kansas State College of Agriculture and Applied Science* (Manhattan: Kansas State College Press, 1940), 10.

92. Allen, "From Mass. to Kansas," 16.

93. Goodnow Diary, April 26, 1855; Wm. Goodnow to Harriet Goodnow, April 29, 1855, KSHS; Isaac Goodnow to Ellen Goodnow, April 8, 1855, KSHS.

94. Goodnow, "Reminiscences," 249.

95. Goodnow Diary, April 30, 1855.

96. Ibid.; Lovejoy Letters from Kanzas, 40.

97. *Lawrence Herald of Freedom*, April 21, May 5, 1855; *Lawrence Kansas Free State*, May 7, 1855; *Howard Report*, 1134.

98. *Atchison Squatter Sovereign*, April 24, 1855.

99. *Lawrence Kansas Free State*, May 7, 1855; John Gihon, *Geary and Kansas* (Philadelphia: J.H.C. Whiting, 1857), 37; Charles Robinson, *The Kansas Conflict* (New York: Harper & Bros., 1892), 130–131.

100. *Atchison Squatter Sovereign*, April 24, 1855.

101. S. Pomeroy to George Park, April 24, 1855, KSHS.

102. *Lawrence Herald of Freedom,* May 5, 1855.

103. Park always retained his house in Parkville and returned for the first time in late 1855, despite his mistreatment at the hands of its proslavery citizens. *New York Times,* November 19, 1855; Allen, "From Mass. to Kansas," 23.

104. "Records of Blue Mont Central College Meetings, 1857–1881," Marlatt Papers, KSU. After several years of moving around, Park returned permanently to Parkville, Missouri, near the end of the Civil War to "bless and enrich the very men who had conspired for his ruin." W. M. Paxson, *Annals of Platte Co., Missouri* (Kansas City: Hudson-Kimberly Publishing Co., 1897), 919.

105. "Reminiscences: Recollections of Ten Years on the Frontier," Marlatt Papers, KSU. Park was given shares "in consideration of the withdrawal of his previous claim to a part of the town, and the erection of a business block and the introduction of a printing press, etc., none of which he ever did, much to the after disgust of the company."

106. J. Denison to "Bro. ___," April 19, 1855, KSHS, referring to the disease as "lung fever."

107. Ibid.

108. Ibid.

109. Sarah Denison to "Sister," April 1855, KSHS.

110. J. Denison to "Bro. ___," April 19, 1855, KSHS.

111. Lovejoy Letters III, 369; Lovejoy Letters from Kanzas, 36.

112. "Diary of Julia Lovejoy," 4; cf. J. Denison to "Bro. ___," April 19, 1855, KSHS: "The Kanzas River has been so low that Boats could not go up. The first one this Spring has attempted to day and we hope will succeed."

113. Lovejoy Letters III, 369; "Diary of Julia Lovejoy," 4.

114. Lovejoy Letters III, 372.

115. "Diary of Julia Lovejoy," 11.

116. Lovejoy Letters III, 368.

117. James Griffing to Augusta Goodrich, May 6, 1855, KSHS.

118. Lovejoy Letters III, 368.

119. *Manhattan Express,* May 5, 1860.

CHAPTER 5. SPRING 1855: BECOMING MANHATTAN

1. In an article inviting pioneers to settle in "the boundless stretch of country in the west," the *Lawrence Herald of Freedom* on December 29, 1855, noted, "There are no towns in reality (except Manhattan, at the mouth of the Blue,) but a great many prospective, or on paper, in the upper country."

2. Craig Miner, *Kansas: The History of the Sunflower State, 1854–2000* (Lawrence: University Press of Kansas, 2002), 54.

3. William Cutler and Alfred Theodore Andreas, *History of the State of Kansas* (Chicago: Western Historical Co., 1883), 1303.

4. George Willard to *Boston Journal,* January 7, 1855, quoted in Louise Barry, "The

Emigrant Aid Company Parties of 1854," *KHQ* (May 1943): 148; see also RCHS, *Log Cabin Days* (Manhattan, KS: RCHS, 1929), 85–86.

5. J. H. Pillsbury to Mary Pillsbury, July 6, 1855, KU.

6. RCHS, *Log Cabin Days*, 25.

7. Ibid.

8. Lovejoy Letters from Kanzas, 41.

9. Isaac Goodnow to Ellen Goodnow, April 21, 1855, KSHS.

10. Isaac Goodnow to unidentified [Ellen Goodnow], April 8, 1855, KSHS.

11. Ibid.

12. Isaac Goodnow to Ellen Goodnow, April 21, 1855, KSHS.

13. "A Brief Sketch of History," Charles H. Lovejoy Collection, KU.

14. Ibid.; Lovejoy Letters III, 379; *Western Kansas Express,* December 15, 1860; Lovejoy Letters from Kanzas, 39.

15. Lovejoy Letters from Kanzas, 38–39.

16. *East Greenwich Weekly Pendulum,* June 30, 1855; Wm. Goodnow to Harriet Goodnow, May 20, 1855, KSHS.

17. RCHS, *Log Cabin Days,* 29.

18. *Lawrence Herald of Freedom,* June 23, 1855.

19. *East Greenwich Weekly Pendulum,* June 30, 1855; see also Isaac Goodnow to unidentified [Ellen Goodnow], April 8, 1855, KSHS.

20. Lovejoy Letters from Kanzas, 39.

21. Wells Letters I, 152.

22. Lovejoy Letters from Kanzas, 38, 42.

23. Wm. Goodnow to Harriet Goodnow, May 25, 1855, KSHS.

24. Amanda Arnold interview, *Topeka Daily Capital,* November 18, 1923; Isaac Goodnow, "Personal Reminiscences and Kansas Emigration, 1855," *Transactions of the KSHS* 4 (1888): 250; Sonie Liebler, *That Splendid Little Steamer Hartford* (Oklahoma City: Kaw River Research, 2003), 9.

25. Donald Parrish, *This Land Is Our Land: The Public Domain in the Vicinity of Riley County and Manhattan, Kansas* (Manhattan, KS: RCHS, 2003), 32; Pillsbury, "Why I Left New York City," KU: "Just why these Ohioans named their Pet New 'Manhattan' I could never learn."

26. *Cincinnati Enquirer,* July 10, 1855, Riley County Clippings, vol. 1, KSHS.

27. *Lawrence Herald of Freedom,* October 13, 1855.

28. Cora Dolbee, "The Second Book on Kansas: An Account of C. B. Boynton and T. B. Mason's 'A Journey through Kansas,'" *KHQ* (May 1935).

29. Parrish, *This Land,* 169.

30. *Daily Cincinnati Gazette,* April 20, 1855; also announcing, "They are all Anti-Slavery and Temperance men."

31. *Daily Cincinnati Gazette,* April 21, 1855; Liebler, *Hartford,* 4–5.

32. *Cincinnati Daily Enquirer,* April 22, 24, 1855.

33. Ibid., April 25, 1855.

34. Ibid., April 27, May 2, 1855.

35. *Daily Cincinnati Gazette*, April 20, 27, 1855; *East Greenwich Weekly Pendulum*, August 25, 1855; *Leavenworth Herald*, May 5, 1855; John Pipher interview, *Manhattan Republic*, February 19, 1897: "The first printing outfit ever brought to Manhattan came with Judge Pipher's Cincinnati colony."

36. *Cincinnati Daily Enquirer*, April 27, 1855.

37. Amanda Arnold interview, *Topeka Daily Capital*, November 18, 1923.

38. "Journal," November 4, 1855, Isaiah Morris Harris Collection, KU.

39. Amanda Arnold interview, *Topeka Daily Capital*, November 18, 1923; Albert R. Greene, "The Kansas River — Its Navigation," *Transactions of the KSHS* 9 (1906): 327–328; W. Hoon letter, *Daily Cincinnati Gazette*, May 25, 1855: "We have had but little sickness on board, and but four deaths; most of the sickness was brought on by intemperance."

40. *St. Louis Missouri Democrat*, May 2, 1855.

41. Greene, "Kansas River," 327.

42. *Daily Cincinnati Gazette*, April 30, 1855.

43. W. Hoon letter, *Daily Cincinnati Gazette*, May 25, 1855; cf. May 14, 1855.

44. *Daily Cincinnati Gazette*, May 14, 19, 25, 1855.

45. Goodnow, "Reminiscences," 244–245; *Chicago Daily Tribune*, April 8, 1856.

46. Greene, "Kansas River," 328.

47. W. Hoon letter, *Daily Cincinnati Gazette*, May 25, 1855.

48. *Lawrence Kansas Free State*, May 21, 1855; see also John Pipher interview, *Manhattan Republic*, February 19, 1897.

49. W. Hoon letter, *Daily Cincinnati Gazette*, July 27, 1855.

50. Greene, "Kansas River," 327–328.

51. *Lawrence Herald of Freedom*, May 26, 1855; cf. W. Hoon letter, *Daily Cincinnati Gazette*, July 27, 1855.

52. *Daily Cincinnati Gazette*, May 25, 1855; John Pipher interview, *Manhattan Republic*, February 19, 1897; Parrish, *This Land*, 32.

53. *Lawrence Herald of Freedom*, May 26, 1855.

54. *Lawrence Kansas Free State*, May 28, 1855; *Lawrence Kansas Tribune*, May 23, 1855; W. Hoon letter, *Daily Cincinnati Gazette*, July 27, 1855.

55. Cutler, *History of Kansas*, 1306; Lowell Jack, *A History of Manhattan, Kansas — Riley County and Ft. Riley* (Manhattan, KS: Hawley Printing, 2003), 2; *Cincinnati Daily Enquirer*, June 14, 1855.

56. W. Hoon letter, *Daily Cincinnati Gazette*, July 27, 1855.

57. MTA Records, June 2, 1855.

58. Lovejoy Letters from Kanzas, 41: "Our 'Association' made them a present of one-half our 'City-site' or one side of 'Main Street,' that runs through the centre, and the privilege of changing the name from 'Boston,' first given to it, to 'Manhattan.'" The BTA had appointed a committee to recommend a name change in any event. MTA Records, May 10, 1855.

59. Greene, "Kansas River," 328.

60. W. Hoon letter, *Daily Cincinnati Gazette*, July 27, 1855.

61. Parrish, *This Land,* 35, 170–172; Goodnow Diary, June 4, 1855.

62. W. Hoon letter, *Daily Cincinnati Gazette,* July 27, 1855.

63. John Pipher Recollections, *Lawrence Western Home Journal,* April 25, 1878.

64. *Manhattan Nationalist,* March 8, 1871.

65. Goodnow, "Reminiscences," 250.

66. *East Greenwich Weekly Pendulum,* August 25, 1855.

67. Four of the prefabricated buildings were apparently unloaded before the boat reached Manhattan. "Cincinnati houses" were noted to exist in Lawrence and Wyandotte City.

68. Elaine Olney and Mary Roberts, eds., *Pioneers of the Bluestem Prairie* (Manhattan, KS: Riley County Genealogical Society, 1976), 361; see also *Salem (MA) Register,* February 25, 1856, quoted in "Bypaths of Kansas History," *KHQ* (November 1938): 414–415: "I stopped also a short time at Manhattan, a Cincinnati settlement on the north side of the river, within ten or twelve miles of the fort. There were there, at that time, six or eight houses built of Cincinnati lumber."

69. Chestina Allen, "Journey from Mass. to Kansas," Pottawatomie County History Collection, KSHS, 19.

CHAPTER 6. BLEEDING KANSAS: "TYRANNY IS NOW IN THE ASCENDANT"

1. MTA Records, June 4, 1855.

2. *Howard Report,* 1035; MTA Records, April 18, 1855.

3. *Daily Cincinnati Gazette,* June 30, 1855; *Cincinnati Enquirer,* July 10, 1855, Riley County Clippings, vol. 1, KSHS.

4. *Daily Cincinnati Gazette,* June 30, 1855; *Cincinnati Enquirer,* July 10, 1855, Riley County Clippings, vol. 1, KSHS; Donald Parrish, *This Land Is Our Land: The Public Domain in the Vicinity of Riley County and Manhattan, Kansas* (Manhattan, KS: RCHS, 2003), 39.

5. *Leavenworth Herald,* June 15, 1855; see also *New York Herald,* June 17, 1855; *New York Daily Times,* June 27, 1855; *Richmond (VA) Daily Dispatch,* June 29, 1855; *New Orleans Daily Picayune,* June 30, 1855. The *Cincinnati Daily Gazette* reprinted the *Herald*'s story on June 28, 1855, but opined at the end, "Knowing the character of the emigrants who left this city, we give little credit to the above statements."

6. *Leavenworth Herald,* June 15, 1855.

7. Ibid.

8. *Howard Report,* 1036; *Daily Cincinnati Gazette,* June 30, 1855.

9. *Daily Cincinnati Gazette,* June 30, 1855; *Cincinnati Enquirer,* July 10, 1855, Riley County Clippings, vol. 1, KSHS.

10. *Howard Report,* 1036.

11. *Daily Cincinnati Gazette,* June 30, 1855.

12. *Leavenworth Herald,* June 15, 1855.

13. Ibid.

14. Ibid.

15. Ibid., June 29, 1855.

16. *Lawrence Herald of Freedom,* October 13, 1855.

17. *Cincinnati Enquirer,* July 10, 1855, Riley County Clippings, vol. 1, KSHS. The June 30, 1855, *Daily Cincinnati Gazette* was more equivocal, writing, "The proceedings of the [Manhattanites], though not such as could be approved of in a country where laws are regularly administered, are sanctioned by the Squatter's Code, and have been practiced for many years on our Western frontier."

18. *Richmond (VA) Daily Dispatch,* June 29, 1855.

19. *New Orleans Daily Picayune,* June 30, 1855.

20. Ibid.

21. John Pipher Recollections, *Lawrence Western Home Journal,* April 25, 1878.

22. *Leavenworth Herald,* June 29, 1855.

23. For reference to claim jumpers, see Lovejoy Letters from Kanzas, 40; Goodnow Diary, March 15, 1857; John Pipher Recollections, *Lawrence Western Home Journal,* April 25, 1878.

24. *Howard Report,* 1035.

25. Goodnow Diary, May 16, 22, 1855; see also W. Hoon letter, *Daily Cincinnati Gazette,* July 27, 1855: Captain Millard of the *Hartford* "vented his spite on a person named Haskel, who had 'jumped' a city claim."

26. Goodnow Diary, May 11, 1855.

27. Ibid., May 9, 1855; June 23, 1855; Parrish, *This Land,* 36.

28. Isaac Goodnow, "Personal Reminiscences and Kansas Emigration, 1855," *Transactions of the KSHS* 4 (1888): 250.

29. Ibid.; Goodnow Diary, June 23, 1855; *Portrait and Biographical Album of Washington, Clay and Riley Counties, Kansas* (Chicago: Chapman Bros., 1890), 550.

30. *Goodnow v. Haskell* file, Goodnow Collection, KSHS; MTA Records, September 25, 1858; Parrish, *This Land,* 38; "Reminiscences: Recollections of Ten Years on the Frontier," Marlatt Papers, KSU.

31. *Howard Report,* 1035.

32. *Lawrence Herald of Freedom,* February 16, 1856.

33. Goodnow, "Reminiscences," 250.

34. James Shortridge, *Cities on the Plains: The Evolution of Urban Kansas* (Lawrence: University Press of Kansas, 2004), 76–78; William McKale and William D. Young, *Fort Riley: Citadel of the Frontier West* (Topeka: KSHS, 2000), 21–24; Wm. Goodnow to Harriet Goodnow, July 1, 1855, KSHS.

35. Marc Parrott to E. A. Parrott, June 11, 1855, KSHS.

36. Wells Letters I, 155; Isaac Goodnow notes entitled "Kansas As It Is," KSHS; Amos Powers, "Old Settlers Stories," Riley County Clippings, vol. 2, KSHS, 46; H. A. Wilcox letter, *Hartford Daily Courant,* October 23, 1855.

37. Goodnow notes, "Kansas As It Is," KSHS.

38. Craig Miner, *Kansas: The History of the Sunflower State, 1854–2000* (Lawrence: University Press of Kansas, 2002), 47.

39. Lovejoy Letters from Kanzas, 43.

40. Powers, "Old Settlers Stories," 46.

41. Lovejoy Letters from Kanzas, 43.

42. Goodnow Diary, June 27, 28, 1855.

43. *Lawrence Herald of Freedom,* July 14, 1855.

44. Ibid., July 21, 1855.

45. Wm. Goodnow to Harriet Goodnow, July 1, 1855, KSHS.

46. Goodnow Diary, July 5, 1855.

47. Old Colorado City also served as a territorial capital for five days, but it was never recognized as such by the federal government.

48. Boston *Post,* January 16, 1856, quoted in George Martin, "Territorial and Military Combine at Fort Riley," *Transactions of the KSHS* 7 (1902): 371.

49. Lovejoy Letters from Kanzas, 43.

50. *Leavenworth Herald,* July 17, 1855.

51. Goodnow notes, "Kansas As It Is," KSHS.

52. *Lawrence Kansas Free State,* July 30, 1855.

53. Charles Robinson, *The Kansas Conflict* (New York: Harper & Bros., 1892), 155.

54. Sara Robinson, *Kansas: Its Interior and Exterior Life* (Boston: Crosby, Nichols & Co., 1856), 79–83; David Reynolds, *John Brown, Abolitionist: The Man Who Killed Slavery, Sparked the Civil War, and Seeded Civil Rights* (New York: Alfred A. Knopf, 2005), 141; Miner, *Kansas,* 63.

55. William Connelley, *A Standard History of Kansas and Kansans* (Chicago: Lewis Publishing Co., 1918), 388.

56. Wells Letters I, 155.

57. *East Greenwich Weekly Pendulum,* August 25, 1855; see also H. A. Wilcox letter, *Hartford Daily Courant,* October 23, 1855.

58. Goodnow notes, "Kansas As It Is," KSHS.

59. Lovejoy Letters from Kanzas, 43.

60. *Howard Report,* 85; *Portrait and Biographical Album,* 549; Goodnow Diary, August 13–15, 1855; Goodnow, "Reminiscences," 251; *Chicago Daily Tribune,* August 5, 1857: "The Territorial taxes . . . have never been collected in Lawrence, Topeka, Quindaro, Manhattan, or in the southern section of the Territory."

61. *Lawrence Herald of Freedom,* August 18, 1855.

62. Shortridge, *Cities on the Plains,* 73; see also Reynolds, *John Brown,* 142: "The Free State convention at Big Springs specified that 'the best interests of Kansas require a population of free white men,' demanding 'stringent laws excluding all negroes, bond and free.'"

63. Miner, *Kansas,* 63; Reynolds, *John Brown,* 137, 143; *Lawrence Kansas Free State,* November 26, 1855. The "Negro Exclusion Clause" was put to a separate vote from the rest of the constitution and passed easily.

64. Reynolds, *John Brown,* 145.

65. Miner, *Kansas,* 64; McKale and Young, *Fort Riley,* 29.

66. Reynolds, *John Brown,* 145.

67. Ibid., 146.

68. Chestina Allen, "Journey from Mass. to Kansas," Pottawatomie County History Collection, KSHS, 23.

69. Goodnow Diary, December 10, 1855.

70. Isaac Goodnow to [unknown], January 1856, KSHS.

71. Wm. Goodnow to Harriet Goodnow, December 16, 1855, KSHS.

72. Robinson, *Kansas*, 190.

73. Reynolds, *John Brown*, 149; Daniel Walker Howe, *What Hath God Wrought: The Transformation of America, 1815–1848* (New York: Oxford University Press, 2007), 577–578.

74. Arrest warrant issued April 14, 1856, KSHS; Reynolds, *John Brown*, 156.

75. Wm. Goodnow to Harriet Goodnow, April 27, 1856, KSHS.

76. *Howard Report*, 34.

77. Ibid., 67.

78. Wells Letters I, 164–165.

79. Reynolds, *John Brown*, 151.

80. Ibid., 156.

81. Wm. Goodnow to Harriet Goodnow, April, 16, 1856, KSHS.

82. Ibid., May 16, 1856; Wells Letters I, 170; Whitehorn, "Historical Sketch"; Goodnow Diary, May 18, 1856; *New York Times*, May 26, 1856.

83. Wm. Goodnow to Harriet Goodnow, May 16, 1856, KSHS.

84. Alberta Prantle, "The Connecticut Kansas Colony: Letters of Charles B. Lines," *KHQ* (Spring 1956).

85. Wells Letters I, 170.

86. Ibid.; Miner, *Kansas*, 64.

87. Reynolds, *John Brown*, 157.

88. Ibid., 159.

89. James Humphrey letter, *Manhattan Nationalist*, March 1, 1878; Whitehorn, "Historical Sketch."

90. Reynolds, *John Brown*, 171–173.

91. Ibid., 185–187.

92. Ibid., 175; Goodnow Diary, June 15, 1856.

93. Wells Letters I, 169–171.

94. Ibid.

95. Miner, *Kansas*, 64.

96. Reynolds, *John Brown*, 192–193.

97. Ibid., 197–198.

98. Wells Letters I, 177.

99. Allen, "From Mass. to Kansas," 29.

100. "Diary of Julia Lovejoy," 18.

101. Reynolds, *John Brown*, 198.

102. Miner, *Kansas*, 57.

103. Reynolds, *John Brown,* 200.

104. Ibid., 204; Wells Letters II, 283; Wm. Goodnow to Harriet Goodnow, September 21, 1856, October 19, 1856, KSHS.

105. Goodnow Diary, November 21, 1856.

106. *Dred Scott v. Sandford,* 60 U.S. 393, 15 L.Ed. 691 (1856).

CHAPTER 7. THE WEARYING WORK OF FRONTIER LIFE

1. *Lawrence Herald of Freedom,* January 10, 1857.

2. *East Greenwich Weekly Pendulum,* August 25, 1855.

3. Wells Letters I, 172; see also Whitehorn, "Historical Sketch"; Wm. Goodnow to Harriet Goodnow, July 6, 1856, KSHS.

4. Eli Thayer, *A History of the Kansas Crusade: Its Friends and Its Foes* (New York: Harper & Bros., 1889), 31.

5. *Lawrence Herald of Freedom,* June 23, 1855.

6. W. Hoon letter, *Daily Cincinnati Gazette,* July 27, 1855.

7. *East Greenwich Weekly Pendulum,* August 25, 1855.

8. Samuel Houston letter, *Manhattan Mercury,* March 18, 1911.

9. A. F. Grow Reminiscences, *Manhattan Nationalist,* April 22, 1887; Federal Writers' Project, *The WPA Guide to 1930s Kansas* (Lawrence: University Press of Kansas, 1984), 65–66.

10. Wm. Goodnow to Harriet Goodnow, June 10, 1855, KSHS; *East Greenwich Weekly Pendulum,* August 25, 1855; Lovejoy Letters from Kanzas, 42; see also Sara Robinson, *Kansas: Its Interior and Exterior Life* (Boston: Crosby, Nichols & Co., 1856), 84.

11. Edward Everett Hale, *Kanzas and Nebraska: The History, Geographical and Physical Characteristics, and Political Position of Those Territories* (Boston: Philips, Sampson & Co., 1854), 255; Lovejoy Letters from Kanzas, 42; Wells Letters III, 391.

12. RCHS, *Log Cabin Days* (Manhattan, KS: RCHS, 1929), 53–54; David Fairchild, *The World Was My Garden: Travels of a Plant Explorer* (New York: Charles Scribner's Sons, 1939), 9; Wells Letters I, 155; Wells Letters II, 312; Wells Letters III, 403; Chestina Allen, "Journey from Mass. to Kansas," Pottawatomie County History Collection, KSHS, 38; Goodnow Diary, October 14, 1861.

13. Lovejoy Letters from Kanzas, 40.

14. Ibid., 41; see also Goodnow notes, "Kansas As It Is," KSHS.

15. Isaac Goodnow to Ellen Goodnow, April 8, 1855, KSHS; cf. Wells Letters I, 148.

16. Reminiscences of Mrs. George Lee, KSHS.

17. "Diary of Julia Lovejoy," 14; see also Thomas Schlereth, *Victorian America: Transformations in Everyday Life, 1876–1915* (New York: HarperPerennial, 1991), 99.

18. Lovejoy Letters from Kanzas, 41.

19. Ibid.

20. *New York Daily Times,* June 27, 1855.

21. Wells Letters I, 155.

22. W. Hoon letter, *Daily Cincinnati Gazette,* July 27, 1855.

23. Lovejoy Letters from Kanzas, 42.

24. Wells Letters I, 155.

25. RCHS, *Log Cabin Days,* 29.

26. Reminiscences of Mrs. George Lee, KSHS.

27. Francis A. Abbott, "Some Reminiscences on Early Days in Deep Creek," *Transactions of the KSHS* 12 (1912): 395.

28. *Manhattan Express,* May 5, 1860.

29. Lovejoy Letters from Kanzas, 44.

30. Whitehorn, "Historical Sketch"; Allen, "From Mass. to Kansas," 19.

31. Wells Letters I, 155–156.

32. Amos Powers, "Old Settlers Stories," Riley County Clippings, vol. 2, KSHS, 44.

33. Allen, "From Mass. to Kansas," 32; Goodnow Diary, March 5, 1856; Abbott, "Some Reminiscences on Early Days in Deep Creek," 395; see also W. Hoon letter, *Daily Cincinnati Gazette,* July 27, 1855.

34. Robinson, *Kansas,* 179.

35. Reminiscences of Mrs. George Lee, KSHS; RCHS, *Log Cabin Days,* 71.

36. Wm. Goodnow to Harriet Goodnow, July 1, 1855, KSHS.

37. Ellen Goodnow to T. Webb, July 10, 1855, KSHS; Ellen Goodnow to Harriet Goodnow, July 21, 1855, KSHS.

38. Ellen Goodnow to Isaac Goodnow, March 24, 1855, KSHS; see also Ellen Goodnow to Isaac Goodnow, April 4, 1855, KSHS.

39. Isaac Goodnow to Ellen Goodnow, April 8, 1855, KSHS; Isaac Goodnow to Ellen Goodnow, April 21, 1855, KSHS; see also Goodnow Diary, April 5, 1855.

40. Ellen Goodnow to Harriet Goodnow, July 21, 1855, KSHS.

41. Notes of Ellen (Denison) Goodnow, RCHM; Isaac Goodnow to Ellen Goodnow, April 8, 1855, KSHS.

42. Ellen Goodnow to Harriet Goodnow, July 21, 1855, KSHS.

43. Isaac Goodnow to mother, December 27, 1863, KSHS.

44. *Lawrence Kansas Free State,* August 13, 1855; George Martin, "Territorial and Military Combine at Fort Riley," *Transactions of the KSHS* 7 (1902): 365; Goodnow Diary, August 4, 1855; Wells Letters I, 157.

45. Goodnow Diary, August 3, 1855; Allen, "From Mass. to Kansas," 20.

46. Wells Letters I, 154.

47. Powers, "Old Settlers Stories," 46.

48. George E. Omer, "An Army Hospital: From Dragoons to Rough Riders — Fort Riley, 1853–1903," *KHQ* (Winter 1957): 341; William McKale and William D. Young, *Fort Riley: Citadel of the Frontier West* (Topeka: KSHS, 2000), 19; Martin, "Military Combine at Fort Riley," 365.

49. Omer, "An Army Hospital," 341.

50. Wells Letters I, 158.

51. John Pipher Recollections, *Lawrence Western Home Journal,* April 25, 1878; Isaac Goodnow to Wm. Goodnow, October 10, 1855, KSHS; Goodnow Diary, October 26, 1855.

52. Isaac Goodnow to Wm. Goodnow, October 10, 1855, KSHS; see also A. F. Grow Reminiscences, *Manhattan Nationalist,* April 1, 1887.

53. Goodnow Diary, January 29, 1857.

54. *Lawrence Herald of Freedom,* December 6, 1856.

55. Ellen Goodnow to Harriet Goodnow, July 21, 1855, KSHS. Ellen Goodnow was much more positive writing for potential newspaper publication that same month: "We are sure judging from what has been done in three months that we shall not be far behind our Eastern friends in improvements, in a short time, and then if we secure Freedom for the territory, what we came expressly for, we shall have a treble reward." Ellen Goodnow to T. Webb, July 10, 1855, KSHS.

56. MTA Records, June 29, August 21, 1855.

57. Abbott, "Some Reminiscences on Early Days in Deep Creek," 393.

58. Manhattan's temperature swings a wide arc: the record high in the town is 116 degrees Fahrenheit, while the record low is –32 degrees. See also *New York Times,* April 7, 1872.

59. Powers, "Old Settlers Stories," 42; Isaac Goodnow to Wm. Goodnow, October 10, 1855, KSHS; Goodnow Diary, October 23, 1855; *Lawrence Kansas Free State,* October 29, 1855.

60. Isaac Goodnow to Wm. Goodnow, April 9, 1855, KSHS; cf. Goodnow Diary, May 26, 1855.

61. MTA Records, October 9, 1855; Isaac Goodnow to Wm. Goodnow, October 10, 1855, KSHS.

62. Goodnow Diary, November 9, 1855; Samuel A. Johnson, "The Emigrant Aid Company in Kansas," *KHQ* (November 1932): 434; Isaac Goodnow to Wm. Goodnow, October 10, 1855, KSHS; *Lawrence Herald of Freedom,* March 15, 1856.

63. Goodnow Diary, October 19, 1855.

64. Isaac Goodnow, "Personal Reminiscences and Kansas Emigration, 1855," *Transactions of the KSHS* 4 (1888): 251.

65. Donald Parrish, *This Land Is Our Land: The Public Domain in the Vicinity of Riley County and Manhattan, Kansas* (Manhattan, KS: RCHS, 2003), 42; MTA Records, November 10, 1855; Minute Books of Early Manhattan City Council Meetings, RCHM (hereafter cited as City Council Minute Books), May 11, 1865: "At the Eastern terminus of Osage Street."

66. Samuel A. Johnson, *The Battle Cry of Freedom: The New England Emigrant Aid Company in the Kansas Crusade* (Westport, CT: Greenwood Press, 1977), 123.

67. Ibid., 122.

68. Wells Letters I, 172; "Manhattan Twenty Years Ago," Marlatt Papers, KSU.

69. Wells Letters I, 159; see also Allen, "From Mass. to Kansas," 15.

70. "Manhattan Twenty Years Ago," Marlatt Papers, KSU.

71. Powers, "Old Settlers Stories," 40.

72. Wells Letters II, 290.

73. Reminiscences of Mrs. George Lee, KSHS.

74. Powers, "Old Settlers Stories," 40.

75. William H. Mackey, "Looking Backwards," *Transactions of the KSHS* 10 (1908): 643.

76. "Letters of Julia Louisa Lovejoy, 1856–1864: 1," *KHQ* (May 1947): 127.

77. Goodnow Diary, December 25, 1855.

78. Goodnow Diary, January 26, 1856; see also *Lawrence Herald of Freedom*, March 15, 1856; Abbott, "Some Reminiscences on Early Days in Deep Creek," 393.

79. Goodnow Diary, January 26, 1856.

80. Goodnow, "Reminiscences," 251.

81. RCHS, *Log Cabin Days,* 50; Goodnow Diary, November 29, 1856.

82. Goodnow, "Reminiscences," 250.

CHAPTER 8. 1856: WAITING OUT THE VIOLENCE

1. Charles Bebee letter, *Lawrence Herald of Freedom*, March 15, 1856.

2. Ibid.; Wells Letters I, 159.

3. MTA Records, January 1, 1856; Isaac Goodnow notes, "Kansas As It Is," KSHS; Donald Parrish, *This Land Is Our Land: The Public Domain in the Vicinity of Riley County and Manhattan, Kansas* (Manhattan, KS: RCHS, 2003), 43; Samuel A. Johnson, *The Battle Cry of Freedom: The New England Emigrant Aid Company in the Kansas Crusade* (Westport, CT: Greenwood Press, 1977), 170.

4. George Willard to *Boston Journal*, January 7, 1855, quoted in Louise Barry, "The Emigrant Aid Company Parties of 1854," *KHQ* (May 1943): 148. For lower estimates of Juniata's population, see *Parkville (MO) Industrial Luminary*, November 28, 1854; and Wells Letters I, 159.

5. Parrish, *This Land,* 21; John Pipher Recollections, *Lawrence Western Home Journal*, April 25, 1878.

6. Chestina Allen, "Journey from Mass. to Kansas," Pottawatomie County History Collection, KSHS, 24; Goodnow Diary, February 26, 1856; Whitehorn, "Historical Sketch."

7. Goodnow Diary, February 27, 1856.

8. Allen, "From Mass. to Kansas," 24.

9. Wm. Goodnow to Harriet Goodnow, May 16, 1856, KSHS; MTA Records, April 20, 1856; Amos Powers, "Old Settlers Stories," Riley County Clippings, vol. 2, KSHS, 43; A. F. Grow Reminiscences, *Manhattan Nationalist*, April 1, 1887; see also *Lawrence Herald of Freedom*, April 5, 1856.

10. Powers, "Old Settlers Stories," 43.

11. Ibid.; *Lawrence Herald of Freedom*, March 15, 1856.

12. MTA Records, April 20, 1856; *Junction Sentinel*, May 14, 1859.

13. RCHS, *Log Cabin Days* (Manhattan, KS: RCHS, 1929), 61.

14. MTA Records, April 20, 1856.

15. *Lawrence Herald of Freedom*, January 3, 1857.

16. Wm. Goodnow to Harriet Goodnow, May 25, 1856, KSHS; see also Wm. Goodnow to Harriet Goodnow, June 15, 1856, KSHS; John Gihon, *Geary and Kansas* (Philadelphia: J.H.C. Whiting, 1857), 203.

17. "Reminiscences: Recollections of Ten Years on the Frontier," Marlatt Papers, KSU.

18. Winifred N. Slagg, *Riley County — Kansas* (Brooklyn: Theo Gaus' Sons, 1968), 75; Parrish, *This Land,* 170; Lovejoy Letters from Kanzas, 41.

19. In 1908 the streets were renamed so that all blocks and numbers progressed more rationally. At that time, the first street by the river, Wyandotte Avenue, essentially became "First Street" for purposes of addresses (although keeping its name), while the second street from the river was changed from First Street to Second Street, and all other numbered blocks followed that pattern. To avoid confusion, I have attempted to convert all addresses in this book from the pre-1908 era to a modern description.

20. MTA Records, May 31, 1856.

21. Daniel Walker Howe, *What Hath God Wrought: The Transformation of America, 1815–1848* (New York: Oxford University Press, 2007), 295–296, 541, 727: Preplanned utopian communities.

22. A. J. Mead, "Reminiscences of Kansas," *Transactions of the KSHS* 7 (1902): 470.

23. *Portrait and Biographical Album of Washington, Clay and Riley Counties, Kansas* (Chicago: Chapman Bros., 1890), 550; Wm. Goodnow to Harriet Goodnow, February 10, 1856, KSHS; Wm. Goodnow to Harriet Goodnow, April 27, 1856, KSHS; *Historical Plat Book of Riley County, Kansas* (Chicago: Bird & Mickle Map Co., 1881), 24.

24. Wm. Goodnow to Harriet Goodnow, April 27, 1856, KSHS; Lowell Jack, *A History of Manhattan, Kansas — Riley County and Ft. Riley* (Manhattan, KS: Hawley Printing, 2003), 22; *Portrait and Biographical Album,* 549–550; A. F. Grow Reminiscences, *Manhattan Nationalist,* April 22, 1887.

25. A. F. Grow Reminiscences, *Manhattan Nationalist,* April 8, 1887; Elaine Olney and Mary Roberts, eds., *Pioneers of the Bluestem Prairie* (Manhattan, KS: Riley County Genealogical Society, 1976), 430; Pipher obituary, *Manhattan Nationalist,* June 15, 1900.

26. "Manhattan Twenty Years Ago," Marlatt Papers, KSU; Whitehorn, "Historical Sketch"; Goodnow Diary, April 28, 1856.

27. David Reynolds, *John Brown, Abolitionist: The Man Who Killed Slavery, Sparked the Civil War, and Seeded Civil Rights* (New York: Alfred A. Knopf, 2005), 190.

28. Wm. Goodnow to Harriet Goodnow, May 25, 1856, KSHS.

29. Manhattan Relief Committee to Thadeus Hyatt, January 1, 1857, Hyatt Collection, KSHS.

30. J. H. Pillsbury to Hobart Pillsbury, January 8, 1857, KU.

31. Letter of J. M. Kimball, April 27, 1856, quoted in *Manhattan Daily Mercury,* April 20, 1914.

32. The house is now known as the Washington Marlatt House. Wells Letters I, 168; Patricia O'Brien, *The Architects and Buildings of Manhattan, Kansas* (Manhattan, KS: RCHS, 2008), 120. Charles Lovejoy reportedly started building a limestone house one year earlier, but there is no indication it was completed (Lovejoy Letters from Kanzas, 38).

33. Wells Letters I, 166.

34. Isaac Goodnow to John Wood, May 11, 1857, KSHS; see also Wells Letters I, 172.

35. Wm. Goodnow to Harriet Goodnow, May 11, 1856, KSHS.

36. Allen, "From Mass. to Kansas," 26; RCHS, *Log Cabin Days,* 60; "Riley County Kansas: 'The Blue Ribbon County,'" supplement to *Manhattan Nationalist,* June 16, 1881, 52.

37. "Blue Ribbon County," 53–54; *Manhattan Independent,* November 22, 1864; A. F. Grow Reminiscences, *Manhattan Nationalist,* April 8, 1887; RCHS, *Log Cabin Days,* 60.

38. *Manhattan Independent,* December 29, 1866; *Manhattan Standard,* February 20, 1869.

39. Allen, "From Mass. to Kansas," 27.

40. W. Marlatt to Isaac Goodnow, June 18, 1860, KSU.

41. Ibid., June 14, 1859; September 29, 1859; October 3, 1860.

42. Wm. Goodnow to Harriet Goodnow, May 4, 1856, KSHS.

43. Ibid., May 25, 1856.

44. Goodnow Diary, May 31, 1856; see also Goodnow Diary, April 18, 1856.

45. Wells Letters II, 286; see also Wells Letters III, 405.

46. Francis A. Abbott, "Some Reminiscences on Early Days in Deep Creek," *Transactions of the KSHS* 12 (1912): 394; see also Federal Writers' Project, *The WPA Guide to 1930s Kansas* (Lawrence: University Press of Kansas, 1984), 65; Wells Letters II, 308.

47. Wells Letters III, 392.

48. Ellen Goodnow to T. H. Webb, July 10, 1855, KSHS; Wells Letters II, 317; Goodnow Diary, November 20, 1855; December 22, 1856; January 9, 1857; Allen, "From Mass. to Kansas," 32.

49. Howe, *What Hath God Wrought,* 567.

50. "Diary of Julia Lovejoy," 17; Wm. Goodnow to Harriet Goodnow, July 6, 1856, KSHS; Goodnow Diary, July 2, 1856.

51. "Diary of Julia Lovejoy," 16–17.

52. Goodnow Diary, August 21, 1856.

53. RCHS, *Log Cabin Days,* 61; see also "Diary of Julia Lovejoy," 17–18.

54. Wm. Goodnow to Harriet Goodnow, May 25, 1856, KSHS.

55. Ibid., May 16, 1856.

56. Ibid., May 25, 1856.

57. *Cincinnati Daily Gazette,* June 21, 1856.

58. Gihon, *Geary and Kansas,* 203; see also Wm. Goodnow to Harriet Goodnow, July 20, 1856, KSHS.

59. Wells Letters II, 282.

60. Parrish, *This Land,* 49–51; MTA Records, November 15, 1856; November 25, 1856.

61. Parrish, *This Land,* 48.

62. MTA Records, November 10, 1855.

63. Parrish, *This Land,* 48; see also *Lawrence Herald of Freedom,* January 3, 1857. The Manhattan Town Association compensated citizens who had previously started down the road to claiming individual plots. Wm. Goodnow to Harriet Goodnow, November 23, 1856, KSHS; Goodnow Diary, December 23, 1856.

64. Gihon, *Geary and Kansas,* 202; see also Goodnow Diary, November 2, 1856.

65. Gihon, *Geary and Kansas,* 202.

66. *Lawrence Herald of Freedom,* January 10, 1857; Wm. Goodnow to Harriet Goodnow, November 16, 1856, KSHS: "Gov. Geary made us a visit here & gave a publick talk — the people liked him very well."

67. Gihon, *Geary and Kansas,* 203.

68. Wells Letters II, 282.

CHAPTER 9. 1857: A TOWN BUILT FROM STONE

1. Goodnow Diary, December 13, 21, 1856; *Lawrence Herald of Freedom,* January 3, 1857; Wells Letters II, 295.

2. Isaac Goodnow to John Wood, May 11, 1857, KSHS.

3. Wells Letters II, 297.

4. Ellen Goodnow to Isaac Goodnow, [1857], KSHS.

5. A. J. Mead, "Reminiscences of Kansas," *Transactions of the KSHS* 7 (1902): 470.

6. Ellen Goodnow to Isaac Goodnow, [1857], KSHS.

7. Mead, "Reminiscences of Kansas," 470.

8. MTA Records, April 23, 1857; J. Denison to Isaac Goodnow, May 6, 1857, KSHS; Samuel A. Johnson, *The Battle Cry of Freedom: The New England Emigrant Aid Company in the Kansas Crusade* (Westport, CT: Greenwood Press, 1977), 248–249.

9. A. F. Grow Reminiscences, *Manhattan Nationalist,* May 6, 1887; MTA Records, January 2, 1860; Johnson, *Battle Cry of Freedom,* 248–249.

10. A. F. Grow Reminiscences, *Manhattan Nationalist,* April 22, 1887.

11. Ibid.; Ellen Goodnow Diary, May 17, 1857, Goodnow Collection, KSHS.

12. Ellen Goodnow Diary, May 17, 1857, Goodnow Collection, KSHS.

13. Ibid., March 28, 1857.

14. Ellen Goodnow to Isaac Goodnow, [1857], KSHS; Ellen Goodnow Diary, July 19, 1857, Goodnow Collection, KSHS.

15. Wells Letters II, 306.

16. *Plat Book of Riley County,* 23, 25; George Martin, "Territorial and Military Combine at Fort Riley," *Transactions of the KSHS* 7 (1902): 382; *Manhattan Independent,* March 2, 1867; *Kansas Kin,* May 1989; A. F. Grow Reminiscences, *Manhattan Nationalist,* April 1, 1887.

17. Elizabeth Shor, *Fossils and Flies: The Life of a Compleat Scientist Samuel Wendell Williston* (Norman: University of Oklahoma Press, 1971), 10–11.

18. Etcheson, "Labouring for the Freedom of This Territory," 69; Wells Letters III, 400.

19. Robert Richmond, "A Free-Stater's 'Letters to the Editor': Samuel N. Wood's Letters to Eastern Newspapers, 1854," *KHQ* (Summer 1957): 185.

20. Ellen Goodnow to Isaac Goodnow, [1857], KSHS; see also Sara Robinson, *Kansas: Its Interior and Exterior Life* (Boston: Crosby, Nichols & Co., 1856), 178–179.

21. Wells Letters II, 311.

22. John Winter Robinson to Hiram Hill, August 17, 1857, KSHS; *Big Blue Union,* August 8, 1863, quoted in "Bypaths of Kansas History," *KHQ* (August 1939): 315.

23. A. F. Grow Reminiscences, *Manhattan Nationalist,* March 25, 1887.

24. *Plat Book of Riley County,* 24; Elaine Olney and Mary Roberts, eds., *Pioneers of the Bluestem Prairie* (Manhattan, KS: Riley County Genealogical Society, 1976), 291; Patricia O'Brien, *The Architects and Buildings of Manhattan, Kansas* (Manhattan, KS: RCHS, 2008), vii.

25. O'Brien, *The Architects and Buildings of Manhattan,* vii.

26. Albert Deane Richardson, *Beyond the Mississippi: From the Great River to the Great Ocean* (Hartford, CT: American Publishing Co., 1869), 554; see also John Winter Robinson to Hiram Hill, August 17, 1857, KSHS; Isaac Goodnow to Ellen Goodnow, March 25, 1855, KSHS.

27. Carolyn Jones, *The First One Hundred Years: A History of the City of Manhattan, Kansas 1855–1955* (Manhattan, KS: privately printed, 1955), 43; *Columbian History of Education in Kansas* (Topeka: Hamilton Printing Co., 1893), 190.

28. A. F. Grow Reminiscences, *Manhattan Nationalist,* April 1, 1887; *Manhattan Express,* December 24, 1859; Whitehorn, "Historical Sketch."

29. City Council Minute Books, February 23, 1861; October 4, 1862.

30. *Manhattan High School Monitor,* November 1873; Jones, *First One Hundred Years,* 43.

31. Thomas Schlereth, *Victorian America: Transformations in Everyday Life, 1876–1915* (New York: HarperPerennial, 1991), 244–253.

32. Wells Letters II, 303; Goodnow Diary, March 30, 1857; *Columbian History of Education in Kansas,* 190; Amanda Arnold interview, *Topeka Daily Capital,* November 18, 1923; Shor, *Fossils and Flies,* 12.

33. Amanda Arnold interview, *Topeka Daily Capital,* November 18, 1923; *Columbian History of Education in Kansas,* 190; *Manhattan Mercury,* March 6, 2005.

34. Wells Letters II, 307.

35. *Manhattan Kansas Express,* May 21, 1859; *Manhattan High School Monitor,* November, December 1873.

36. Edward B. Smythe to Hiram Hill, August 31, 1857, KSHS; see also John Winter Robinson to Hiram Hill, August 17, 1857, KSHS.

37. *Manhattan High School Monitor,* November 1873; Shor, *Fossils and Flies,* 12–13.

38. Whitehorn, "Historical Sketch"; Leonard Pillsbury, "My Experiences As a Schoolmaster," Pillsbury Family Papers, KU; Shor, *Fossils and Flies,* 13.

39. Wells Letters II, 314; Goodnow Diary, November 26, 1857; City Council Minute Books, June 23, 1859; November 22, 1862; *Manhattan High School Monitor,* December 1873; A. F. Grow Reminiscences, *Manhattan Nationalist,* April 1, 1887.

40. James Humphrey, "The Country West of Topeka Prior to 1865," *Transactions of the KSHS* 4 (1888): 294.

41. Shor, *Fossils and Flies,* 12.

42. Ibid.; Daniel Walker Howe, *What Hath God Wrought: The Transformation of America, 1815–1848* (New York: Oxford University Press, 2007), 449–455.

43. James Shortridge, *Cities on the Plains: The Evolution of Urban Kansas* (Lawrence: University Press of Kansas, 2004), 216–217; see also Humphrey, "West of Topeka," 292: "While its material progress was carefully attended to and watched with solicitude and interest, it early became the scene of much mental activity."

44. Donald Parrish, *This Land Is Our Land: The Public Domain in the Vicinity of Riley County and Manhattan, Kansas* (Manhattan, KS: RCHS, 2003), 57–58; MTA Records, January 2, 1860; City Council Minute Books, May 30, 1857.

45. City Council Minute Books, June 27, 1857.

46. Whitehorn, "Historical Sketch."

47. *Leavenworth Daily Times,* July 29, 1863.

48. Parrish, *This Land,* 68–69.

49. Simeon Fox to Anne Young, December 1, 1929, RCHM.

50. James Humphrey letter, *Manhattan Nationalist,* March 1, 1878.

51. Goodnow Diary, December 11, 1856.

52. John Winter Robinson to Hiram Hill, August 17, 1857, KSHS; Parrish, *This Land,* 57; *Topeka Kansas Tribune,* July 11, 1857; A. F. Grow Reminiscences, *Manhattan Nationalist,* March 25, 1887.

53. John Winter Robinson to Hiram Hill, August 17, 1857, KSHS; Wells Letters II, 307; J. Denison to Isaac Goodnow, May 6, 1857, KSHS; cf. *Leavenworth Daily Times,* July 19, 1863.

54. L. H. Pillsbury to Lavina Pillsbury, September 13, 1857, KU; Ellen Goodnow Diary, June 1, 1857, Goodnow Collection, KSHS.

55. *New York Daily Times,* August 21, 1857.

56. John Winter Robinson to Hiram Hill, August 17, 1857, KSHS.

57. *Lawrence Herald of Freedom,* September 26, 1857.

58. A. F. Grow Reminiscences, *Manhattan Nationalist,* April 15, 1887.

59. Wells Letters II, 315.

60. Ibid., 314.

61. *Lawrence Herald of Freedom,* September 26, 1857.

62. Jones, *First One Hundred Years,* 43.

63. Whitehorn, "Historical Sketch"; William Cutler and Alfred Theodore Andreas, *History of the State of Kansas* (Chicago: Western Historical Co., 1883), 1305.

64. Craig Miner, *Kansas: The History of the Sunflower State, 1854–2000* (Lawrence: University Press of Kansas, 2002), 72; Wells Letters II, 315.

65. Ibid.

66. Miner, *Kansas,* 72.

67. *Plat Book of Riley County,* 17.

68. *Manhattan Independent,* December 8, 1866; February 23, 1867; Whitehorn, "Historical Sketch."

69. Goodnow Diary, November 18, 1857.

70. Ibid., November 19, 1857.

71. City Council Minute Books, October 31, 1857.

72. Humphrey, "West of Topeka," 294; Statement of Dr. Daniel L. Chandler, quoted in Henry Shindler, "The First Capital of Kansas," *Transactions of the KSHS* 12 (1912): 336n7.

73. Cutler, *History of Kansas,* 1304; John Pipher interview, *Manhattan Republic,* February 19, 1897.

74. Cutler, *History of Kansas,* 1304.

75. John Pipher interview, *Manhattan Republic,* February 19, 1897; "Statement of Theodore Weichselbaum," *Transactions of the KSHS* 11 (1910): 562n1; *Plat Book of Riley County,* 17.

76. Cutler, *History of Kansas,* 1304.

77. Ibid.; Goodnow Diary, December 14, 1857; see also City Council Minute Books, January 29, 1859 *(Manhattan City v. Ogden Town Company).*

78. Cutler, *History of Kansas,* 1304.

79. "Statement of Theodore Weichselbaum," *Transactions of the KSHS* 11 (1910): 562n1.

80. RCHS, *Log Cabin Days* (Manhattan, KS: RCHS, 1929), 55; Whitehorn, "Historical Sketch."

81. RCHS, *Log Cabin Days,* 44, 50.

82. Wells Letters III, 407.

83. Ibid.

84. RCHS, *Log Cabin Days,* 50.

85. Ibid., 44.

86. Ibid., 50.

87. George Willard to *Boston Journal,* January 7, 1855, quoted in Louise Barry, "The Emigrant Aid Company Parties of 1854," *KHQ* (May 1943): 148.

88. William McKale and William D. Young, *Fort Riley: Citadel of the Frontier West* (Topeka: KSHS, 2000), 35.

89. Shor, *Fossils and Flies,* 17.

90. Amos Powers, "Old Settlers Stories," Riley County Clippings, vol. 2, KSHS, 45.

91. RCHS, *Log Cabin Days,* 64; Goodnow Diary, May 10, 1856; November 8, 1858; see also Powers, "Old Settlers Stories," 45.

92. Ibid.; see also RCHS, *Log Cabin Days,* 50.

93. Shor, *Fossils and Flies,* 11–12; see also Powers, "Old Settlers Stories," 45.

94. Chestina Allen, "Journey from Mass. to Kansas," Pottawatomie County History Collection, KSHS, 37–38; Jones, *First One Hundred Years,* 22

95. Ellen Goodnow to T. H Webb, July 10, 1855, KSHS; see also Ellen Goodnow to Harriet Goodnow, July 21, 1855, KSHS: "they are perfectly civil if treated civilly."

96. Jones, *First One Hundred Years,* 22.

97. Ibid.

98. Ibid.

99. *New York Daily Times,* August 21, 1857.

100. Ibid.

101. Jones, *First One Hundred Years,* 22.

102. David Reynolds, *John Brown, Abolitionist: The Man Who Killed Slavery, Sparked the Civil War, and Seeded Civil Rights* (New York: Alfred A. Knopf, 2005), 168.

103. Lowell Jack, *A History of Manhattan, Kansas—Riley County and Ft. Riley* (Manhattan, KS: Hawley Printing, 2003), 40–41.

104. Powers, "Old Settlers Stories," 47. Powers calls the man Jim Fisher, but other sources agree his name was Bishop, and a James Bishop is listed on the 1855 census for the area.

105. Ibid.; RCHS, *Log Cabin Days,* 86; Goodnow Diary, September 3, 1855.

106. Miner, *Kansas,* 95.

107. Benjamin Dixon, "Furthering Their Own Demise: How Kansa Indian Death Customs Accelerated Their Depopulation," *Ethnohistory* (Summer 2007), 473–476, 496.

108. *Manhattan Express,* October 29, 1859; see also George Morehouse, "History of the Kansa or Kaw Indians" *Transactions of the KSHS* 10 (1908): 357.

CHAPTER 10. 1858: "WE DO NOT DESPAIR OF A FREE STATE YET"

1. Goodnow Diary, January 4, 1858.

2. Craig Miner, *Kansas: The History of the Sunflower State, 1854–2000* (Lawrence: University Press of Kansas, 2002), 73.

3. Goodnow Diary, April 15, 1858.

4. Wells Letters III, 384.

5. Goodnow Diary, April 2, February 27, 1858; Miner, *Kansas,* 73.

6. Daniel Walker Howe, *What Hath God Wrought: The Transformation of America, 1815–1848* (New York: Oxford University Press, 2007), 648–651, 839, 848.

7. Goodnow Diary, April 2, 1858.

8. "Address of the Constitutional Convention to American Public," April 1858, Goodnow Collection, KSHS.

9. Wells Letters III, 391.

10. W. Marlatt to Isaac Goodnow, June 14, 1859, KSU.

11. *Kansas Constitutional Convention: A Reprint of the Proceedings and Debates of the Convention Which Framed the Constitution of Kansas at Wyandotte in July, 1859* (Topeka: Kansas State Printing Plant, 1920), 73, 232–233, 257–258; see also Calvin W. Gower, "Kansas Territory and Its Boundary Question: 'Big Kansas' or 'Little Kansas,'" *KHQ* (Spring 1967): 1–12. The irascible Houston was the only Free-State delegate to insist on keeping the Rocky Mountains in Kansas, and the other delegates "ridiculed" him for this. *Manhattan Kansas Express,* September 3, 1859.

12. Miner, *Kansas,* 77.

13. Isaac Goodnow Notes from 1858, KSHS.

14. David Reynolds, *John Brown, Abolitionist: The Man Who Killed Slavery, Sparked the Civil War, and Seeded Civil Rights* (New York: Alfred A. Knopf, 2005), 269.

15. Ibid., 276; see also Miner, *Kansas,* 73–75; Wm. Goodnow to *Oxford Democrat,* July 24, 1858, KSHS.

16. *Manhattan Nationalist,* January 25, 1884: "He arrived quietly, departed silently, and very few knew of his presence. Those who were told he was here were cautioned to keep the fact secret."

17. Wells Letters III, 384.

18. Lovejoy Letters III, 379.

19. Ibid.

20. Wells Letters III, 393.

21. Wells Letters II, 307; Goodnow Diary, June 6, 1858.

22. Liebler, *Hartford,* 18.

23. Wells Letters III, 391.

24. *Manhattan Nationalist,* January 21, 1876.

25. Wells Letters III, 401; *Manhattan Kansas Express,* July 27, 1859; W. Marlatt to Isaac Goodnow, June 14, 1859, KSU.

26. Wells Letters II, 299–300.

27. Wells Letters III, 394; see also Chestina Allen, "Journey from Mass. to Kansas," Pottawatomie County History Collection, KSHS, 33.

28. Miner, *Kansas,* 73; Donald Parrish, *This Land Is Our Land: The Public Domain in the Vicinity of Riley County and Manhattan, Kansas* (Manhattan, KS: RCHS, 2003), 103; Isaac Goodnow to E. E. Hale, February 10, 1859, KSHS.

29. Isaac Goodnow to E. E. Hale, February 10, 1859, KSHS.

30. Goodnow Diary, February 8, 14, 1857.

31. Goodnow Diary, April 17, 1857; Wells Letters II, 303; "Kansas Reminiscences: Bluemont Central College," Marlatt Papers, KSU; J. T. Willard, "Bluemont Central College," *KHQ* (May 1945): 326–327; Parrish, *This Land,* 99–100.

32. *Private Laws of the Territory of Kansas, Passed at the Fourth Session of the Legislative Assembly* (Lecompton, KS: S. W. Driggs & Co, 1858), 75–76.

33. Thomas Webb to Isaac Goodnow, July 21, 1858, KSHS.

34. Allen, "From Mass. to Kansas," 30.

35. Ibid., 39.

36. Amos Powers, "Old Settlers Stories," Riley County Clippings, vol. 2, KSHS, 42.

37. J. Denison to Isaac Goodnow, May 6, 1857, KSHS; Ellen Goodnow Diary, April 21, 1857, Goodnow Collection, KSHS.

38. Goodnow Diary, December 22, 1857; January 13, 1858.

39. Ibid., August 20, 1858.

40. Ellen Goodnow Diary, May 16, 1857, Goodnow Collection, KSHS.

41. Ibid., June 3, 1857.

42. Goodnow Diary, May 7, July 6, 1855.

43. Alberta Prantle, "The Connecticut Kansas Colony: Letters of Charles B. Lines," *KHQ* (Spring 1956).

44. *Manhattan Independent,* August 17, 1863.

45. Allen, "From Mass. to Kansas," 17.

46. Wells Letters II, 285.

47. Goodnow Diary, June 10, 1858; February 18, 1859.

48. Wells Letters III, 382.

49. RCHS, *Log Cabin Days* (Manhattan, KS: RCHS, 1929), 53; see also W. Hoon letter, *Daily Cincinnati Gazette,* July 27, 1855; Allen, "From Mass. to Kansas," 13.

50. Prantle, "Letters of Charles Lines."

51. RCHS, *Log Cabin Days,* 53.

52. Powers, "Old Settlers Stories," 44; A. F. Grow Reminiscences, *Manhattan Nationalist,* May 20, 1887.

53. Powers, "Old Settlers Stories," 46; A. F. Grow Reminiscences, *Manhattan Nationalist,* March 25, 1887.

54. RCHS, *Log Cabin Days,* 29; see also A. F. Grow Reminiscences, *Manhattan Nationalist,* May 27, 1887; Wm. Goodnow to Harriet Goodnow, June 15, 1856, KSHS; Ellen Goodnow Diary, May 16, 1857, Goodnow Collection, KSHS; May 26, 1857; Goodnow Diary, January 10, 1856.

55. "Manhattan Twenty Years Ago," Marlatt Papers, KSU.

56. Carolyn Jones, *The First One Hundred Years: A History of the City of Manhattan, Kansas 1855–1955* (Manhattan, KS: privately printed, 1955), 45; *Manhattan Express,* May 12, 1860; Mrs. Henry Strong letter, *Manhattan Nationalist,* July 7, 1876.

57. Howe, *What Hath God Wrought,* 641–643.

58. Goodnow Diary, August 1, 1857.

59. RCHS, *Log Cabin Days,* 85; see also W. Marlatt to Isaac Goodnow, June 14, 1859, KSU: "Don't forget to bring that girl out with you, as I'm very lonesome and can't get any one here."

60. Wells Letters II, 292; "Manhattan Twenty Years Ago," Marlatt Papers, KSU; *Manhattan Express,* December 24, 1859; see also Howe, *What Hath God Wrought,* 619–620.

61. "Manhattan Twenty Years Ago," Marlatt Papers, KSU; A. F. Grow Reminiscences, *Manhattan Nationalist,* March 25, 1887.

62. "Manhattan Twenty Years Ago," Marlatt Papers, KSU; A. F. Grow Reminiscences, *Manhattan Nationalist,* March 25, 1887.

63. Parrish, *This Land,* 40.

64. Joseph Collins, ed., *Natural Kansas* (Lawrence: University Press of Kansas, 1985), 76.

65. Wells Letters I, 155.

66. Ibid., 154; Allen, "From Mass. to Kansas," 18; Reminiscences of Mrs. George Lee, KSHS; W. Hoon letter, *Daily Cincinnati Gazette,* July 27, 1855.

67. Lovejoy Letters from Kanzas, 39.

68. Powers, "Old Settlers Stories," 47–48.

69. W. Marlatt to Isaac Goodnow, May 16, 1859, KSU; see also Chas. Blood to Isaac Goodnow, May 16, 1859, RCHM; A. F. Grow Reminiscences, *Manhattan Nationalist,* May 6, 1887.

70. Chas. Blood to Isaac Goodnow, May 16, 1859, RCHM; see also Henry Denison to Isaac Goodnow, June 26, 1859, RCHM.

71. Elizabeth Shor, *Fossils and Flies: The Life of a Compleat Scientist Samuel Wendell Williston* (Norman: University of Oklahoma Press, 1971), 15.

72. RCHS, *Log Cabin Days,* 87.

73. A. F. Grow Reminiscences, *Manhattan Nationalist,* May 13, 1887.

74. William Least Heat-Moon, *PrairyErth* (Boston: Houghton Mifflin Co., 1991), 40; see also Goodnow Diary, April 14, 1855; Wm. Goodnow to Harriet Goodnow, April 29, 1855, KSHS; Wm. Goodnow to Harriet Goodnow, April 27, 1856, KSHS; Ellen Goodnow to Isaac Goodnow, April 14, 1857, KSHS: Men working outside wore "goggles to keep the wind and dust from their eyes."

75. Prantle, "Letters of Charles Lines"; see also *Manhattan Standard,* September 4, 1869.

76. Powers, "Old Settlers Stories," 41.

77. *Lawrence Herald of Freedom,* April 12, 1856.

78. *New York Times Magazine,* November 20, 1949.

79. Ibid.

80. Wells Letters III, 412, 414; Miner, *Kansas,* 80; Shor, *Fossils and Flies,* 15.

81. Kenneth Davis, *River on the Rampage* (Garden City, NY: Doubleday & Co., 1953), 23.

82. Ibid., 24–25; Karl Detzer, "Manhattan Rises from the Mud," *Reader's Digest,* July 1953.

83. *Salem (MA) Register,* February 25, 1856, quoted in "Bypaths of Kansas History," *KHQ* (November 1938): 414.

84. U.S. Geological Survey, "Kansas: Earthquake History," http://earthquake.usgs.gov/earthquakes/states/kansas/history.php.

85. *Manhattan Independent,* March 27, 1867.

86. B. F. Mudge to John Parker, April 30, 1867, John Parker Collection, KU.

87. *Manhattan Nationalist,* January 11, 1906; *Manhattan Mercury,* January 10, 1906.

CHAPTER 11. 1859: "A FLOURISHING YANKEE SETTLEMENT"

1. John Gihon, *Geary and Kansas* (Philadelphia: J.H.C. Whiting, 1857), 203.

2. *Manhattan Kansas Express,* May 21, 1859; Wells Letters III, 416; A. Mead to John Halderman, March 14, 1859, KSHS.

3. *Manhattan Kansas Express,* May 21, 1859.

4. Elliot West, *The Contested Plains: Indians, Goldseekers and the Rush to Colorado* (Lawrence: University Press of Kansas, 1998), 120.

5. A. F. Grow Reminiscences, *Manhattan Nationalist,* April 1, 1887.

6. Wells Letters III, 395; see also Ellen Goodnow to Isaac Goodnow, May 29, 1859, KSHS; Goodnow Diary, April 10, 1859.

7. *Manhattan Kansas Express,* May 21, 1859.

8. Henry Denison to J. Denison, May 11, 1859, KSHS.

9. West, *Contested Plains,* xv, 145.

10. Ibid., 124; Lovejoy Letters III, 401; George A. Root and Russell K. Hickman, "Pike's Peak Express Companies," *KHQ* (November 1944): 211–213; cf. Wells Letters III, 398.

11. Ibid., 395; see also Goodnow Diary, April 15, 1859.

12. *Manhattan Kansas Express,* May 21, 1859; Carolyn Jones, *The First One Hundred Years: A History of the City of Manhattan, Kansas 1855–1955* (Manhattan, KS: privately printed, 1955). 67. The Kansas Stage Company also began running stages through Manhattan in 1859. Henry Tisdale, "Travel by Stage in the Early Days," *Transactions of the KSHS* 7 (1902): 460.

13. *New York Times,* August 22, 1866.

14. George Martin, "Territorial and Military Combine at Fort Riley," *Transactions of the KSHS* 7 (1902): 381.

15. City Council Minute Books, April 6, 1859. The prior year, in 1858, the *Minnie Bell* stopped in Manhattan at least three times. Wells Letters III, 391; Whitehorn, "Historical Sketch."

16. *Lawrence Republican,* May 16, 1859, quoted in "Bypaths of Kansas History," *KHQ* (August 1940): 315; see also Goodnow Diary, May 8, 1859; W. Marlatt to Isaac Goodnow, May 16, 1859, KSU; Martin, "Military Combine at Fort Riley," 380.

17. Wells Letters III, 392, 395.

18. A. Mead to John Halderman, March 14, 1859, KSHS.

19. Wells Letters III, 395.

20. *Manhattan Kansas Express,* May 21, 1859.

21. Ibid.; Albert Deane Richardson, *Beyond the Mississippi: From the Great River to the Great Ocean* (Hartford, CT: American Publishing Co., 1869), 161.

22. *Manhattan Express,* June 9, 1860.

23. *Junction Sentinel,* May 14, 1859.

24. Ibid.; Wells Letters III, 399; Henry Denison to J. Denison, May 11, 1859, KSHS; Chas. Blood to Isaac Goodnow, May 11, 1859, RCHM.

25. W. Marlatt to Isaac Goodnow, May 16, 1859, KSU.

26. Chas. Blood to Isaac Goodnow, May 11, 1859, RCHM. The college building would be visible from the town, but during that era of horse-and-wagon travel, the location was far enough away that it was called a suburb of Manhattan proper. *Leavenworth Daily Times,* July 29, 1863; Isaac Goodnow to E. E. Hale, February 10, 1859, KSHS.

27. Parrish, *This Land,* 101; *Hartford (CT) Daily Courant,* September 18, 1860; Goodnow Diary.

28. George S. Park to Isaac Goodnow, June 7, 1859, KSHS.

29. "Minutes of Meetings from 1857–1881," Marlatt Papers, KSU.

30. W. Marlatt to Isaac Goodnow, May 16, 1859, KSU.

31. Goodnow Diary, June 9, 1859; see also *Hartford (CT) Daily Courant,* September 18, 1860; W. Marlatt to Isaac Goodnow, September 14, 1859, KSU: "Do not trouble yourself particularly about the 'Endowment.' Colleges are not the growth of a *year,* but a *century.*"

32. Isaac Goodnow to E. E. Hale, February 10, 1859, KSHS.

33. Parrish, *This Land,* 102; "Minutes of Meetings from 1857–1881," October 20, 1858, Marlatt Papers, KSU.

34. Ibid.; Julius Terrass Willard, *History of the Kansas State College of Agriculture and Applied Science* (Manhattan: Kansas State College Press, 1940), 11; *Manhattan*

Mercury, June 6, 2005; Ellen Goodnow Diary, May 14, 1857, Goodnow Collection, KSHS; George S. Park to Isaac Goodnow, June 7, 1859, KSHS; cf. J. Denison to Isaac Goodnow, May 6, 1857, KSHS.

35. Samuel A. Johnson, *The Battle Cry of Freedom: The New England Emigrant Aid Company in the Kansas Crusade* (Westport, CT: Greenwood Press, 1977), 250; Craig Miner, *Kansas: The History of the Sunflower State, 1854–2000* (Lawrence: University Press of Kansas, 2002), 74; E. E. Hale to Isaac Goodnow, September 15, 1858, KSHS. Blue Mont College also acquired at least fifty shares of NEEAC stock. NEEAC Stock Certificates, Goodnow Collection, KSHS.

36. Parrish, *This Land,* 99; Goodnow Diary, April 1, 1857; MTA Records, March 31, 1857.

37. Parrish, *This Land,* 99; Goodnow Diary, April 1, 1857; MTA Records, March 31, 1857; "Minutes of Meetings from 1857–1881," Marlatt Papers, KSU; John D. Walters, *History of the Kansas State Agricultural College* (Manhattan: Kansas State Agricultural College, 1909), 17: "The Cincinnati Town Company promised liberal aid in town lots and town stock, but coupled their promise with the illiberal clause that the aid should not be delivered until the college association could show property in the amount of $100,000."

38. W. Marlatt to Isaac Goodnow, June 18, 1860, KSU.

39. Ibid., June 14, 1859.

40. Ibid., June 18, 1860.

41. Ibid., August 5, 1860.

42. Ibid., September 14, 1859.

43. Wells Letters III, 393; Henry Denison to Isaac Goodnow, June 26, 1859, RCHM; *Manhattan Express,* October 1, 1859; W. Marlatt to Isaac Goodnow, September 26, 1859, KSU; Wells Letters III, 404.

44. Parrish, *This Land,* 116; *Big Blue Union,* August 8, 1863, quoted in "Bypaths of Kansas History," *KHQ* (August 1939): 315.

45. Parrish, *This Land,* 116; *Big Blue Union,* August 8, 1863, quoted in "Bypaths of Kansas History," *KHQ* (August 1939): 315; Andrew Stark, *Kansas Register for the Year 1864* (Leavenworth, KS: State Agricultural Society, 1864), 81–82.

46. *Leavenworth Daily Times,* July 29, 1863.

47. City Council Minute Books, May 1859; George Wells, "A Series of Articles Published in *The Mercury* in 1913," Riley County Genealogical Society.

48. City Council Minute Books, March 18, 1859. J. M. Russell, George Park, and Sanders Johnston had previously departed. By 1859 Horace A. Wilcox, who since 1855 had gone back and forth escorting parties of New England emigrants, had moved permanently back to New England (Goodnow Diary, July 12, 1859; August 3, 1860). Reverend Blood, who had lived in Juniata in 1854, continued to live in Manhattan until 1861, and Seth Child, who had never lived inside the town's borders, remained living in the area until his death in 1913.

49. *Historical Plat Book of Riley County, Kansas* (Chicago: Bird & Mickle Map Co., 1881), 25.

50. Horace Greeley, *An Overland Journey* (New York: C. M. Saxton, Barker & Co., 1860), 58.

51. Ibid., 70.

52. Richardson, *Beyond the Mississippi*, 161.

53. Greeley, *Overland Journey*, 58–59.

54. The only known copy of the first issue is in the Library of Congress. Cutler's *History of Kansas* improperly states that the *Express* was the westernmost newspaper published in Kansas Territory at the time; the *Junction City Sentinel* began publishing in August 1858, and Denver's *Rocky Mountain News* began publishing on April 23, 1859.

55. *Manhattan Kansas Express,* July 13, 1859; W. Marlatt to Isaac Goodnow, June 14, 1859, KSU.

56. Chas. Blood to Isaac Goodnow, June 28, 1859, KSHS; see also Chas. Blood to Isaac Goodnow, May 11, 1859, RCHM; Henry Denison to Isaac Goodnow, June 26, 1859, RCHM.

57. Wells Letters III, 394.

58. John Pipher interview, *Manhattan Republic,* February 19, 1897.

59. *Lawrence Herald of Freedom,* January 10, 1857.

60. John Winter Robinson to Hiram Hill, August 17, 1857, KSHS; Goodnow Diary, March 6, May 25, 1858; January 13, 22, 1859; Wells Letters III, 394; see also Wm. Goodnow to Harriet Goodnow, June 10, 1855, KSHS.

61. Goodnow Diary, June 17, 18, 1858; January 9, 10, 1859; Parrish, *This Land,* 64.

62. MTA Records, February 11, June 29, 1859.

63. Isaac Goodnow to Charles Blood, May 5, 1859, KSHS; see also Charles Blood to Isaac Goodnow, August 4, 1859, KSHS: "The paper does well. The Editor is encouraged."

64. *Smoky Hill and Republican Union,* September 26, 1861; see also *Manhattan Express,* July 12, 1862: Notice of lawsuit *Humphrey v. De Vivaldi.*

65. *Manhattan Mercury,* February 8, 2009.

CHAPTER 12. 1860–1865: DROUGHT, VIOLENCE, AND VICTORIES

1. A. F. Grow Reminiscences, *Manhattan Nationalist,* April 22, 1887.

2. Wells Letters III, 405.

3. Donald Parrish, *This Land Is Our Land: The Public Domain in the Vicinity of Riley County and Manhattan, Kansas* (Manhattan, KS: RCHS, 2003), 75.

4. It seems likely that there were sixty-three inhabited buildings in Manhattan in 1860, and the census recorded 260 people living with the first sixty-three families it surveyed, each of which was recorded as within the "City of Manhattan." However, William Goodnow wrote to his wife on December 4, 1859, that "one man, C. Barnes, visited 63 families in Manhattan containing 381 souls & found only 3 destitute of the Bible." Wm. Goodnow to Harriet Goodnow, December 4, 1859, KSHS; see also City Council Minute Books, June 23, 1865. The 1860 census showed that

somewhere between 600–640 people were served by the Manhattan post office, out of a total of 1,224 in Riley County.

5. Wells Letters III, 395; see also William Least Heat-Moon, *PrairyErth* (Boston: Houghton Mifflin Co., 1991), 55–56.

6. City Council Minute Books, July 12, 1858; November 20, 1858; February 26, April 6, 1859; see also *Manhattan Express*, December 24, 1859.

7. *Manhattan Kansas Express*, May 21, 1859.

8. Ibid., September 3, 1859.

9. Ibid., December 24, 1859.

10. J. T. Willard, "Bluemont Central College," *KHQ* (May 1945): 337. Enrollment soon increased to fifty-three in the first term. Julius Terrass Willard, *History of the Kansas State College of Agriculture and Applied Science* (Manhattan: Kansas State College Press, 1940), 12.

11. "Constitution of Bluemont Central College Association," Marlatt Papers, KSU.

12. Isaac Goodnow to Ellen Goodnow, July 31, 1857, KSHS; see also Goodnow Diary, January 11, 1857: "One [newspaper] has a drawing of the Wilberforce Cottage at Xenia Springs, Ohio, for colored Youth. I have been querying whether I would become a Prof. in this Institution, should an opening present itself. I feel an interest for our poor persecuted Blacks."

13. *Rocky Mountain News*, May 14, 1859; Calvin W. Gower, "The Pike's Peak Gold Rush and the Smoky Hill Route: 1859–1860," *KHQ* (Summer 1959); Elliot West, *The Contested Plains: Indians, Goldseekers and the Rush to Colorado* (Lawrence: University Press of Kansas, 1998), 155–157.

14. RCHS, *Log Cabin Days* (Manhattan, KS: RCHS, 1929), 33.

15. Craig Miner, *Kansas: The History of the Sunflower State, 1854–2000* (Lawrence: University Press of Kansas, 2002), 80; Wm. Goodnow to Isaac Goodnow, May 14, 1860, RCHM; Chas. Blood to Isaac Goodnow, July 14, 1860, RCHM; RCHS, *Log Cabin Days*, 28.

16. Miner, *Kansas*, 80; *Manhattan Express*, July 21, 1860.

17. Wells Letters III, 415.

18. Henry L. Denison to J. Denison, August 2, 1860, KSHS; see also W. Marlatt to Isaac Goodnow, August 5, 1860, KSU.

19. Miner, *Kansas*, 80.

20. John Winter Robinson to Thaddeus Hyatt, October 6, 1860, KSHS.

21. *Manhattan Express*, March 24, 1860.

22. Isaac Goodnow to John Wood, May 11, 1857, KSHS; see also Wells Letters II, 315; Goodnow Diary, October 18, 1858; Wells Letters III, 403; J. H. Pillsbury to Stephen Pillsbury, April 15, 1860, KSU.

23. *Western Kansas Express*, November 24, 1860.

24. John Winter Robinson to Isaac Goodnow, November 12, 1860, KSHS; Wells Letters III, 415.

25. Parrish, *This Land*, 76–77.

26. Wells Letters III, 410.

27. RCHS, *Log Cabin Days*, 53.

28. John Winter Robinson to Isaac Goodnow, November 12, 1860, KSHS; see also Wm. Goodnow to Isaac Goodnow, December 22, 1860, KSHS.

29. W. Marlatt to Isaac Goodnow, June 26, 1860, KSU; W. Marlatt to Isaac Goodnow, August 5, 1860, KSU; cf. Simeon Fox to Annie Young, December 1, 1929, RCHM.

30. *Western Kansas Express,* May 18, April 20, 1861; Amos Powers, "Old Settlers Stories," Riley County Clippings, vol. 2, KSHS, 39.

31. Goodnow Diary, November 21, 1857; February 11, 1858; March 11, 1859.

32. William McKale and William D. Young, *Fort Riley: Citadel of the Frontier West* (Topeka: KSHS, 2000), 40.

33. Ibid.; City Council Minute Books, May 28, 1860; Wm. Goodnow to Isaac Goodnow, September 24, 1860, RCHM.

34. *Manhattan Kansas Express,* September 24, 1859.

35. John Winter Robinson to Isaac Goodnow, November 12, 1860, KSHS.

36. Amanda Arnold interview, *Topeka Daily Capital,* November 18, 1923; cf. Wells Letters III, 415.

37. Miner, *Kansas,* 83.

38. *Western Kansas Express,* March 16, 1861.

39. W. Marlatt to Isaac Goodnow, October 3, 1860.

40. David Dary, *True Tales of Old Time Kansas* (Lawrence: University Press of Kansas, 1984), 252–256.

41. *Leavenworth Daily News,* April 26, 1861. De Vivaldi went to Washington, D.C., on March 13, 1861, seeking appointment as a foreign consul. Goodnow Diary, March 13, 1861; *Manhattan Western Kansas Express,* March 16, 1861; *Kansas Kin,* May 1989.

42. *Manhattan Western Kansas Express,* May 4, 1861.

43. *Report of the Adjutant General of the State of Kansas,* vol. 1, *1861–1865* (1867); Chestina Allen, "Journey from Mass. to Kansas," Pottawatomie County History Collection, KSHS, 41; C. A. Kimball, "A Kansas Pioneer: Biographical Sketch of J. M. Kimball" (1922), reprinted in *The Manhattan Tribune,* March 23, 1922; Whitehorn, "Historical Sketch."

44. RCHS, *Log Cabin Days,* 36.

45. *Report of Adjutant General;* Whitehorn, "Historical Sketch"; *Manhattan Independent,* November 15, 1864; Goodnow Diary, November 13, 1864.

46. E. L. Prentice to Isaac Goodnow, March 2, 1863, KSHS.

47. David Ballard, "The First State Legislature, 1861," *Transactions of the KSHS* 10 (1908): 253; *Manhattan Independent,* February 15, 1864.

48. Powers, "Old Settlers Stories," 45; see also Goodnow Diary, October 16, 1864: "Manhattan Regt. behind, will be here [Topeka] tomorrow. War times! Bound to checkmate Gen. Price."

49. *Manhattan Express,* October 5, December 14, 1861; see also *Manhattan Express,* October 19, 1861; January 23, 1862.

50. David Reynolds, *John Brown, Abolitionist: The Man Who Killed Slavery, Sparked the Civil War, and Seeded Civil Rights* (New York: Alfred A. Knopf, 2005), 281; McKale and Young, *Fort Riley,* 56.

51. *Manhattan Independent,* August 17, 1863.

52. Ibid., August 24, 1863.

53. Elizabeth Shor, *Fossils and Flies: The Life of a Compleat Scientist Samuel Wendell Williston* (Norman: University of Oklahoma Press, 1971), 16–17.

54. McKale and Young, *Fort Riley,* 52.

55. *Manhattan Independent,* August 24, September 14, 1863.

56. Goodnow Diary, June 5, 15, 1861.

57. Ibid., May 19, 1862; *Manhattan Express,* May 17, 24, 1862.

58. Goodnow Diary, May 13, 1862. Troops from Fort Riley also marched Confederate prisoners of war through Manhattan. *Smoky Hill and Republican Union,* July 3, 1862; McKale and Young, *Fort Riley,* 50.

59. Ballard, "First State Legislature," 240.

60. *Plat Book of Riley County,* 17, 23.

61. *Manhattan Independent,* August 17, 1863.

62. Goodnow helped draft resolutions that served as instructions for the delegates from the area. *Manhattan Express,* August 23, 1862; see also Goodnow Diary, January 15, April 4, April 10, May 7, 1861.

63. James Shortridge, *Cities on the Plains: The Evolution of Urban Kansas* (Lawrence: University Press of Kansas, 2004), 83; Walters, *History of the Kansas State Agricultural College,* 18; see also *Manhattan Express,* October 19, 1861: "Now it is of some importance that we cooperate with those who will help us. . . . By helping Topeka against Lawrence, we are at the same time promoting indirectly our own interests, and forming the only combination which is possible to sustain the claims of the west."

64. Isaac Goodnow to Ellen Goodnow, May 13, 1861, KSHS: "The City of Lawrence opposed with all their power."

65. C. S. Griffin, "The University of Kansas and the Years of Frustration, 1854–64," *KHQ* (Spring 1966): 16.

66. Willard, "Bluemont Central College," 344; Shortridge, *Cities on the Plains,* 87.

67. *Manhattan Express,* June 1, 1861.

68. Parrish, *This Land,* 112; Willard, *Kansas State College,* 12.

69. Daniel Walker Howe, *What Hath God Wrought: The Transformation of America, 1815–1848* (New York: Oxford University Press, 2007), 457.

70. Miner, *Kansas,* 87, 124.

71. The *Manhattan Express* opined on January 18, 1862: "Had not local interests ruled most disgracefully the Executive, at the last session of the Legislature, Kansas would have had established in her midst an institution of this character to which she might have pointed with pride and pleasure . . . all the State is asked to do at present is to take charge of an institution already prepared for it, and send here her youth to be educated."

72. Miner, *Kansas,* 87, 124; Griffin, "The University of Kansas and the Years of Frustration," 19–20; see also *Manhattan Express,* September 16, 1862.

73. Isaac Goodnow to Ellen Goodnow, March 4, 1862, KSHS.

74. Parrish, *This Land,* 157.

75. Isaac Goodnow to Ellen Goodnow, February 15, 1863, KSHS.

76. Invitations were sent out for a "Regent's Dinner" at the school, noting that it would be free to attend. See also *Big Blue Union,* August 8, 1863, quoted in "Bypaths of Kansas History," *KHQ* (August 1939): 315; Willard, "Bluemont Central College," 350.

77. Isaac Goodnow to Ellen Goodnow, February 19, 1863, KSHS.

78. Willard, *Kansas State College,* 24.

79. Stark, *Kansas Register for the Year 1864,* 80–81.

80. Cf. *Manhattan Independent,* June 29, 1867: "This is not only the first class graduated by this College, but in the State, and it is the only Agricultural College in the United States which admits both sexes to its instructions hence there was not a little curiosity among the visitors to see how the young lady candidates for the honorary degree, would compare in scholarship and genius with their male class-mates."

81. *Manhattan Independent,* December 15, 1866.

82. Albert Deane Richardson, *Beyond the Mississippi: From the Great River to the Great Ocean* (Hartford, CT: American Publishing Co., 1869), 555; Nupur Chaudhuri, "The Afro-American Community in Manhattan, Kansas 1865–1940" (Ph.D. diss., Kansas State University, 1986), 17.

83. *Manhattan Independent,* August 17, 1863.

84. Ibid., December 7, 1863.

85. Griffin, "The University of Kansas and the Years of Frustration," 25–27.

86. Ibid.

87. Ibid.

88. Whitehorn, "Historical Sketch."

89. Goodnow Diary, March 1, 1859.

90. *Western Kansas Express,* October 22, 1860.

91. Goodnow Diary, February 23, 1861.

92. Ibid., December 7, 1861; Whitehorn, "Historical Sketch."

93. *Manhattan Express,* December 14, 1861.

94. Ibid.

95. Whitehorn, "Historical Sketch."

96. Ibid.

97. *Kansas: A Cyclopedia of State History* (Chicago: Standard Publishing Co., 1912), vol. 3, pt. 2, 825.

98. *Manhattan Express,* December 14, 1861.

99. *Kansas City Star,* November 25, 1906.

100. Ibid.

101. City Council Minute Books, January 18, 1860; July 30, 1860; August 27, 1860; January 24, 1861.

102. Ibid., December 29, 1860.

103. *Manhattan Express,* April 5, 1862.

104. *Manhattan Independent,* December 21, 1863.

105. Harriett Lee to Isaac Goodnow, May 24, 1863, KSHS: "I am sorry to say that religion is at too low an ebb with us all."

106. *Manhattan Express*, December 14, 1861.

107. Genevieve Yost, "History of Lynchings in Kansas," *KHQ* (May 1933): 210–219.

108. Whitehorn, "Historical Sketch."

109. *Manhattan Express*, October 4, 1862.

110. Goodnow Diary, December 18, 1862.

111. *Smoky Hill and Republican Union*, August 1, 1863; *Manhattan Independent*, August 17, 1863; cf. *Manhattan Independent*, May 30, 1864: "Our Code of Criminal Law is well enough, we presume, but its execution or observance has not yet become as effectual or general as we hope it soon will be."

112. *Smoky Hill and Republican Union*, May 14, 1864; Yost, "Lynchings in Kansas," 213.

113. *Smoky Hill and Republican Union*, May 14, 1864.

114. Ibid.

115. *Manhattan Independent*, May 23, 1864.

116. Ibid., May 30, 1864.

117. Whitehorn, "Historical Sketch."

118. Ibid.

119. McKale and Young, *Fort Riley*, 50. Additional counties were organized on Riley County's western border between 1857 and 1860.

120. *Manhattan Independent*, April 7, 1866.

121. *Manhattan Express*, June 21, 1862; City Council Minute Books, January 26, February 2, 1867.

122. City Council Minute Books, December 1, 1866. Councilman B. F. Palmer was removed under this ordinance in 1867. *Manhattan Independent*, February 2, 1867.

123. Ibid., August 11, 1866.

124. Ibid., March 10, 1866.

125. The vote in Riley County for the Prohibition amendment in 1880 was 1,178 in favor and 828 against. Cf. *Manhattan Nationalist*, July 18, 1879: "James Reynolds, arrested for keeping a tippling house without a license, was discharged for want of sufficient evidence. Sherriff Houghton refused to answer questions on the ground that his testimony might criminate himself, and the other witnesses swore they had drunk nothing but ice water, lemonade, or something equally harmless."

126. *Manhattan Independent*, June 15, 1867: Senators Lyman Trumbull, Zachariah Chandler, Timothy Howe, Alexander Cattell, John Creswell, Samuel Pomeroy, and Edmund Ross.

127. *Manhattan Independent*, July 6, 1867.

CHAPTER 13. POST–CIVIL WAR: TRIUMPH OF THE YANKEES

1. City Council Minute Books, April 13, 1865. The celebration, scheduled for April 20, 1865, was postponed after news of President Lincoln's assassination reached Manhattan on April 17. *Manhattan Independent—Extra*, April 17, 1865.

2. *Junction City Union*, May 20, 1865.

3. Fifty-two percent were from "Northern culture" states; only the unincorporated settlement of Waubaunsee had a higher percentage. James Shortridge, *Peopling the*

Plains: Who Settled Where in Frontier Kansas (Lawrence: University Press of Kansas, 1995), 26–27.

4. *Manhattan Kansas Radical,* July 21, 1866; James Humphrey, "The Country West of Topeka Prior to 1865," *Transactions of the KSHS* 4 (1888): 292.

5. *Manhattan Independent,* December 15, 1866: Advertisement headlined "ATTENTION! YANKEES!!"

6. *Manhattan Express,* June 7, 1862.

7. Wells Letters II, 290; Whitehorn, "Historical Sketch"; "Slavery in Kansas," *Transactions of the KSHS* 7 (1902): 241.

8. 1865 Kansas Census; Geraldine Baker Walton, *140 Years of Soul: A History of African-Americans in Manhattan, Kansas* (Manhattan: KS Publishing, 2008), 1–2.

9. "Some Early Black Families in Manhattan, Kansas," *Kansas Kin,* February 1987; "History of the Manhattan Black Community," ibid., May 1986.

10. Nupur Chaudhuri, "'We All Seem Like Brothers and Sisters': The Afro-American Community in Manhattan, Kansas, 1865–1940" *Kansas History* (Winter 1991–1992): 280; cf. *Manhattan Nationalist,* March 24, 1871.

11. *Manhattan Independent,* January 4, 1868.

12. Ibid., August 17, 1863.

13. James Shortridge, *Cities on the Plains: The Evolution of Urban Kansas* (Lawrence: University Press of Kansas, 2004), 104, 106; *Manhattan Express,* April 19, 1862; Goodnow Diary, July 3, 1862; Eli Thayer to Isaac Goodnow, December 12, 1862, KSHS; *Manhattan Independent,* November 22, 1864.

14. The railroad followed closely the route of David Butterfield's old Overland Despatch stagecoach line. Shortridge, *Cities on the Plains,* 128.

15. City Council Minute Books, July 26, 1865.

16. *Manhattan Independent,* June 23, 1866.

17. *Manhattan Kansas Radical,* July 14, August 11, 1866: "Good bye dusty roads and crowded stages."

18. *Manhattan Kansas Radical,* August 18, 1866; City Council Minute Books, November 15, December 4, 1865.

19. *Topeka Capital Journal,* February 24, 1997.

20. Simeon Fox to Annie Young, December 1, 1929, RCHM. The city council granted permission for the Kansas Pacific to build the track through Manhattan on any street, and the railroad selected Riley Street, six blocks south of Poyntz Avenue. City Council Minute Books, November 15, December 4, 1865.

21. Ibid., December 4, 1865.

22. *Manhattan Independent,* August 11, 1866; *Manhattan Kansas Radical,* August 18, September 1, 1866; Donald Parrish, *This Land Is Our Land: The Public Domain in the Vicinity of Riley County and Manhattan, Kansas* (Manhattan, KS: RCHS, 2003), 146.

23. *New-York Times,* August 22, 1866.

24. Ibid.

25. *Manhattan Independent,* August 25, 1866.

26. Ibid., August 11, 1866; February 9, 1867.

27. Ibid., August 4, 1866; Elizabeth Shor, *Fossils and Flies: The Life of a Compleat Scientist Samuel Wendell Williston* (Norman: University of Oklahoma Press, 1971), 17.

28. *Manhattan Independent,* July 28, 1866. It had taken more than two full days for news of the assassination of President Abraham Lincoln to reach Manhattan in April 1865. *Manhattan Independent — Extra,* April 17, 1865.

29. *Manhattan Independent,* August 4, 1866.

30. *Manhattan Kansas Radical,* August 18, 1866.

31. A. F. Grow Reminiscences, *Manhattan Nationalist,* May 13, 1887: "Not till about the close of the war and the advent of the railroad, did the city begin to grow in earnest."

32. *Manhattan Independent,* October 6, 1866.

33. Ibid., May 19, June 23, 1866; *Manhattan Kansas Radical,* July 14, 1866; *Junction City Union,* March 24, 1866.

34. *Manhattan Kansas Radical,* July 28, 1866.

35. *Manhattan Standard,* October 23, 1869.

36. Ibid., September 4, October 23, November 13, 1869.

37. Ibid., May 8, 1869.

38. *Manhattan Independent,* August 11, 1866.

39. Ibid., January 26, June 22, August 17, 1867; January 18, 1868; *Manhattan Standard,* September 4, 1869.

40. *Manhattan Independent,* June 23, August 11, 1866.

41. Simeon Fox to Annie Young, December 1, 1929, RCHM.

42. *Manhattan Independent,* May 19, 1866: "business houses reach" to Fourth Street on old map and Fifth Street on present grid.

43. City Council Minute Books, November 15, 1865; April 28, 1866; *Manhattan Independent,* May 19, 1866; June 1, 1867; *Manhattan Kansas Radical,* July 28, 1866.

44. City Council Minute Books, November 17, 1866.

45. Shortridge, *Peopling the Plains,* 30–31.

46. *Manhattan Independent,* February 16, 1867.

47. *Manhattan Nationalist,* December 30, 1870.

48. Manhattan's "progress during the past ten years has been slight, when compared with what it should have been" (*Manhattan Nationalist,* March 3, 1871). By May 2, 1868, the *Independent* seemed chastened, advising its readers to "Be Kind to Strangers": "Strangers who have just arrived among us from a far country, complain of us that our bearing is cold and indifferent; that no one inquires for their welfare, or pays them the least attention; that if one of their number sickens and dies among us, no one appears to know or care anything about it."

49. *Manhattan Independent,* April 6, August 31, September 7, 1867.

50. Ibid., January 13, 1866.

51. Ibid., August 18, 1866.

52. Ibid., April 27, September 14, 1867.

53. *Manhattan Kansas Radical,* September 14, 1867: "Susan B. Anthony has a remarkable amount of impudence in her composition."

54. *Manhattan Independent,* October 19, 1867.

55. Ibid., November 9, 1867: the vote in favor of black suffrage was 351–227; the vote against women's suffrage was 378–218. Allen, Ottawa, and Wabaunsee counties also voted for suffrage for blacks, but only Ottawa County voted for female suffrage. William Cutler and Alfred Theodore Andreas, *History of the State of Kansas* (Chicago: Western Historical Co., 1883), 1303.

56. *Manhattan Independent,* November 9, 1867.

57. Whitehorn, "Historical Sketch."

58. William McKale and William D. Young, *Fort Riley: Citadel of the Frontier West* (Topeka: KSHS, 2000), 61–72.

59. Craig Miner, *Kansas: The History of the Sunflower State, 1854–2000* (Lawrence: University Press of Kansas, 2002), 113.

60. *Manhattan Standard,* April 17, 1869.

61. Joseph B. Herring, "The Chippewa and Munsee Indians: Acculturation and Survival in Kansas, 1850s–1870," in Napier, *Kansas and the West,* 83–85.

62. Harry Sinclair Drago, *Wild, Wooly and Wicked: The History of the Kansas Cow Towns and the Texas Cattle Trade* (New York: Clarkson N. Potter, 1960), 31–32.

63. Miner, *Kansasy,* 135–136; Shortridge, *Cities on the Plains,* 136.

64. Drago, *Wild, Wooly and Wicked,* 14–15.

65. *Manhattan Independent,* December 7, 1867.

66. Ibid.; see also February 9, 1867.

67. *Manhattan Standard,* August 7, 1869.

68. Ibid., July 24, 1869.

69. Ibid., June 12, 1869.

70. Ibid., July 3, 10, 1869; see also August 21, 1869.

71. Ibid., September 11, 1869.

72. Ibid., February 27, 1869.

73. McKale and Young, *Fort Riley,* 135.

74. *Manhattan Kansas Radical,* July 14, August 11, 1866.

75. *Manhattan Nationalist,* March 8, 1871; see also Clinton Carter Hutchinson, *Resources of Kansas: Fifteen Years Experience* (Topeka, KS: C. C. Hutchinson, 1871), 219.

76. Patricia O'Brien, *The Architects and Buildings of Manhattan, Kansas* (Manhattan, KS: RCHS, 2008), 8; *Manhattan Nationalist,* March 31, 1871.

77. Lowell Jack, *A History of Manhattan, Kansas — Riley County and Ft. Riley* (Manhattan, KS: Hawley Printing, 2003), 9.

78. *Manhattan Nationalist,* May 30, 1884; *Manhattan Mercury,* May 10, 1981.

79. *Manhattan Nationalist,* April 28, 1871; "Riley County Kansas: 'The Blue Ribbon County,'" supplement to *Manhattan Nationalist,* June 16, 1881, 46.

80. Purcell purchased Pipher's store in conjunction with George W. Higinbotham. *Manhattan Independent*, October 20, November 24, 1866; March 21, 1868; *Manhattan Standard*, December 12, 1868; August 21, 1869; "Blue Ribbon County," 46.

81. *Manhattan Nationalist*, July 2, 1875; June 30, July 7, 1876 (letter of Mrs. Henry Strong).

82. *Manhattan Mercury*, January 20, 1927; O'Brien, *The Architects and Buildings of Manhattan*, 9.

83. *Manhattan Nationalist*, March 7, 1873; RCHS, *Log Cabin Days* (Manhattan, KS: RCHS, 1929), 70.

84. RCHS, *Log Cabin Days*, 70.

85. "Blue Ribbon County," 51.

86. Ibid.

87. Elaine Olney and Mary Roberts, eds., *Pioneers of the Bluestem Prairie* (Manhattan, KS: Riley County Genealogical Society, 1976), 435; *Manhattan Republican*, March 10, 1887.

88. *Manhattan Mercury*, April 17, 2005.

89. Ibid.

90. *Manhattan Daily Republic*, August 7, 1887; *Manhattan Nationalist*, May 18, 1888; November 3, 1893.

91. *Manhattan Nationalist*, September 16, 1880; Carolyn Jones, *The First One Hundred Years: A History of the City of Manhattan, Kansas 1855–1955* (Manhattan, KS: privately printed, 1955), 68.

92. *Manhattan Mercury*, April 17, 2005.

93. Ibid.

94. *Chicago Daily Tribune*, April 9, 1890; *Topeka Capital*, April 9, 1890; Louise Barry, "A British Bride in Manhattan, 1890–1891: The Journal of Mrs. Stuart James Hogg," *KHQ* (August 1951): 271–272.

95. *Chicago Daily Tribune*, April 9, 1890.

96. *Manhattan Standard*, June 12, August 14, October 23, 1869; *Topeka Journal*, December 20, 1933.

97. O'Brien, *The Architects and Buildings of Manhattan*, 8.

98. *Manhattan Independent*, November 24, 1866.

99. Goodnow Diary, March 25, 1866; *Manhattan Standard*, February 27, 1869.

CHAPTER 14. 1870S: "A LIVELY TOWN, FULL OF BUSINESS"

1. Albert Deane Richardson, *Beyond the Mississippi: From the Great River to the Great Ocean* (Hartford, CT: American Publishing Co., 1869), 554.

2. *Manhattan Nationalist*, June 6, 1873; Charles R. Tuttle, *A New Centennial History of the State of Kansas* (Madison, WI: Inter-State Book Co., 1876), 645.

3. *Manhattan Nationalist*, June 7, 1878.

4. *Manhattan Standard*, July 17, 1869.

5. Wm. Goodnow to Mrs. Reed, January 20, 1872, KSHS; Wayne Griswold, *Kansas: Her Resources and Developments* (Cincinnati: Robert Clarke & Co., 1871), 66.

6. The 1875 and 1880 censuses are broken down by birthplace at the Riley County Genealogical Library.

7. Whitehorn, "Historical Sketch"; *Manhattan Nationalist*, February 24, March 10, 24, 1871.

8. *Manhattan Nationalist*, March 31, 1871.

9. Ibid., April 21, 1871.

10. Ibid., February 24, 1871.

11. Whitehorn, "Historical Sketch."

12. Ibid.; Tuttle, *Centennial History of the State,* 554, 645.

13. *Manhattan Nationalist*, February 6, 1880; October 20, 1881. The line was completed to Marysville in 1886.

14. *Manhattan Nationalist*, July 29, 1880.

15. Percy Ebbutt, *Emigrant Life in Kansas* (London: Swan Sonnenschein & Co., 1886), 193, 203.

16. *Manhattan Kansas Radical,* August 15, 1866; *Manhattan Independent,* March 9, 1867; *Manhattan High School Monitor,* March 1874; *Manhattan Nationalist,* July 12, 1878.

17. *Manhattan Republican,* March 10, 1887.

18. *Manhattan Nationalist,* March 24, 1873; Thomas Schlereth, *Victorian America: Transformations in Everyday Life, 1876–1915* (New York: HarperPerennial, 1991), 135, 211.

19. David Fairchild, *The World Was My Garden: Travels of a Plant Explorer* (New York: Charles Scribner's Sons, 1939), 8.

20. *Manhattan Independent,* July 20, 1867; January 11, 1868.

21. William Cutler and Alfred Theodore Andreas, *History of the State of Kansas* (Chicago: Western Historical Co., 1883), 1307.

22. Elizabeth Shor, *Fossils and Flies: The Life of a Compleat Scientist Samuel Wendell Williston* (Norman: University of Oklahoma Press, 1971), 55.

23. *Manhattan Nationalist,* May 13, 1887.

24. Ibid., August 20, 1875.

25. Ebbutt, *Emigrant Life in Kansas,* 204; see also *Manhattan Nationalist,* July 8, 1880.

26. *First Biennial Report of the (Kansas) State Board of Agriculture* (Topeka: Kansas State Board of Agriculture, 1878), 392; *Manhattan Enterprise,* August 15, 1877; *Manhattan Nationalist,* February 24, 1881.

27. Ebbutt, *Emigrant Life in Kansas,* 203.

28. *Manhattan High School Monitor,* November 1873.

29. Ibid., February 1874; *Manhattan Nationalist,* July 18, August 29, 1873.

30. Ibid.

31. *Manhattan High School Monitor,* February 1874. Earlier references to a high school do exist. *Manhattan Independent,* June 30, 1866: "The exhibition of the High School last evening was a complete success."

32. *Manhattan Nationalist,* November 14, 1873.

33. "Fifty Years of Progress," *Manhattan Nationalist,* June 16, 1910; ibid., July 5, 12, 1878.

34. *Manhattan High School Monitor,* December 1873.

35. "Fifty Years of Progress," *Manhattan Nationalist,* June 16, 1910; *Manhattan Free Press,* July 14, 2005; Patricia O'Brien, *The Architects and Buildings of Manhattan, Kansas* (Manhattan, KS: RCHS, 2008), 11, 21; *Manhattan Nationalist,* May 17, 1878; May 25; September 14, 1882.

36. Donald Parrish, *This Land Is Our Land: The Public Domain in the Vicinity of Riley County and Manhattan, Kansas* (Manhattan, KS: RCHS, 2003), 118.

37. *Manhattan Nationalist,* December 30, 1870.

38. Ibid., January 21, 1876.

39. Julius Terrass Willard, *History of the Kansas State College of Agriculture and Applied Science* (Manhattan: Kansas State College Press, 1940), 49, 547.

40. Ibid., 59.

41. Ibid., 65, 547.

42. *Manhattan Nationalist,* March 4, 1887.

43. Ibid., August 27, 1875; Willard, *Kansas State College,* 42; see also Tuttle, *Centennial History of the State,* 529.

44. J. T. Willard, "Bluemont Central College," *KHQ* (May 1945): 353–355; O'Brien, *The Architects and Buildings of Manhattan,* 2; *Manhattan Nationalist,* December 28, 1883.

45. Dee Brown, *Bury My Heart at Wounded Knee: An Indian History of the American West* (New York: Henry Holt & Co., 1991), 352.

46. Ibid.

47. Ibid.

48. Ibid., 356.

49. Ibid., 357; *Manhattan Nationalist,* June 29, 1877.

50. *Manhattan Nationalist,* June 29, 1877.

51. Ibid.

52. William McKale and William D. Young, *Fort Riley: Citadel of the Frontier West* (Topeka: KSHS, 2000), 72.

53. *Historical Plat Book of Riley County, Kansas* (Chicago: Bird & Mickle Map Co., 1881), 15.

54. *Manhattan Nationalist,* April 25, 1879.

55. *Kansas City Mail,* April 14, 17, 22, 1879.

56. Ibid., April 24, 1879.

57. Nupur Chaudhuri, "'We All Seem Like Brothers and Sisters': The Afro-American Community in Manhattan, Kansas, 1865–1940" *Kansas History* (Winter 1991–1992): 275.

58. Ibid.

59. *Manhattan Nationalist,* May 2, 1879.

60. Chaudhuri, "'We All Seem Like Brothers and Sisters,'" 273–275.

61. Jill Watts, *Hattie McDaniel: Black Ambition, White Hollywood* (New York: Amistad, 2005), 14–15.

62. *Manhattan Nationalist,* January 30, 1880.

63. Chaudhuri, "'We All Seem Like Brothers and Sisters,'" 276.

64. Ibid., 17.

65. *Manhattan Nationalist*, March 5, 1875.
66. Randall Bennett Woods, *A Black Odyssey: John Lewis Walker and the Promise of American Life, 1878–1900* (Lawrence: Regents of Kansas, 1981), 67.
67. *Manhattan Nationalist*, March 5, 1875.

CHAPTER 15. 1880–1894: INTO THE MODERN ERA

1. *Manhattan Nationalist*, May 6, 1887 (quoting *Leonardville Monitor*); *Topeka Capital*, July 31, 1888.
2. *Manhattan Nationalist*, November 4, 1887.
3. *Topeka Capital*, July 31, 1888.
4. Joseph Collins, ed., *Natural Kansas* (Lawrence: University Press of Kansas, 1985), 3–4; RCHS, *Log Cabin Days* (Manhattan, KS: RCHS, 1929), 24–25; Federal Writers' Project, *The WPA Guide to 1930s Kansas* (Lawrence: University Press of Kansas, 1984), 116.
5. "Riley County Kansas: 'The Blue Ribbon County,'" supplement to *Manhattan Nationalist*, June 16, 1881, 32.
6. *Topeka Capital*, July 31, 1888.
7. A. F. Grow Reminiscences, *Manhattan Nationalist*, March 25, 1887.
8. Patricia O'Brien, *The Architects and Buildings of Manhattan, Kansas* (Manhattan, KS: RCHS, 2008), 11, 14.
9. *Manhattan Mercury*, August 3, 1887.
10. Louise Barry, "A British Bride in Manhattan, 1890–1891: The Journal of Mrs. Stuart James Hogg," *KHQ* (August 1951): 275.
11. William Cutler and Alfred Theodore Andreas, *History of the State of Kansas* (Chicago: Western Historical Co., 1883), 1308.
12. *Manhattan Nationalist*, September 22, 1882.
13. "Blue Ribbon County"; Cutler, *History of Kansas*, 1307.
14. *Manhattan Republican*, March 10, 1887.
15. *Manhattan Nationalist*, October 14, 1887.
16. Ibid.
17. *Manhattan Republican*, March 10, 1887.
18. The record is even thinner for Asian Americans and other minorities in Manhattan. For example, censuses show no Asian Americans in Manhattan during this era, although the *Manhattan Nationalist* reported on February 11, 1887, that a Chinese man called Fung Lee moved his Laundromat from Manhattan to Junction City.
19. Cutler, *History of Kansas*, 1306.
20. *Topeka Capital*, November 25, 1906.
21. *Manhattan Nationalist*, September 23, 1880: "We understand that some white men and boys have been misbehaving themselves at the colored church. This is contemptible, cowardly and ungentlemanly, and we are glad to hear that, if it is not stopped, the parties will be arrested."
22. *Manhattan Nationalist*, October 12, 1882; Nupur Chaudhuri, "'We All Seem Like Brothers and Sisters': The Afro-American Community in Manhattan, Kansas 1865–1940" *Kansas History* (Winter 1991–1992): 283.

23. Chaudhuri, "'We All Seem Like Brothers and Sisters,'" 284; see also James E. Butler, "A Black History of Manhattan," *Flint,* February 21, 1979.

24. Chaudhuri, "'We All Seem Like Brothers and Sisters,'" 279.

25. Ibid., 27–28.

26. Ibid.

27. The African American population in Manhattan was 307 in 1890; 314 in 1900; 303 in 1910; 289 in 1920; 332 in 1930; and 270 in 1940. Ibid., 287.

28. 1950 U.S. Census; "Manhattan's Changing Complexion," *Manhattan Mercury,* March 13, 2011.

29. "A Century Ago Electric Lights Came to Manhattan," *Kansas Kin,* August 1989; *Manhattan Daily Republic,* January 2, 1890.

30. "A Century Ago Electric Lights Came to Manhattan," *Kansas Kin,* August 1989; *Manhattan Daily Republic,* January 2, 1890.

31. *Topeka Capital,* July 31, 1888.

32. Barry, "British Bride in Manhattan," 275.

33. Julius Terrass Willard, *History of the Kansas State College of Agriculture and Applied Science* (Manhattan: Kansas State College Press, 1940), 547.

34. Thomas Schlereth, *Victorian America: Transformations in Everyday Life, 1876–1915* (New York: HarperPerennial, 1991), xii, 35.

35. Ibid., 174.

36. *Manhattan Mercury,* December 27, 1893.

37. Ibid., February 14, 1894.

38. *Manhattan Nationalist,* January 27, 1893; see also *College Symposium of the Kansas State Agricultural College* (Topeka, KS: Hall & O'Donald Litho Co., 1891).

39. *Students' Herald,* September 14, 1899.

40. *Manhattan Nationalist,* June 3, 1887.

41. *Manhattan Mercury,* January 31, 1894.

42. *Manhattan Nationalist,* March 23, 1894.

43. *New York Times,* March 21, 1894.

44. Goodnow Diary, May 12, September 2, October 25, 26, 1857; June 7, July 6, November 5, 1860; January 10, 1861.

45. William Connelley, *A Standard History of Kansas and Kansans* (Chicago: Lewis Publishing Co., 1918), 1853–1854; Goodnow Diary, August 10, 1864; *American Journal of Education* 14 (1864).

46. Isaac Goodnow to Ellen Goodnow, February 19, 1862, KSHS.

47. *Manhattan Express,* October 19, 1861.

48. Goodnow Diary, February 11, 1857.

49. *Portrait and Biographical Album of Washington, Clay and Riley Counties, Kansas* (Chicago: Chapman Bros., 1890), 549.

50. Carolyn Jones, *The First One Hundred Years: A History of the City of Manhattan, Kansas 1855–1955* (Manhattan, KS: privately printed, 1955), 52.

51. Simeon Fox to Annie Young, December 1, 1929, RCHM.

52. Charles Robinson, *The Kansas Conflict* (New York: Harper & Bros., 1892), xvii;

cf. *New York Times,* October 28, 1894: "Mr. Goodnow's contribution to the book, while extremely laudatory of Robinson, is silent on the subject of his own efforts in the Free Soil interest, which were not inconsiderable."

53. *Manhattan Nationalist,* May 4, June 22, 1894.

54. Wareham died on July 13, 1939. *Manhattan Mercury,* July 13, 1939.

55. Ibid.

56. Ruth Wareham, "The Life and Times of Harry Pratt Wareham" (privately printed); *Manhattan Nationalist,* February 3, 1871; August 27, 1875; June 7, 1878.

57. Ibid., October 31, 1884; Schlereth, *Victorian America,* 220.

58. Wareham, "Harry Pratt Wareham"; *Manhattan Nationalist,* August 25, 1893; *Manhattan Mercury,* August 23, 30, 1893; July 13, 1939.

59. Jones, *First One Hundred Years,* 16.

60. Wareham, "Harry Pratt Wareham."

61. Ibid.; "Fifty Years of Progress," *Manhattan Nationalist,* June 16, 1910.

62. Wareham, "Harry Pratt Wareham"; *Manhattan Mercury,* July 13, 1939.

63. Wareham, "Harry Pratt Wareham"; *Kansas City Star,* May 7, 1911.

64. Wareham, "Harry Pratt Wareham."

65. Schlereth, *Victorian America,* 223.

66. Mark Stallard, *Wildcats to Powercats: K-State Football Facts and Trivia* (Lenexa, KS: Addax Publishing Group, 2000), 30.

67. *Manhattan Mercury,* December 6, 1893.

68. Willard, *Kansas State College,* 497; *Manhattan Nationalist,* June 1, 1894.

69. Willard, *Kansas State College,* 497; Schlereth, *Victorian America,* 223.

70. *Manhattan Nationalist,* March 14, 1873; see also May 10, 1878.

71. Willard, *Kansas State College,* 510.

72. Schlereth, *Victorian America,* 15, 171–174.

73. *Manhattan Nationalist,* January 27, 1893.

74. A. F. Grow Reminiscences, *Manhattan Nationalist,* April 22, 1887.

75. "Manhattan 150," supplement to *Manhattan Mercury,* May 29, 2005.

EPILOGUE

1. Federal Writers' Project, *The WPA Guide to 1930s Kansas* (Lawrence: University Press of Kansas, 1984), 249.

2. *New York Times,* January 9, 1946.

3. *Christian Science Monitor,* March 11, 2002.

4. Stephen E. Ambrose, *To America: Personal Reflections of an Historian* (New York: Simon & Schuster, 2002), 139–140.

5. *Christian Science Monitor,* March 11, 2002.

6. Ambrose, *To America,* 228.

7. Calvin Trillin, "U.S. Journal: Manhattan and Atcheson, Kan. — The Maes Family," *New Yorker,* June 12, 1971.

8. *Manhattan Mercury,* November 5, 2008.

9. William Stevens, "Superhighway System in 20 Years Has Tied a Vast Nation

Together," *New York Times,* November 14, 1976; James Shortridge, *Cities on the Plains: The Evolution of Urban Kansas* (Lawrence: University Press of Kansas, 2004), 323–324.

10. *Christian Science Monitor,* March 11, 2002.
11. Ibid.
12. *Manhattan Historic Preservation Clearance* (June 1981), KSHS.

SELECTED BIBLIOGRAPHY

The following is a partial list of published works and archival material that provided significant help in making this book, and that might prove relevant to readers interested in further pursuing information on early Kansas history, or on the general history of the eras covered here. A large portion of the material relied upon in this book was derived directly from primary sources, including Manhattan settlers' letters and diaries, together with contemporary newspaper accounts. The latter sources are too voluminous to list in this bibliography, but direct citations to all sources are provided in the notes.

Barry, Louise. "The Emigrant Aid Company Parties of 1854." *KHQ* (May 1943): 115–155.
———. "The New England Emigrant Aid Company Parties of 1855." *KHQ* (August 1943): 227–268.
Boston Town Association and Manhattan Town Association Records. KSHS, microfilm reel MS 123.01. (Cited in notes as "MTA Records.")
Boynton, C. B., and T. B. Mason. *A Journey through Kansas; with Sketches of Nebraska.* Cincinnati: Moore, Wilsach, Keys & Co., 1855.
Connelley, William E. *A Standard History of Kansas and Kansans.* Chicago: Lewis Publishing Co., 1918.
Cutler, William G., and Alfred Theodore Andreas. *History of the State of Kansas.* Chicago: Western Historical Co., 1883.
Fairchild, David. *The World Was My Garden: Travels of a Plant Explorer.* New York: Charles Scribner's Sons, 1939.
Federal Writers' Project of the Work Projects Administration for the State of Kansas. *The WPA Guide to 1930s Kansas.* Lawrence: University Press of Kansas, 1984.
Foveaux, Jessie Lee Brown. *Any Given Day: The Life and Times of Jesse Lee Brown Foveaux.* New York: Warner Books, 1997.
Goodnow, Isaac. *Diary.* KSHS, transcribed by RCHM. (Cited in notes as "Goodnow Diary.")
———. "Personal Reminiscences and Kansas Emigration, 1855." *Transactions of the KSHS* 4 (1888): 244–253.
Howe, Daniel Walker. *What Hath God Wrought: The Transformation of America, 1815–1848.* New York: Oxford University Press, 2007.
Humphrey, James. "The Country West of Topeka Prior to 1865." *Transactions of the KSHS* 4 (1888): 289–297.
Jack, Lowell. *A History of Manhattan, Kansas — Riley County and Ft. Riley.* Manhattan, KS: Hawley Printing, 2003.

Jones, Carolyn. *The First One Hundred Years: A History of the City of Manhattan, Kansas 1855–1955*. Manhattan, KS: privately printed, 1955.

Lovejoy, Julia. "Diary of Julia Lovejoy." Charles and Julia Lovejoy Collection, KSHS.

———. "Letters from Kanzas." *KHQ* (February 1942): 29–44. (Cited in notes as "Lovejoy Letters from Kanzas.")

———. "Letters of Julia Louisa Lovejoy, 1856–1864: Part 3." *KHQ* (November 1947): 368–403. (Cited in notes as "Lovejoy Letters III.")

Manhattan City Council. *Minute Books of Early Meetings*. RCHM. (Cited in notes as "City Council Minute Books.")

McKale, William, and William D. Young. *Fort Riley: Citadel of the Frontier West*. Topeka: Kansas State Historical Society, 2000.

Miner, Craig. *Kansas: The History of the Sunflower State, 1854–2000*. Lawrence: University Press of Kansas, 2002.

O'Brien, Patricia J. *The Architects and Buildings of Manhattan, Kansas*. Manhattan, KS: Riley County Historical Society, 2008.

Olney, Elaine, and Mary Roberts, eds. *Pioneers of the Bluestem Prairie*. Manhattan, KS: Riley County Genealogical Society, 1976.

Parrish, Donald. *This Land Is Our Land: The Public Domain in the Vicinity of Riley County and Manhattan, Kansas*. Manhattan, KS: RCHS, 2003.

Reynolds, David S. *John Brown, Abolitionist: The Man Who Killed Slavery, Sparked the Civil War, and Seeded Civil Rights*. New York: Alfred A. Knopf, 2005.

Richardson, Albert Deane. *Beyond the Mississippi: From the Great River to the Great Ocean*. Hartford, CT: American Publishing Co., 1869.

Riley County Historical Society. *Log Cabin Days*. Manhattan, KS: RCHS, 1929.

Robinson, Sara. *Kansas: Its Interior and Exterior Life*. Boston: Crosby, Nichols and Co., 1856.

Schlereth, Thomas J. *Victorian America: Transformations in Everyday Life, 1876–1915*. New York: HarperPerennial, 1991.

Shortridge, James R. *Cities on the Plains: The Evolution of Urban Kansas*. Lawrence: University Press of Kansas, 2004.

Thayer, Eli. *A History of the Kansas Crusade: Its Friends and Its Foes*. New York: Harper & Bros., 1889.

U.S. Congress. *Report of the Special Committee Appointed to Investigate the Troubles in Kansas; with the Views of the Minority of Said Committee*. 1856. (Cited in notes as *Howard Report*.)

Walton, Geraldine Baker. *140 Years of Soul: A History of African-Americans in Manhattan, Kansas*. Manhattan: KS Publishing, 2008.

Wells, Thomas C. "Letters of a Kansas Pioneer: Thomas C. Wells Part I." *KHQ* (May 1936): 143–179. (Cited in notes as "Wells Letters I.")

———. "Letters of a Kansas Pioneer: Thomas C. Wells Part II." *KHQ* (August 1936): 282–318. (Cited in notes as "Wells Letters II.")

———. "Letters of a Kansas Pioneer: Thomas C. Wells Part III." *KHQ* (November 1936): 381–418. (Cited in notes as "Wells Letters III.")

Whitehorn, Samuel. "Historical Sketch of Riley County." *Manhattan Nationalist*, July 7, 1876. (Cited in notes as "Whitehorn, 'Historical Sketch.'")

INDEX